Holy Cow

Holy Cow

The Hare Krishna Contribution
to Vegetarianism and Animal Rights

STEVEN J. ROSEN

Lantern Books • New York
A Division of Booklight Inc.

2004
Lantern Books
One Union Square West, Suite 201
New York, NY 10003

Library of Congress Cataloging-in-Publication Data

Printed in the United States of America

Rosen, Steven, 1955–
Holy cow : the Hare Krishna contribution to vegetarianism and animal rights / Steven J. Rosen.
p. cm.
ISBN 1–59056–066–3 (alk. paper)
1. International Society for Krishna Consciousness. 2. Vegetarianism—Religious aspects—Vaishnavism. 3. Vegetarianism. 4. Animal rights movement. I. Title.
BL1285.842.R67 2004
294.5'48693—dc22
2004005483

Dedication

To my three pairs of mothers and fathers:

To my biological parents, Sylvia and Hyman Rosen,
for giving me life and for nurturing in me a sense of compassion;

To Mother Cow and Father Bull,
for sustaining me through my sojourn in the material world;

And to my spiritual parents,
the Vedic literature and His Divine Grace A. C. Bhaktivedanta Swami Prabhupada,
for allowing me the insight with which to write this book.

Acknowledgments

Many people deserve credit for the substance of this work, especially devotees of Krishna worldwide. If several names must be given, both devotees and non-devotees have benefited this work. In no special order, they are: The ISKCON Foundation, Inc., Martin Rowe, Mukunda Goswami, Rynn Berry, Frank Korom, Patrick Olivelle, Edwin Bryant, Luis Gonzalez-Reimann, Lance Nelson, Jayadvaita Swami, Yamaraja Dasa and *Back to Godhead* magazine, Ganga and *Hare Krishna World*, Paramananda, Gaura Hari, Balabhadra, Chaya Dasi, Paul Turner and Food for Life Global, Hare Krishna Dasi, Yamuna Devi, Kurma, David Shapiro, Joshua Greene, Gerald Surya, Richard Schwartz, Norm Phelps, Herman Tull, Christopher Chapple, Knut Jacobsen, Saul Porecki, Jeffrey Moy, Apurva Dasa, Madan Mohan, Luke Hoverman, Mother Sudharma, Tapapunja, and Jerry Abrams.

Contents

List of Illustrations

FIG. 9. Devotees distribute *prasadam* around the world. Regular festivals are held in various strategic locations, such as the yearly one in Poland (as depicted here).

FIG. 10. Massive *prasadam* distribution initiatives are underway in India, Africa, Australia, and Eastern Europe.

FIG. 11. Millions of plates of sacred vegetarian food have been distributed thus far.

FIG. 12. Devotees have opened restaurants in all parts of the globe. Here we find two happy customers at Chez Govinda in Montreal, Canada.

FIG. 13. Swami Prabhupada's motto was "simple living and high thinking." To implement this ideal, many devotees went back to a more agrarian lifestyle, establishing farm communities around the world.

FIG. 14. Devotees of the Lord love not only Krishna but His world, His nature, His people, and His animals, particularly the cow.

FIG. 15. The Deities of Radha-Govinda. It was this manifestation of Krishna who inspired the name "Govinda's" for ISKCON restaurants around the world.

FIG. 16. Lord Krishna the cowherd, lovingly embracing a calf.

Preface
By Chrissie Hynde

Although this book appears to be about the Hare Krishna move-ment—and, indeed, this is its main focus—it is also a universal-ly sound, non-sectarian guide for all true seekers. It should prove invaluable to anyone looking for answers to the following questions:

- What makes an ordinary person raised in a meat-eating society become vegetarian?

- How is animal rights related to the welfare of the human race?

- Why do so many of the world's great religions (Christianity, Judaism, Islam, Buddhism, and so on) seemingly condone animal slaughter?

- Does vegetarianism affect one's spiritual development?

- What is the true relationship between man and the animal kingdom?

And most importantly:

- What would life on earth be like if the killing, torture and exploita-tion of animals came to an end?

While other books have dealt with these questions, Steven Rosen's meticulously researched answers are fascinating, illuminating, and right on! Full of good food for thought, this is the book I've been wait-ing for my entire life. Read in good health, brothers and sisters.

Chrissie Hynde's reputation as a singer-songwriter with the Pretenders has in recent years been eclipsed by her animal rights work. She visits India once a year to further her studies of Vaishnava culture.

Foreword

By Mukunda Goswami

Having joined the Hare Krishna movement before its inception in 1966 cements me squarely in the crustacean category. But because even fossils have functions, I've been called upon to write this foreword. I'm plunking it out on my ergonomic Microsoft keyboard not only because Rosen's book has opened my aging eyes to a part of the movement I've given my life to, but because it's a part of it that I've seldom fully seen. This book's been a sort of wake-up call to a sleeping souvenir.

Before I rattle on, you should know that Rosen, the author, assumes that most readers of his book will already be familiar with the health benefits of a vegetarian diet, and so he has instead focused on the ethical and spiritual aspects. These are, after all, the aspects of the diet emphasized by the Hare Krishna movement, and that's what his book's about.

But just to fill you in—just in case—leading researchers are now calling for a plant-based diet to lower the risk of illnesses such as cancer and heart disease. We are told that antioxidants found in leafy green vegetables may help protect blood vessels, and other studies have found that diets rich in fruits, vegetables and grains significantly reduce high blood pressure and lower incidence of heart disease. Dr. T. Colin Campbell of Cornell University in the U.S. has reported that plant-based diets can prevent the great majority of cancers, cardiovascular diseases, and other types of degenerative diseases. And Dr. Dean Ornish of the University of California has demonstrated that artery blockages can be reversed with regular low-fat vegetarian fare.

Meat, eggs and dairy products are bogged down with fat and cholesterol, which lead to obesity, heart attacks, cancer, strokes, and so on.

Another thing to remember is that vegetarianism is finally reach-
ing its stride. The cover story in the July 15, 2002 issue of *Time* magazine was "Should You Be a Vegetarian?" Subtitle: "Millions of people
are going meatless. Is that a healthy thing?" Cover artwork: top and
bottom burger buns stuffed with only vegetarian fare. The article
praised vegetarianism as a viable, even preferable, alternative to a diet
containing meat. In a similar vein, the June 2001 issue of *Time Out
New York* ran a cover story called "Fake Meat and Other Vegetarian
Delights," extolling the virtues of a veggie diet. This is one of New
York's most popular magazines. Add to these articles the fact that the
Boston Globe and even *Better Homes and Gardens* both ran prominent,
positive stories on the veggie diet in November, 2003, and it becomes
evident that something's brewing here: Vegetarianism is good for you,
and people are recognizing that fact.

Holy Cow's unique contribution, however, is that it explains the
spiritual dimensions of vegetarianism, with a special focus on the
Hare Krishna diet—a diet that may not be as obscure as some might
think. One way to understand this is to hear how the diet is related to
sacraments like the Eucharist of the Christian tradition, a connection
that Rosen makes quite eloquently. He describes the idea of *prasadam*,
the Sanskrit word for food offered to God and spiritualized through a
sacrificial offering that includes devotional mantras. By making food
prasadam, one might say it becomes *Krishna*ized. This offering
process characterizes the entire range of Krishna cuisine, from flat
breads of whole wheat called *chapatis* to deep-fried-in-clarified-butter
avocado flower *pakoras* (vegetable fritters) to mint-flavored fruit
drinks made with honey, strawberries, orange juice and *dahi* (yogurt).
All Krishna food is *prasadam*, from simple raw fruit to the meticulously prepared *tali* in a Maharaja's palace.

Now, regarding the main course of the book: the Hare Krishna
contribution to vegetarianism and animal rights. People today are
obsessed with measuring all things from planets and microbes to
health and happiness. One may question the precision of these calcu-
lations. Similarly, gauging the impact the Hare Krishnas have had on

vegetarianism and animal rights might be considered an almost futile effort. Sure, people in the know are aware that Krishna devotees were forerunners of the modern vegetarian movement in the West, but the details of this history are vague, lost in a barrage of facts and figures.

Nonetheless—and it's a really big NONETHELESS—Rosen brings many little-known facts to the table, and these may cause some heads to turn, and even raise an eyebrow or two. At minimum, *Holy Cow* describes the Hare Krishna contribution in considerable detail. But, more than this, it describes general principles for spiritual living—suggesting the attributes of a good, wholesome life, the best foods to put in your mouth, and sensible approaches to our relationship with the world around us and all the creatures in it. The story makes for intriguing reading, especially the Krishna contribution, which, as you will see, is colorful—it may be referred to as "the pleasure principle of vegetarianism," or what Rosen sometimes refers to as "the kitchen religion," "gastro-hyberbole" and "synesthesia." He speaks of senses being "transformed—heightened—by active engagement in Krishna consciousness."

The Hare Krishna gift to the animal rights movement, among other things, has certainly been the concept of *karma*, which tells us that the things we do to others—even animals—are going to come right back at us. If we look at the creatures around us carefully, we can see their connection to humankind. Animals, especially companion animals, yelp, scratch, sneeze, have sex, defecate, stand up, sit down, eat and sleep. Many like to be patted and some display love and loyalty to their human guardians. It's obvious that they feel pain and pleasure in response to many of the same things we do. In fact, part of the reason companion animals exist, and that we domesticate animals, is for companionship and camaraderie. Rosen argues that we should offer the same sensitivity we have for dogs and cats to cows, chickens and pigs, usually thought of as *livestock*.

As we will see here, from both theoretical and practical points of view, the Hare Krishna movement has worked hard to bring a certain awareness to the world—an awareness of Krishna consciousness but no less of its related vegetarianism and animal rights. The movement has been a part of (perhaps a major force in) this global trend. But let's call it what it is. It's more than a trend—it's a necessary way of life. Without it, we may exist, but will we flourish? Let's see what you think after reading this book. I'm proud to say that this "harmless" way of life is central to our philosophy, as Rosen shows, and as a philosophical underpinning for vegetarianism and animal rights it has been an integral and essential part of the movement's efforts from the start.

As an almost lifelong Krishna practitioner, I would recommend reading this book entirely (and if you like cooking or chemistry, try the recipes as well). It's a story that needs to be told, and one that you should hear. I too am a storyteller, and if I had to tell you just one story, this would be it.

Mukunda Goswami joined the International Society for Krishna Consciousness (ISKCON) before it was formally incorporated in 1966 and was initiated by its founder, His Divine Grace A. C. Bhaktivedanta Swami Prabhupada, in the first initiation ceremony, which was held in that same year. In 1982, he was awarded sannyasa, the highest order of monastic renunciation in the Vaishnava tradition. He has served his teacher's institution as Food for Life Director (1985–1998); a Governing Body Commissioner (1981–1999); Global Director of Communications (1985–2000); and as the author of several books, including Divine Nature: A Spiritual Perspective on the Environmental Crisis *(1995) and* Inside the Hare Krishna Movement *(2001).*

Introduction

The Spiritual Master was asked . . . how to obtain enlightenment.
"Like this," he replied, and popped a piece of *prasadam* [sacred vegetarian food] into his mouth.

—Quoted in *Back to Godhead* magazine

If the way to a person's heart is through the stomach, then access
to the soul may be found in dietary practices. So believe members
of the International Society for Krishna Consciousness
(ISKCON), more commonly known as the Hare Krishna movement, a
familiar sight in most major cities of the Western world. Krishna
devotees parade through the streets in distinctly Indian dress, chanting and singing and proclaiming the glory of God. They show up at
rock concerts, baseball games, airports, and other public venues distributing their books and making their message of love for God,
Krishna, available to all. Their message includes the importance of
vegetarianism and animal rights, for they teach a form of love that is
all-encompassing—extending from each member of the movement to
Krishna and to the entire created world.

Indeed, the devotees see every living being as "part and parcel of
Krishna" and thus worthy of their highest affections. This is elaborated upon by His Divine Grace A. C. Bhaktivedanta Swami Prabhupada
(1896–1977), the founder and spiritual preceptor of the Hare Krishna
movement, while commenting on a particular Sanskrit verse:

He [the devotee of Krishna] is merciful because he is the well-
wisher of all living entities. He is not only a well-wisher of

human society, but a well-wisher of the animal society as well. It is said here, *sarva dehinam*, which indicates all living entities who have accepted material bodies. Not only does the human being have a material body, but other living beings, such as cats and dogs, also have material bodies. The devotee of the Lord is [thus] merciful to everyone—the cats, dogs, trees, etc. He treats all living entities in such a way that they can ultimately get salvation from this material entanglement.[1]

Prabhupada was often quoted as saying, "Real philosophy is nothing more than this: 'friendliness to all living entities.' " Naturally, this sense of universal camaraderie and compassion has far-reaching implications, mandating not only welfare work among humans but also vegetarianism and kindness to animals. On a practical level, this manifests in the lives of all ISKCON members as a vow to abstain from eating meat. It also manifests as a plethora of vegetarian food programs, where devotees freely distribute sacred edibles (*prasadam*) to needy people throughout the world. This is called Food for Life (FFL) and has been honored as one of the most important free food initiatives the world has yet seen, on a par with the work of Mother Teresa. This same food distribution technique also benefits the rest of society through ISKCON's well-established Sunday Love Feast, where literally hundreds of thousands of plates of delicious vegetarian food are distributed weekly. Devotees also own and manage many successful vegetarian restaurants around the world, and they are the authors of numerous award-winning cookbooks. In addition, they have established successful farm communities, cow protection (and adoption) programs, and have given the world an elaborate theology of eating—explaining the science of how to determine what is proper food for human consumption, and how to turn ordinary vegetarian delights into energizing and sumptuous spiritual fare.[2] These are some of the subjects this book will cover.

The growth of ISKCON in the 1960s coincided with the growth of vegetarianism as an expression of nonviolence in a time of objectionable warfare. That is, ISKCON and vegetarianism enjoyed a contemporary as well as historical synchronicity. In fact, it will become evident here that ISKCON in many ways spearheaded the widespread appreciation of vegetarianism and animal rights in the United States and Europe. Thus, this book will focus on ISKCON's pioneering and even visionary efforts in popularizing vegetarian cuisine and the compassionate treatment of animals in the West—how they did so from the days of their first Sunday Love Feast (in 1966) and how they continue to do so in the present day.

The Origins of the Hare Krishna Movement

The movement that brings us this precious fruit of India's spiritual heritage was incorporated in New York City in 1966, though it sprouted from the seeds of a religious and cultural system that is thousands of years old. These seeds were brought West by Swami Prabhupada, mentioned above, who was instructed to do so by his own spiritual master, Srila Bhaktisiddhanta Saraswati Thakur (1874–1937). Now, an instruction is one thing, and executing it is another. Prabhupada did more than merely take this instruction seriously—he took it to unimaginable places, with a vision and strategic excellence that is the stuff of legend.[3] Colorful ISKCON flowers made themselves visible by the 1970s and continued to blossom into a formidable tree of love of God, offering the world the few fruits mentioned above and so much more.

ISKCON's theological roots can be understood in terms of two historical paradigms, one modern and one ancient. The modern form of the movement reaches back into sixteenth-century Bengal, when Chaitanya Mahaprabhu (1486–1533)[4]—the revered religious ecstatic who fully embodied the movement's teachings, practices, and goals—vibrated a song of universal love. This song's main chorus centered on the chanting of the holy names of God, especially the Maha-mantra, or "the Great Chant for Deliverance": Hare Krishna, Hare Krishna, Krishna Krishna, Hare Hare / Hare Rama, Hare Rama, Rama Rama, Hare Hare.

What does the mantra mean? The word "Hare" is the vocative form of "Mother Hara," another name for Radha, Krishna's eternal consort and the very embodiment of devotional service (*bhakti*). Rama is another name for Krishna, meaning "He who gives His devotees the highest pleasure." Thus, in brief translation, the chant may be rendered as follows: "O Lord! O energy of the Lord (Radha)! Please engage me in Your divine service!" This practice of reciting mantras is rooted in earlier Vedic texts—Vedic literature constitutes the scriptural legacy of ancient India—where glorification of God's names is recommended as the most effective form of yoga for the modern age. Historically, such chanting has been embraced by all Vaishnavas (devotees of Vishnu, or Krishna), particularly Gaudiya Vaishnavas, or the particular Bengali branch that descends from Lord Chaitanya.[5]

In the late fifteenth century, European kings sent their heroic explorers in search of new routes to treasure-filled India. Many returned home on ships laden with silks, spices, artwork, and magnificent jewels. But they bypassed India's real treasure, which was just then being widely distributed by Lord Chaitanya. Prior to Chaitanya's time, a reawakening of Krishna-*bhakti*, or devotion to Krishna, had swept the subcontinent, drawing on centuries-old Sanskrit texts and vernacular poetry composed by Chaitanya's immediate predecessors. Now Chaitanya and his followers were filling in the missing pieces by showing how to put this deep theology into practice and by emphasizing the power of the holy name. In this way, Chaitanya pioneered a great social and spiritual movement that continues to spread its profound influence worldwide. At the very least, he transformed India in four respects: philosophically, by establishing the logic of a personal Absolute named Krishna and the need for rendering loving service to Him; socially, by opposing the blindly rigid caste system and setting in place a universal doctrine that is open to all; politically, by organizing India's first civil disobedience movement against a repressive government; and, most important, spiritually, by teaching and demonstrating that love for Krishna is the secret meaning behind all Vedic texts, the cooling balm to heal all the world's woes, and the ultimate nonsectarian truth for which everyone is searching.

Again, Chaitanya's movement came to be called Gaudiya (Bengali) or Chaitanyaite Vaishnavism, but, as stated, it was deeply rooted in the much older tradition of Krishna-*bhakti*. To this end, it makes use of standard classical texts, like the Upanishads, *Bhagavad-gita*, and the *Srimad Bhagavatam*. And, in this sense, it is quite orthodox. It claims affiliation with the prestigious Brahma-Madhva-Sampradya (lineage), and can trace its teaching to Brahma, the father of the created universe. This is the second historical paradigm by which ISKCON can be understood. In this context, it is called *Sanatana-dharma*, or "the eternal function of the soul." To briefly elaborate: Chaitanya did not begin his mission to teach something new. Rather, his purpose was to reveal deeper, esoteric truths found at the core of the ancient Vedic tradition. Moreover, his teaching embodies the original spiritual truth found in all religion. Thus, it is not merely Hindu dogma, but, rather, a transcendental science that benefits everyone, regardless of religious or sectarian affiliation.

This, in fact, is what the Hare Krishna movement teaches about its own tradition. Prabhupada faithfully carried on in this same spirit, claiming that his only credit was that he did not change anything, but delivered the teaching "as it is." God's revealed word, Prabhupada told his followers, is the Absolute Truth—"For our part," he said, "we can only follow this Truth and convey it to others, without interpolation or change." Moreover, unlike other gurus and God-men from India, Prabhupada was adamant that a human being should not be identified with God—he claimed that he was merely God's humble servant, and that he was ready, willing, and able to teach others how to serve in this same capacity.

The Movement's Philosophy in Relation to Vegetarianism and Animal Rights

The basic philosophy of Chaitanya's movement is summed up by Bhaktivinode Thakur (1838–1914), father of Prabhupada's guru and one of the premier theologians of the tradition:

> Give up the shackles of matter slowly. Cultivate your spirit inwards. . . . Be humble in yourself and learn to respect those who work towards spiritual attainments, no matter what their tradition. Do these with your heart, mind, and strength in the company of spiritual people alone, and you will see Krishna in no time.
>
> Spiritual cultivation is the main object of life. Do every-

thing which helps it and abstain from doing anything which thwarts the cultivation of the spirit. Have a strong faith that Krishna, God, alone protects you and none else. Admit Him as your only guardian. Do everything which you know that Krishna wishes you to do, and never think that you do a thing independently of the holy wish of Krishna. Do all that you do with humility. Always remember that you are a sojourner in this world and you must be prepared for your own home. Do your duties and cultivate *bhakti* as a means to obtain the great end of life, Krishna *priti* [love of God]. Employ your body, mind, and spirit in the service of the Deity. Chant His name always. In all your actions, worship your great Lord.[6]

It should be clear from the above that Krishna—famous throughout India as a playful, all-attractive divinity, a dark-hued charmer with a special fondness for cows—is the vision of God in the Chaitanya Vaishnava tradition, and thus the vision adopted by the Hare Krishna movement. It should also be obvious that abundant humility and its concomitant kindness to all living creatures are central to the Vaishnava path of religiosity. These factors weigh heavily, as we shall see, in determining the way Hare Krishna devotees view animals.

A modern-day representative of the Chaitanyaite Vaishnava tradition elaborates on the divine love preached by Chaitanya Mahaprabhu, and emphasizes its role in true *ahimsa*, or harmlessness, which is essential in the philosophy of Krishna consciousness:

Lord Chaitanya propagated the all-embracing philosophy of divine love, irrespective of caste, creed, and religion. Many spiritual paths follow the principle of *ahimsa*, which means to abstain from doing harm to others. But better than merely renouncing the negative is to be engaged in the positive act of love, which means to do good to others. All animated beings are interconnected and parts of the potency of one all-pervading supersoul, or God. We should realize that our real self is neither our physical body, nor subtle body [mind, intelligence, or sense of identity], but an eternally existing blissful particle of consciousness. Realization of our common relation to the Supreme will foster in us love and affection for each other.[7]

Here we see the fundamental Hare Krishna teaching that we are not our bodies but spirit-soul, quite apart from the material body. But, more, we see the basis for true love, i.e., that we are all related spiritual beings with the same universal Father in heaven. The usual understanding of *ahimsa* is here expressed as a given, implying that a believing Vaishnava would never cause intentional harm to any living entity. Interestingly, however, *ahimsa* is now brought further: A Vaishnava is one who feels love for all living entities, and performs positive acts of devotion to help them in any way he or she can. The implications in relation to our subject should be self-evident.

The movement's specific perspective on vegetarianism and animal rights is clearly brought out in a conversation between Prabhupada and Roman Catholic Cardinal Jean Danielou. In a recent academic volume on the implications of vegetarianism and religion, this conversation is considered in depth:

> The two religious leaders are speculating about why Christians typically refuse to extend the Commandment against killing to animals. At one point in their conversation, Cardinal Danielou wonders, "But why does a [loving] God create some animals who eat other animals?" His answer to his own question is both haunting and poignant: "There is a fault in the creation, it seems."
>
> Swami Prabhupada quickly dismisses this possibility. "It is not a fault," he insists. "God is very kind. If you want to eat animals, then He'll give you full facility. God will give you the body of a tiger in your next life so that you can eat flesh very freely. . . . The animal eaters become tigers, wolves, cats, and dogs in their next life." The Swami's point is that if there is a "fault in creation," it exists nowhere but in the devourer of animal flesh and will be reprimanded and redeemed in the working out of karmic necessity. Restless rapacity is the destiny of the meat-eater.[8]

Prabhupada's perspective tells us much about the philosophy of Krishna consciousness in relation to vegetarianism, and even something about the nature of God and the logic of reincarnation as well. First of all, according to Prabhupada, the world behaves according to certain karmic laws, that is, for every action, there is an equal and commensurate reaction. We will explore this in greater depth later. For now, let us understand that God, by definition, is perfect and complete, and His creation reflects this same perfection, if in a distorted way. Prabhupada clearly asserts this faith in God's perfect nature, and he points out that God is inherently kind as well. The logic here is simple: if God is perfect and complete, He needs nothing from anyone else, has no envy, and thus has no need to exploit or to be unkind. Thus, being all-good, God desires our happiness, and He is pleased when we perform acts that are for our own ultimate benefit.

If, due to a poor fund of knowledge, we desire to eat the flesh of animals—or to engage in any other low-grade sense enjoyment, which harms ourselves and others as well—He allows us to do it. In fact, He creates the various species of life—each equipped with a particular sensuous strength (e.g., the bear sleeps six months at a time, the pigeon has hundreds of sexual encounters each day)—to facilitate various forms of sense pleasure. As Prabhupada says, "If you want to eat meat, become a tiger." In this way, Prabhupada sees rhyme and reason in creation—the various forms we see around us exist for a reason. More, if we are not at the level of a human pursuing spiritual matters in earnest, we are in effect preparing our next body according to our peculiar desires for sense enjoyment. The goal, Prabhupada informs us, is to learn the true standard of enjoyment—spiritual enjoyment. By engaging in this higher pleasure, he says, our endless repetition of bodily incarnations will end and we can return to Krishna in the spiritual world.

Devotees of Krishna: Aesthetic Ascetics

While ISKCON shares with other forms of Eastern religion a sense of demarcation between spiritual and material worlds—and clearly asserts the living being's identity as a spiritual being encased within a material body—it differs from most other Indic traditions in that its teaching is not otherworldly. Rather, devotees of Krishna exult in the here and now. True, they shun "sense gratification"—meaning that, as spiritual beings, they prefer not to engage in material pleasures—but they nevertheless enjoy these same senses in a spiritual way. This is based on the precedent set in the *Bhagavad-gita*, where the warrior Arjuna wants to forsake the world and his duties as an administrative officer. Krishna tells him that such weakness of heart does not become him, and that common people depend upon him to do his duty. Before the time of the *Gita*, Indian philosophy favored the way of renunciation, glorifying the yogi who goes off to the forest and leaves aside the world for higher goals. The *Gita* teaches something different. It tells us to *spiritualize* not only our goals but also the actions that lead to these goals. No more should one embrace "renunciation *of* action." Rather, the *Gita* teaches us to embrace "renunciation *in* action." The implications here should be clear. We need not shy away from the material world—we need only learn its proper utilization in Krishna's service. This, according to the *Gita*, is true yoga, or "linking with God."

The virtues of ISKCON's "this-worldly" philosophy have been observed by many but are most succinctly and articulately conveyed, perhaps, by Steven J. Gelberg, a Harvard scholar and long-time observer of ISKCON:

One can see this spiritual and material utilitarianism in practice in ISKCON in its unabashed willingness to employ the fruits of material technology in spreading its message (vehicles, computers, printing presses, communications technology). It involves not only the use of material objects as such, but also of the body, the senses, and the creative instinct. One can witness this sacralizing of sense activity in the proliferating (and increasingly sophisticated) use among devotees of artistic media such as painting, sculpture, music, dance, and drama to express and communicate the many images, moods, and themes of Krishna Consciousness and Vaishnava culture. This aesthetic dimension is also evident in the construction of lavishly designed temples (such as those in Bombay, Vrindavan, and New Vrindavan), in the use of exquisitely designed dress and ornamentation in the decoration of the temple deities, and in the use of various sensory stimuli such as sound (bells, conch shells, *kirtana* music), taste (sumptuous food offerings), and aroma (incense, camphor) in the ceremonial worship of the deities. Krishna Consciousness calls not for an extinguishing of senses and sense activity, but rather their purification and elevation through devotional activity. Devotees are *aesthetic ascetics.*[9]

What is being described, then, is a form of inverse yoga, if you will, wherein divinity is not experienced by suppressing the senses, as in India's many ascetic traditions, but rather by activating them in a unique way. In relation to food, this is clearly a reversal of the traditionally understood need for austerity. It is, rather, a form of "gastrohyperbolism," wherein the pleasures of the tongue are enhanced, but only in service to Krishna. This focus on sensorial engagement leads to one's becoming a connoisseur (*rasika*), of sorts, developing a certain expertise in determining what is sublime, and what is not. In other words, through the process of Krishna consciousness, one develops both aesthetic and gustatory "taste"—a word with multiple meanings. In the Sanskritic tradition, its various nuances are found in the words *rasa*, *ruchi*, and *asvada*, all with differing connotations. In short, "the taster tastes the taste with taste." Vaishnavism has thus been called "the kitchen religion," both because its adherents imbibe a distinguished taste for preparing and devouring sacred vegetarian edibles and because it develops in one a taste for Krishna consciousness.

Clearly, this Vaishnava philosophy of spiritual utilitarianism has led devotees into worlds of sights, sounds, tastes, smells, and touch that would be the envy of gross hedonists. It is a realm of synesthesia, where the senses are transformed—heightened—by active engagement in Krishna consciousness. Such a transformation is a razor's edge, no doubt, and many a practitioner has slipped, cutting off his or her connection to spiritual life. But those who remain ensconced in the world of the spirit learn of a higher pleasure, one that, again, makes the material variety pale by comparison. As Rupa Goswami, one of Lord Chaitanya's immediate successors and the main systematizer of the Gaudiya Vaishnava tradition, writes in his *Bhakti-rasamrita-sindhu* (1.2.39), "My dear friend, if you are at all attached to the material world, do not look at the smiling face of Govinda [Krishna], as He stands on the bank of the Yamuna at Keshi-ghat. Casting sidelong glances, He places His flute to His eager red lips, which seem like newly blossomed twigs. His spiritual body is radiant, and it enhances the beauty of the moon."

If one chooses to look at Krishna's beautiful, smiling face, one cannot simultaneously look into the eyes of a cow that is about to be slaughtered.

Writing on behalf of the entire Hindu world, the late *Hinduism Today* guru, Satguru Shivaya Subramuniyaswami, explains Hindu vegetarianism, and, though not affiliated with the Hare Krishna movement, he clearly articulates many of their reasons for adhering to a vegetarian diet:

Hindus teach vegetarianism as a way to live with a minimum of hurt to other beings, for to consume meat, fish, fowl or eggs is to participate indirectly in acts of cruelty and violence against the animal kingdom. The abhorrence of injury and killing of any kind leads quite naturally to a vegetarian diet, *sakahara* [which is the Sanskrit word for vegetarianism]. The meat-eater's desire for meat drives another to kill and provide that meat. The act of the butcher begins with the desire of the consumer. Meat-eating contributes to a mentality of violence, for with the chemically complex meat ingested, one absorbs the slaughtered creature's fear, pain and terror. These qualities are nourished within the meat-eater, perpetuating the cycle of cruelty and confusion. When the individual's consciousness lifts and expands, he will abhor violence and not be able to even digest the meat, fish, fowl and eggs he was formerly consuming. India's greatest saints have confirmed that one cannot eat meat and live a peaceful, harmonious life. Man's appetite for meat inflicts devastating harm on Earth itself, stripping its precious forests to make way for pastures. The *Tirukural* candidly states, "How can he practice true compassion who eats the flesh of an animal to fatten his own flesh? Greater than a thousand *ghee* offerings consumed in sacrificial fires is not to sacrifice and consume any living creature."[10]

The Importance of *Prasadam*

The central reason for Hare Krishna vegetarianism is that, according to scripture, Krishna Himself is a vegetarian—and devotees do not eat anything without first offering it to Krishna as a religious sacrifice. In other words, devotees of Krishna naturally prefer to offer Him those foods that He Himself says he would like to eat, and then they accept the remnants as His mercy (*prasadam*). This, say Vaishnava texts, is "the yoga of eating."

According to the *Bhagavad-gita* (9.27), the entire process of Vaishnavism may be summarized as follows, "All that you do, all that you eat, all that you offer and give away, as well as all austerities that you may perform, should be done as an offering unto Me [Krishna]." Thus, offering food to Krishna is an integral part of Vaishnava piety. Observing ISKCON and its relationship to food for many years, Eliot Singer writes,

> The act of offering and the prayer which precedes the meal serve to acknowledge that all food is rightfully Krishna's and that the devotees may eat it only due to His "causeless mercy." Offering is a means of expressing subservience. Yet it is also the prime method through which Krishna's "humanity" is revealed. Krishna does eat, although He does not have to do so. In this way, He is explicitly contrasted with the Judeo-Christian God, that "stuffy old man who certainly needs nothing like food." This enables the devotees to feel an accessibility to and intimacy with their God which better allows them to develop the love for Him which is conducive to their concentration.

Offering *prasadam* is meant to show that man's relationship to God is one of servitude; the devotees receive His leftovers only out of His kindness. Krishna's willingness to accept offerings which are certainly not of divine opulence is also a kindness. This willingness to accept offerings, no matter how humble, is what enables the devotees to develop their personal relationship with God.[11]

In the West, one would wonder why we should offer food to God at all. As mentioned above, He doesn't need our meager offerings—He sustains Himself just fine without them. So what exactly is the point of *prasadam?* Vaishnava tradition tells us that while *God* does not need our food offerings, as Singer notes, *we* need the intimacy and deep-rooted connection that comes from offering food to Him. In most religious systems, God is asked for food ("Give us this day our daily bread"), but in Vaishnavism, the devotee offers food to God as an expression of love. Even in ordinary dealings, someone might offer us a meal as a sign of warmth and affection. It isn't only the meal itself that is appreciated, but the thoughtfulness and consideration that goes into it. In the same way, the process of offering food to God is intended to help us increase our love and devotion toward Him.

When discussing *prasadam*, Vaishnava texts explain a three-tiered approach to mercy, involving exchange, reciprocity and redistribution. To make this clear: Offering *prasadam* is at the heart of a loving exchange with the Lord. It helps us recognize that He initially offers food to us, through the earth and through mother cow, i.e., through nature, and that we can show our appreciation by making a gesture— by offering it back to Him in love and devotion (reciprocity). He then allows us to imbibe the remnants as His special mercy (redistribution).

All religious adherents, East or West, recite prayers over food— and this is certainly an important component in offering *prasadam*— but a closer Western parallel would be the Christian idea of transubstantiation, in which bread and wine are mystically transformed into the body and blood of Christ. The notion of *prasadam* is similar, but it goes much further. *Prasadam* is the essence of the entire spiritual world—it is Radha and Krishna, *and* their loving exchange.[12] It is spirituality in edible form. Moreover, as opposed to the Eucharist, it is not merely a once-a-week wafer—it is every morsel that goes into one's mouth, making it an "all-consuming" act of devotion.

The wafer, it is to be remembered, is not an entire meal, but only an edible symbol. So while the Eurcharist and *prasadam* both represent the reception of God through one's lips, offering spiritual nourishment to all who partake, only *prasadam* actually nourishes the body as well. Thus, *prasadam* is more holistic in that it fully sustains its eaters, whereas the Christian Eucharist is a solitary event, the ingestion of a small wafer and a sip of wine—only once a week or every morning, at best. This distinction is important. *Prasadam* is fully incorporated into the daily life of the devotee, facilitating an acute awareness of God's mercy, through food and through nature. Eliot Singer remarks on *prasadam*'s all-encompassing symbolism, which reflects the very essence of Vaishnavism. He perceptively notes how this sacred food resolves the central paradoxes of devotional religion:

> *Prasadam* is a *dominant symbol*, a symbol which sums up and epitomizes the essential and [apparently] contradictory concepts in Krishna Consciousness: austerity and indulgence, servitude and intimacy, omnipotence and accessibility, suffering and bliss. *Prasadam* symbolizes simultaneously the austere control of the senses and the celebration of taste in association with the divine. It expresses the duality of Krishna as eater and feeder and of His devotees as givers and receivers.[13]

For those who doubt that *prasadam* is fully spiritual, the devotees remind us that Krishna is supremely powerful. Anything that comes in contact with Him, they say, is overwhelmed by His holy presence. By such contact, even matter becomes completely pure and spiritual, just as He is. Even in the realm of the physical, certain things have the ability to purify various substances. For instance, the sun, with its powerful rays, can distill fresh, pure water from a lake contaminated with pollutants. If a material object like the sun can act in this way, then we can only imagine the purifying potency of the supreme Lord, who has effortlessly created millions of suns.

Thus, Vaishnava tradition tells us that Krishna, by His immense transcendental energies, can actually convert matter into spirit. The traditional example is that of placing an iron rod in fire. If one so places an iron rod, before long the rod takes on all the essential qualities of fire, such as heat, smoke, light—it will burn you if you touch it. In the same way, material foodstuffs offered to Krishna become completely spiritualized by lovingly placing them in His presence. This is accomplished by preparing the food with a joyful heart, offering the appropriate prayers, and devotionally offering back to Krishna the foods He mercifully bestowed upon us to begin with. Food offerings are one of the few commodities that we can share in this way. As one practitioner insightfully says,

> Unfortunately, we can hold onto money, but food cannot be hoarded. It will spoil if it is not shared. A single person can only eat so much food; the rest needs to be shared or it will spoil. Food, then, is the most shareable form of wealth. Food is among the best things that we can offer to God. Whatever we think is best, we offer to Krishna as *bhoga*. Money is not a form of *bhoga*. Krishna is a divine child. If you give him sweets, milk, or other such things, he will be pleased. *Bhoga* is defined as those things that give pleasure to the Lord. Our sect's wealth is concentrated in food. In the Shastras it states that whatever God gives us, we must give back in return, as an offering. Food should never be prepared for its own sake; to do so is a sin. Why? Because everything we see belongs to God—it cannot be enjoyed by us unless it is first offered to Him. *Prasada[m]* or food is the grace by which Krishna helps us to live our lives. Next to air and water, food is the most essential thing in life. All our necessities, luxuries, everything in short, must first be offered to Krishna, as they rightfully belong to him. We use Krishna's things through his grace.[14]

When vegetarian food is thus offered back to God, it takes on a special quality, purifying all who devour it and all who share it with others. Accomplished devotees can actually taste the difference. Lord Chaitanya himself glorified *prasadam* in this way:

> Everyone has tasted these material substances before. However, in these [now offered] ingredients there are extraordinary tastes and uncommon fragrances. Just taste them and see the difference in the experience. Apart from the taste, even the fragrance pleases the mind and makes one forget any other sweetness besides its own. Therefore it is to be understood that the spiritual nectar of Krishna's lips has touched these ordinary ingredients and transferred to them all their spiritual qualities.[15]

The above might serve as a brief introduction to Vaishnava philosophy, a mere taste of the Hare Krishna worldview. To reiterate what we have learned this far about ISKCON and our subject at hand: Perceiving God as a loving cowherd naturally evinces appreciation for cows and for the entire natural world; the vision of all beings as part of God fosters a mood of respect and love for every living creature; the doctrine of universal compassion does the same; understanding the distinction between the body and the actual self helps one to realize that both animal and human bodies house the same spiritual substance; the doctrines of karma and reincarnation tell us that today's human may be tomorrow's animal, and vice versa; humility enables one to see the virtue of all creatures, without securing a special place for oneself; and the notion of *ahimsa* speaks for itself—deeply considered, all of this points to an appreciation of the natural world and to an understanding of the spiritual and genetic bonding we as humans share with all who live. Add to this the principle of *prasadam*, and a clear picture emerges colorfully illustrating why the Hare Krishnas are vegetarians and strong supporters of animal rights.

A Brief History of Vegetarianism in India

If people are to be educated in the path back to Godhead, they must be taught first and foremost to stop the process of animal-killing.

—Swami Prabhupada

A sia is the continent of superlatives: It has the largest land area, the highest mountains, the greatest number of people, the first civilization, and the oldest religions in the world. "Hinduism"—which is actually a medley of several religious traditions, such as Shaivism, Shaktism, and Vaishnavism—is the oldest of all Asian religions and the earliest and strongest supporter of *ahimsa* (harmlessness) and vegetarianism. Of course, Buddhism[1] and Jainism[2] are usually recognized as more emphatic when it comes to *ahimsa*. Nonetheless, these two Indic paths are offshoots of Hinduism, and their *ahimsa* sensibility has its roots in the earlier tradition. The great religious epic the *Mahabharata* (Anu. 116.37) is clear on harmlessness as a central tenet of early Hinduism: *ahimsa paramo dharma*—"nonviolence is the ultimate form of religion." Still, one of the reasons Buddhism broke off from its parent faith was because of the latter's involvement in animal sacrifice, which was an integral part of the ancient Vedic religion (the root tradition that sprouted into the Hindu complex of religions).

To understand the Hare Krishna view of vegetarianism—and that of Buddhism and Jainism as well—it is necessary to understand its context in the earlier Vedic-Hindu tradition, the tradition against which Buddhism rebelled and with which the Hare Krishna movement is identified. That the earlier tradition was a strong supporter of *ahimsa* and its concomitant vegetarianism is cited above and is evident from a careful reading of the Vedic scriptures and supplementary Indic texts. The following are but a few of the thousands of injunctions against meat-eating:

> One who partakes of human flesh, the flesh of a horse or of another animal, and deprives others of milk by slaughtering cows, O King, if such a fiend does not desist by other means, then you should not hesitate to cut off his head. (*Rig Veda*, 10.87.16)

> You must not use your God-given body for killing God's creatures, whether they are human, animal or whatever. (*Yajur Veda*, 12.32)

> One should be considered dear, even by those born in the animal kingdom. (*Atharva Veda*, 17.1.4)

> Those noble souls who practice meditation and other yogic ways, who are ever careful about all beings, who protect all animals, are the ones who are actually serious about spiritual practices. (*Atharva Veda*, 19.48.5)

> A person who kills an animal for meat will die a violent death as many times as there are hairs on the body of that killed animal. (*Manusmriti*, 5.38)

> Having well considered the origin of flesh-foods, and the cruelty of fettering and slaying corporeal beings, let man entirely abstain from eating flesh. (*Manusmriti*, 5.49)

> By not harming any living being, one becomes fit for salvation. (*Manusmriti*, 6.60)

> God, Keshava [another name for Krishna], is pleased with a person who does not harm or destroy other non-speaking creatures or animals. (*Vishnu Purana*, 3.8.15)

The purchaser of flesh performs *himsa* [violence] by his wealth; he who eats flesh does so by enjoying its taste; the killer does *himsa* by actually tying and killing the animal. Thus, there are three forms of killing. He who brings flesh or sends for it, he who cuts off the limbs of an animal, and he who purchases, sells, or cooks flesh, and, of course, there is a fourth: he who devours it—all of these are to be considered meat-eaters. (*Mahabharata, Anu.*, 115:40)

He who desires to augment his own flesh by eating the flesh of other creatures lives in misery in whatever species he may take his birth. (*Mahabharata, Anu.*, 115:47)

Those who are ignorant of real dharma [religious duty] and, though wicked and haughty, account themselves virtuous, kill animals without any feeling of remorse or fear of punishment. Further, in their next lives, such sinful persons will be eaten by the same creatures they have killed in this world. (*Srimad Bhagavatam*, 11.5.14)

Animal Sacrifices

Although the above verses—and many others like them—clearly advocate vegetarianism, the Vedic tradition permitted another stream of thought as well, one that accommodated animal sacrifice. Recently, a spate of literature has focused on this latter dimension of Vedic dharma.

The Myth of the Holy Cow, to cite one such book, garnered enough interest to be reviewed by *The New York Times* (Saturday, August 17, 2002). The work focuses on Sanskrit texts—texts that point to ancient Vedic sacrifices and to the Brahmins who partook of their fleshy spoils. Professor D. N. Jha, the author of this book, gathered substantial evidence to support his case. As a result, his work created a certain discomfort in Hindu society, for it challenged long-standing beliefs that Brahmins were always pacifists and vegetarians.

What the book does not tell us is that the animal sacrifices mentioned in the Vedas were meant for a previous age, and only then were they properly executed, as we will soon explain. Moreover, the book refuses to reveal that even in the later period, when certain Brahmins began to eat the flesh of animals offered in sacrifice, the majority of Brahmins were still averse to eating meat—and scrupulously avoided it.

Along these lines, many scholars of Hinduism are taken aback by books like *The Myth of the Holy Cow*, and they point out that animal sacrifices were a departure from the overall spirit of Vedic dharma, even if these sacrifices are mentioned in the Vedas themselves. Such sacrifices, they say, were even contested by many Brahmins in the Vedic era:

> It is a common misconception that the entire ancient Hindu tradition supported animal sacrifice and meat-eating as part of the sacrificial process. The Vedic or Hindu tradition as a whole never supported animal killings in sacrifice. Animal sacrifice was vehemently opposed by Upanishadic sages, philosophers, social thinkers, intellectuals, and literary persons from ancient times. . . . [H]owever, the followers of ritualism known as *mimamsakas* or *karmakandins* supported and practiced this animal sacrifice in the name of attaining heaven. When this ritualistic class became very powerful, they influenced the ancient Hindu lawmakers to accept killing animals in sacrifice and, ironically, to declare it equal to nonviolence. . . . These bloody animal sacrifices did not fail to arouse criticism and protest. Even [the] ancient *Samaveda* opposed this cruel act (I.II.IX.2). . . . In [the] *Mahabharata* we find opposition to animal sacrifice: "Man loses merit earned from other penance by resorting to sacrificial killing. Men who are engaged in killing animals deserve to go to hell." (*Anushasanaparva*, XIII.68; *Shantiparva*, 272.18)[3]

So, while animal sacrifices are clearly found in the Vedas, Brahmins themselves looked for an alternative Vedic model, one that espoused compassion for all living things—and indeed they found it. A careful look at Indian history reveals that, in addition to Buddhists and Jains, Brahmin priests also sought legitimacy in harmlessness, even while adhering to the principle of Vedic sacrifice. As Henk W. Bodewitz points out, "Hinduism also replaced the bloody rituals. . . . And the Brahmins, the authorities of Vedism . . . became the champions of vegetarianism."[4] Some, like the Vaishnava theologian Madhva, accommodated the requirement for animal sacrifices with *pishta-pashu*, or "an animal made of dough." Others went further, finding legitimization in Vedic and post-Vedic texts to do away with such sacrifices altogether. In the earliest of these, we find acknowledgment that animal sacrifices are unduly harsh, with one hymn even telling us that certain mantras should be chanted so as to help the poor animals avoid pain and be promoted to heaven (*Rig Veda*, 1.162.21). The *Sama Veda* tells us more: "Ultimately, we endorse no sacrificial stake, no slaying of human or non-human victims—we endorse only worship that makes use of sacred mantras" (1.2.92). Another striking example may be found in the *Mahabharata* (12.174–365), in which a sage named Kapila eloquently expresses his distaste for animal sacrifice, and points out that while such sacrifices, as part of the Veda, must be honored, there are higher forms of sacrifice—those that do not require the killing of animals.

All of this points to one simple truth: Brahminhood has little meaning without activity in the mode of goodness as defined in the *Bhagavad-gita*. Such goodness includes cleanliness, austerity, and mercy—with special emphasis on qualities like harmlessness and vegetarianism. In ancient Vedic society, the Brahmins were expected to be *sattvik*, i.e., to refrain from passionate and ignorant action. Vedic texts are clear that meat-eating is the result of both passion (i.e., killing) and ignorance (i.e., death). Hence, a true Brahmin would never eat meat.

The Brahmins who supported animal sacrifices were largely Shaivite and Shakta Brahmins (worshipers of Shiva, the demigod in charge of universal destruction, or Shakti, the universal goddess)—many of whom find justification for fleshy fare to this day—as opposed to Vaishnava Brahmins, who always valued the vegetarian way of life. The word "Vaishnava" is never mentioned in Vedic texts in conjunction with animal sacrifice. Rather, from studying these texts closely, one gets the feeling that it was a Proto-Shakta cult that engaged in the bloody sacrifices. Thus, the Hare Krishna movement, as inheritors of the Vaishnava tradition, does not have meat-eating or animal sacrifice in its past, though there are isolated cases, especially among those in the military castes, who did engage in meat-eating. It

should also be pointed out that when the meat-eating aberration finally grew to epidemic proportions—when even a segment of the
Vaishnava priesthood may have come under its sway—the situation
was eventually rectified by a plan set into motion by Vishnu through
the agency of Lord Buddha, the founder of Buddhism, and Shankara,
the eighth-century theologian who emphasized the impersonal
dimension of the Absolute Truth.

Vegetarianism and the Long-Term Vedic Restoration Paradigm

From the Vaishnava point of view, the original Vedic system was highly monotheistic; it supported vegetarianism and basically extolled the
Vaishnava way of life (as now seen in the Hare Krishna movement). It
was described in esoteric texts, such as those of the Vaikhansa of
South India, and existed side by side with the more exoteric texts
promulgating animal sacrifice and external religious observance. This
inner dimension of Vedic knowledge, say the Vaishnavas, was lost
over the course of time, but it was eventually rediscovered through a
lengthy Vedic restoration process. Briefly, that process unfolded as follows: In ancient times, there was a period when Vedic texts were mis-
interpreted by an unscrupulous Brahmin class as supporting animal
sacrifice and meat-eating (along with polytheism, the caste system,
and a host of other non-Vaishnava ideas). In response, the Buddha
appeared in our world and preached the simple truths of nonviolence
and the suffering of man. In addition, he repudiated the Vedas altogether, saying that people in general did not need religious scriptures
and elaborate sacrifices in order to perceive the highest truth. They
needed only a simple heart and a developed state of consciousness.

But there was more to the Buddha's teaching than meets the eye.
Ancient Indic texts and Jayadeva's *Gita-govinda*, a medieval poem
deeply revered in the Vaishnava tradition, specifically say that the
Buddha's central purpose in this world was to bring an end to the animal sacrifices mentioned in the Vedas. According to scriptural histories—many of which predate the Buddha and even predict his birth
and mission—the Buddha was an incarnation of Vishnu with a long-
term plan. He represented the first link in the major Vedic restoration
process, a centuries-long strategy that would continue with the teach-

ings of Shankara and then with that of the great Vaishnava teachers. By rejecting Vedic texts and preaching *ahimsa*, he would get his followers and others to stop eating meat, because their justification for meat-eating, i.e., the guidelines for sacrifice laid down in Vedic texts, would be devalued. In this pious enterprise, however, the people of India would also lose access to the scriptures at the base of their entire theological heritage. For this reason, Buddhism in India gradually came to be identified as a heterodox or even atheistic tradition.

The Vedic restoration process was carried forward by Shankara, who appeared centuries after the Buddha. Shankara reestablished Vedic texts, but in a way that his then predominantly Buddhist audience could understand. He de-emphasized the personal Absolute and focused instead on the impersonal aspects of reality. This appealed to his Buddhist and quasi-Buddhist students, who could more relate to amorphous existential truths than to the worship of a supreme personality of Godhead. Shankara's contribution to the long-term strategy worked, driving Buddhism out of India and into neighboring countries. More importantly, Vedic texts were now again regarded as sacred and became a significant part of India's burgeoning intellectual traditions.

The final step in the Vedic restoration process began in the tenth century with Ramanuja, the great Vaishnava reformer, continued on into the thirteenth with his successor Madhva, mentioned earlier, and climaxed in the sixteenth with Sri Chaitanya, who is considered the father of the modern-day Hare Krishna movement. With Sri Chaitanya, the original monotheism of the Vedic literature was fully reestablished, as was the vegetarianism of the Brahmins.

The Myth of the Holy Cow—and other books like it—fails to mention this Vedic restoration process. It also neglects to reveal the underlying purpose of the animal sacrifices—they were originally intended to attract meat-eaters to a more holy way of life by encouraging them to follow scriptural rules and regulations. In other words, if a certain class of people felt that they absolutely had to eat flesh, then, ran the thought, let them at least do it as a religious sacrifice. Even then, unlike other world scriptures that temporized in regard to meat-eating, the Vedic literature was quite clear that animal sacrifice was an inferior form of worship; it was meant to elevate those in the mode of ignorance to progressively higher levels of spiritual attainment.

Indic texts endeavor to accommodate all people—at whatever stage they may be in their spiritual evolution. Thus, while the *Laws of Manu*, for example, prohibit the eating of meat for Brahmins (intellectuals, philosophers, priests), these *Laws* merely discourage meat-eating for the remaining classes of society. In other words, the traditional Indian law books take a hard stance for those who are able to follow this prohibition. But they adopt a more gentle approach for others who may need to make concessions, either because of conditioning or because of their station in life. However, Manu's *Laws* conclude by firmly discouraging the eating of meat: "The merit of not eating meat, which involves killing, is equal to the merit of performing hundreds of horse sacrifices" (5.53).

Looking at the Sacrifices More Closely

Since Vedic animal sacrifices have become the subject of recent studies—and since the Hare Krishna tradition is often associated with the texts that endorsed these sacrifices—let us look at them a little more closely. A primary example of an animal sacrifice was the Ashvamedha, a ritual in which a horse was offered to God in a sacrificial arena. The clearly stated purpose of these rituals was not to sanctify the eating of horse flesh. Rather, it was to prove the efficacy of the Vedic mantra (mystical sound vibration): An old horse would be led into a fire of sacrifice, qualified Brahmins would chant the sacred mantra, and the horse would then emerge in a rejuvenated body. The animal was never harmed, only reanimated. Today, of course, there are no qualified priests to perform such a complicated, mystical sacrifice, and the Vedas themselves specify that these rituals were only for an earlier age. According to the *Brahma-vaivarta Purana* (*Krishna-janma-khanda*, 185.180), such killing of sacrificial animals is described as *kali-varjya*, or prohibited in the Kali-yuga, our current age of quarrel and hypocrisy. The Hare Krishna tradition makes frequent use of this verse and it is repeated in one of their central texts, the *Chaitanya-charitamrita* (*Adi*, 17.164).

Another type of animal sacrifice mentioned in the Vedas involved goats, which were to be killed in the presence of the goddess Kali (again indicating that the Brahmins who ate meat were Shaktas, or worshipers of the goddess, as opposed to Vaishnavas). This procedure is also described in the *Markandeya Purana*, a scripture that prescribes rituals for the gradual elevation of the spiritually challenged. Those who were more spiritually evolved would offer red flowers to the goddess instead of a blood sacrifice, and in this way appease her with the facsimile of color.[5] It is interesting, too, that these texts describing the goat sacrifice only sanctioned the eating of flesh offered on the altar. Much like early Judaism, which originally only granted the eating of meat offered sacrificially at the first Temple, the Vedic and Puranic literature never endorsed the wholesale slaughter of animals so prevalent today. It was solely in the context of religious sacrifice.

Also as in Judaism, Vaishnava scriptures teach that in the earliest days—in the Edenic state—there was no violence of any kind, no animal sacrifices, and no meat-eating. This idea is found in all world cultures. As stated in the encyclopedic *History of Food*,

> In all myths of a lost Golden Age, or a state of grace to be recovered, vegetarianism, i.e. abstention from meat, has connotations of purity and virtue. Milk, which is permitted, is white and thus pure. It is represented as good in Buddhism and Brahmanism, systems of thought to the forefront of Gandhi's mind, in the writings of Rousseau and Saint-Just, who hoped to feed the new generations of Republicans on bread, milk, and water, and in "cleansing" diets and popular therapies, and it also features in ritual fasts or those of initiation ceremonies.[6]

India's great epic, the *Mahabharata*, tells us that in the Satya-yuga, the first of the four world ages (characterized by peace and prosperity), animals were not killed in sacrifice. Rather, such sacrifices were introduced in the Treta-yuga, the following age, when people began to resort to violence as a means to adjudicate disharmonious situations (*Shanta* 34.82–84). The *Skandha Purana* (*Vasudeva Mahatmya*, 7–9) further describes the origin of animal sacrifice: Early in the Treta-yuga, due to a Brahmin's curse, the universe was afflicted by famine. The common people slaughtered animals to satisfy their hunger, but those who knew the progressive values of life did not, even though many of them would die of starvation. The sages told the people in general that they could sacrifice animals to the gods and eat their remains, but only if they did so as a religious sacrifice and not merely for personal survival. "After this allowance was put in place," the Purana tells us, "gods, kings, and men performed animal sacrifices and ate the meat that resulted from them. But those who were truly wise ate no meat, even if calamity resulted from it. Soon, however, the famine abated . . . ." The *Matsya Purana* concurs with this remote origin of animal sacrifice, and gives elaboration on how the followers of Kali, specifically, were to perform these sacrifices.

Worshipers of Kali were obliged to chant the Sanskrit word for meat (*mamsa*) into the goat's ear before slitting its throat. The word carries deep meaning. Etymologically, *mamsa* is broken down into *mam* ("me") and *sa* ("he"). According to traditional Indian philology, the implication is as follows: "As I eat him now, so he will eat me in the future."[7] This is an example of the law of karma: for every action, there is an equal and commensurate reaction. While the word *karma* literally means "act," it also implies causality.

The complete Sanskrit verse in which *mamsa* originally appears is as follows:

mamsa sa bhakshayitamutra
yasya mamsam ihadmy aham
etan mamsaya mamsatvam
pravadanti manisinaha

"That creature whose flesh I am eating here and now will consume me in the next life. Thus, meat is called mamsa, as described by learned authorities."

The Sanskrit noun *pashu-ghna* ("he who kills the body"), a word also associated with meat-eating and allied concepts, can apply to both "meat-eater" and "one who commits suicide." This, too, reinforces the notion that a severe reaction awaits anyone who eats meat. In fact, the earliest Vedic texts endorse the idea that those who sacrifice animals in this life will be eaten by these same creatures in the next. (See *Kausheetaki Brahmana*, 11.3; *Shatapatha Brahmana*, 11.6.1; and *Jaimaniya Brahmana*, 1.42–44.) The *Laws of Manu* (5.55) echoes the same idea.

Narada Muni, cosmic sage revered in the Hare Krishna tradition and throughout the Vaishnava world, lays bare the karmic reaction to meat-eating in his instructions to King Prachinabarhi, an ancient prince who was enamored by opulent animal sacrifices: "O ruler of the citizens, my dear King, please see in the sky those animals that you have sacrificed, without compassion and without mercy, in the sacrificial arena. All these animals are awaiting your death so that they can avenge the injuries you have inflicted upon them. After you die, they will angrily pierce your body with iron horns and then eat your flesh" (*Srimad Bhagavatam*, 4.25.7–8). This, again, is consistent with the traditional understanding of the word *mamsa*.

For the Good of All Creatures

Despite popular knowledge of meat-eating's adverse effects—and scriptural injunctions against such eating—the non-vegetarian diet has become widespread among Hindus in the modern world, just as it had in the early part of the Vedic restoration process. After two major invasions by foreign powers—the Muslim and later the British incursions into India—meat-eating again took hold among the common people, who developed the desire to be "civilized," to eat as did "the *saheeb*." Those actually trained in Vedic knowledge, however, never adopted a meat-oriented diet—either in days of old or in modern India—and the pious Hindu still observes vegetarian principles as a matter of religious duty. A full 83 percent of India's one billion people are Hindu, the majority of whom are vegetarian.[8] India is largely a vegetarian country, plain and simple.

The facts behind the statistics, however, are not that simple. India is changing fast. With the encroachment of Western culture, McDonald's and other meat-centered food chains are opening at whirlwind speed. The Anthropological Survey of India (ASI) recently released a 46,000-page survey, entitled, "The Life of the People of India." This survey—the end result of more than 500 sociologists engaging in fieldwork and some 3,000 other researchers analyzing contemporary Indian culture for nearly eight years—has uncovered surprising findings: A staggering 88 percent of India's Hindu population say that they would eat meat if they could afford it—this includes everything from beef and mutton to baby crocodiles, jackals and field rats, depending on their means. Many of those surveyed in the middle and upper classes reported that they already eat meat on a daily basis. Poor people admitted to eating meat too, but not daily. The report concluded by saying that while many hold on to values and traditions of the past, an increasing number of Indians are now eating meat.

Interestingly, the converse is true in the West. The Vegetarian Resource Group (VRG) estimates that there are nearly six million strict vegetarians in the United States alone—which is a significant increase within the last 10 years—with many millions more in European countries, and still more if one includes those who are occasional or less strict vegetarians (allowing eggs and dairy in their diets). These statistics are supported by more conservative research and consulting firms as well, such as the well-known Harris Interactive Group. A 2002 *Time*/CNN Harris Interactive survey backs up these results, as does the Natural Marketing Institute and a recent series of Zogby polls.[9] The growth of vegetarianism in the West is evidenced, too, by the increased number of vegetarian products on the market—Burger King offers a vegetarian burger, and most supermarkets now carry soy milk and vegetable alternatives to meat. Thus, the principle of supply and demand is a sure way of ascertaining the rise of vegetarianism in the West. It is the contention of this book—and the real irony behind the increasing popularity of the non-meat diet on Western shores—that the Hare Krishna movement, a movement identified with the East, has had a large hand in waving the vegetarian banner in the Occidental world.

But to return for a moment to the disarmingly poor show of vegetarian support in India, it should be pointed out that the majority of those participating in the above survey were secularists—the believing Vaishnavas, who comprise a good portion of the Hindu world, Jain and Buddhist monks, and other Brahmin priests were not called upon to be part of the study. Moreover, the sociologists and anthropologists conducting the research would likely find themselves interviewing India's peasant majority, many of whom associate meat-eating with a life of luxury and who would thus indeed eat meat if they could afford it. Thus, it might be argued that the survey results cited above do not give an accurate view of vegetarianism in the subcontinent. After all, a similar survey[10], asking how many Indians stand behind their ancient traditions—including vegetarianism—produced overwhelming results in the positive. This National Indian Survey (NIS), conducted in 2003, took place largely in Hindu temples, where the pulse of India still vibrates most loudly. Here it was found that literally millions still endorse their vegetarian heritage. In truth, vegetarianism in India is complicated. While Brahmins and those of the mercantile class (Vaishya) are traditionally vegetarian, the warrior or administrative (Kshatriya) and laborer (Shudra) classes were and are given to eating meat. Ultimately, however, most of India understands and endorses the vegetarian way of life.

This ultimate acceptance of vegetarianism among Hindus can be attributed, in great measure, to the very clear teaching of universal compassion found in India's sacred texts. The *Mahabharata* (*Shanti*, 109.10), in defining religious duty (*dharma*), acknowledges that in its best form, religion takes into account all of God's creatures:

Dharma exists for the general welfare (*abhyudaya*) of all living beings. Thus, that by which the welfare of the greatest number of living beings is sustained, that for certain is Dharma.

This idea is echoed throughout the tradition, which divides ethical consideration into two distinct categories: *sarva-bhuta-hita* ("devotion to the good of all creatures") and *loka-hita* ("devotion to the good of humanity"). The first ethical system, say Vaishnava texts, includes the second. If one cares for all living creatures, then one naturally cares for humanity as well. Accordingly, *sarva-bhuta-hita* is the superior code of ethics delineated in the scriptures and remains a central tenet of modern-day Hinduism.

The Vaishnava viewpoint is that a person should see the same life force in all living entities—regardless of "outer dress" (the body). The

Bhagavad-gita (5.18) sums it up as follows: "The wise see the same essence in a Brahmin endowed with culture and learning, a cow, an elephant, a dog, and a dog-eater." Since those who are wise see the same essence in all beings, say Vaishnava commentators, then how could one with such equal vision treat any living creature inequitably? To underline the point: Eating any of God's creatures would be a form of inequitable treatment and go against the spirit of this verse from the *Gita*. Further, those who cannot understand the principle of life in lesser beings may then eventually misunderstand what the life force is altogether and lose their sense of humanity. Thus, the *Bhagavad-gita* (6.32) gives us its own version of the Golden Rule: "The perfect yogi is one who considers all beings as dear as his own self." The true follower of the *Gita*, then, would uphold the principle of nonviolence in all its forms.

Vegetarianism and Nonviolence

In India, nonviolence has always been closely associated with vegetarianism. This was observed by the ancient traveler Megasthenes and also by Fa-hsien, a Chinese Buddhist monk who, in the fifth century, traveled to India in order to obtain authentic copies of the Vedic scriptures. These scriptures, Fa-hsien wrote, unambiguously support the meatless way of life, and they base their predilection toward this diet on the importance of nonviolence.[11] The monk cites the *Mahabharata* (*Anu.*, 114.11): The great warrior Bhishma, he says, explains to Yudhishthira, eldest of the Pandava princes, that the meat of animals is like the flesh of one's own son, and that the foolish person who eats meat must be considered the vilest of human beings. The *Mahabharata* (*Shanti*, 141.88) indeed emphasizes this point. The eating of "dirty" food, it warns, is not as terrible as the eating of flesh. (It must be remembered that the Brahmins of ancient India exalted cleanliness to a divine principle.)

The *Mahabharata* is often associated with another epic work, the *Ramayana*. Together, these two texts are considered the greatest literary works of Asia, each strong in its support of vegetarianism. The *Ramayana* (5.31.4) informs us that elevated souls, such as descendants of the demigod Ikshvaku, shun meat-eating and violence in any form. Of course, the Ikshvaku dynasty, and other great dynasties of India, were not impractical: When necessary, they employed Kshatriya (military) methods to defend their kingdom. But it should be noted that the true Kshatriya was never violent in an antagonistic sense. Rather, he "protected others from violence," as the etymology of the word implies (from the root *kshat*, which means "hurt," and *trayate*, "to give protection.").[12] Regarding the *Ramayana*, D. N. Jha, in *The Myth of the Holy Cow*, cites numerous instances of Rama's Kshatriya tendency run amok[13]—killing animals for food and sacrifice. But as an incarnation of Vishnu, his behavior is necessarily extraordinary, and not to be followed by the common people. The *Ramayana*'s tenor is quite clear about the preferred behavior of ordinary human beings—that they should be vegetarian and compassionate toward animals. The *Ramayana* shows us, however, that the *ahimsa* ideal can only subsist in a certain environment, and that, outside of that environment, certain ideals must sometimes be suspended.

Indeed, the *Bhagavad-gita* teaches that one should not be fanatical about nonviolence and that total nonviolence is in fact impossible. Material nature forces us to commit violence, for even breathing necessitates the killing of countless microorganisms. Or, as the *Mahabharata* (Shanti, 15.25–26) puts it, "There are many creatures in water, in soil, and in fruit. Indeed, there are many creatures that are so minute that their existence can only be inferred. With the falling of the eyelids alone, they are destroyed." Thus, it is clearly impossible to live in a world without some form of violence. "Nonviolence in politics may work in terms of diplomacy," the *Gita* teaches, "but it can never be an absolute factor or principle."[14]

Mahatma Gandhi also acknowledged that nonviolence may exist within violence—albeit in very rare exceptions. "I have come to see," wrote Gandhi, "what I did not so clearly before, that there is nonviolence in violence. . . . I had not fully realized the duty of restraining a drunkard from doing evil, of killing a dog in agony or one infected with rabies. In all these instances, violence is in fact nonviolence."[15]

In other words, in the Vaishnava tradition, nonviolence has to be practiced with common sense, with guidance from scriptures and qualified teachers. Discussing the implications of the *Gita*'s teachings in this regard, Indian historian S. Dasgupta asks: If a dangerous beast enters a cattle shed, should one kill the beast or allow it to destroy the valuable cattle? Kill the beast, he concludes, for the principal objective is to maintain social order and the well-being of the people.[16]

Higher forms of nonviolence may include being "violent" for a greater good. This is the Kshatriya principle. According to the *Gita*, this principle supersedes any abstraction, such as unqualified nonviolence that may result in more harm done than good. True *ahimsa*, then, might more accurately be understood as "non-aggression" rather than "nonviolence." An extension of this idea is found in the Sanskrit word *anrishamsya*, which refers to "non-cruelty," and there is much scholarship these days about the implications of this word in connection to true *ahimsa*.[17]

The bottom line here is that while violence may at times be unavoidable, one should never be unnecessarily aggressive or unkind. Rather, to become truly advanced in spiritual life—and this should be obvious—one must be kind and compassionate. The Vaishnava scriptures merely extend this sense of kindness to all living beings—toward all of God's creatures. Those with truly kind hearts cannot help but extend their mercy in this way, toward those who may be weaker. In fact, one of the last of the great Vedic kings, Maharaja Pariksit, is quoted as saying that "only the animal-killer cannot relish the message of the Absolute Truth" (*Srimad Bhagavatam*, 10.1.4). Therefore, India's scriptures inform us, to obtain spiritual knowledge, one must begin with being vegetarian. This correlates well with Prabhupada's statement at the opening of this chapter.

The fundamental principle of all Vaishnava injunctions is that everything must be done in pursuit of God's will. For example, even the action of hunting (*mrigaya*), which is considered sinful, can be counteracted by austerity (*tapas*) and surrender to God (*Srimad Bhagavatam*, 10.51.63). This surrender is the crucial point in Vaishnava religion. To give some indication of its importance, the *Varaha Purana* (8.26–30) relates a story in which an ignorant but sincere hunter kills only one animal a day and ritually offers part of the flesh to God, for it is his misguided belief that his offering purifies the killing. In the story there is also a vegetarian forest dweller, a farmer who harvests grain. The Vashnavas recognize grain as a lower yet conscious life form, and in the process of accumulating grain, the farmer kills more living beings (in the form of seeds and plants) than the hunter. The farmer, however, never offers anything to God. The story concludes that he was therefore more sinful than the hunter and guilty of *maha-himsa*, the highest violence, for he is one "who eats food without ritual offering." This story, the Purana tells us, is not to endorse meat-eating, which is sinful, but to eulogize offering food to God, which eradicates all sin.[18]

"The Lord's Mercy"

As mentioned in the previous chapter, Vaishnavas believe that one should offer all foods as a sacrifice to God: "[A]ll that you do, all that you eat, all that you offer and give away, as well as all austerities that you may perform, should be done as an offering unto Me" (*Bhagavad-gita*, 9.27). One should not conclude from this, however, that everything is offerable (as our simple hunter wrongly believed). The *Gita* (9.26) specifies exactly what should be offered: "If one offers Me with love and devotion a leaf, a flower, fruit or water, I will accept it." There are other references in Vaishnava texts confirming that fruits, vegetables, grain, nuts and dairy products are fit for human consumption. Followers of the *Gita* thus refrain from offering meat, fish, poultry or eggs, for these are not sanctioned by either the scriptures or the Vaishnava prophets. According to the Krishna tradition, then, submission to God's word and the words of His true devotees invariably leads to vegetarianism.

The *Bhagavad-gita* (3.13) further declares that one who lovingly offers his food to God, according to scriptural guidelines, is freed from all sinful reactions and consequent rebirth in the material world: "The devotees of the Lord are released from all kinds of sins because they eat food which is offered first in sacrifice. Others, who prepare food for personal sense enjoyment, verily eat only sin."

The remnants of such devotional offerings are called *prasadam* (literally, "mercy"), a concept to which we were introduced in the previous chapter. What needs to be pointed out here is that *prasadam* is not peculiar to the modern-day Hare Krishna movement. Rather, it is a phenomenon that exists throughout India, and can be found in Vaishnava and many non-Vaishnava temples. And this has been going on for centuries. The largest shrines, such as Sri Rangam in South India and Jagannath Mandir, the main temple in Puri (state of Orissa), all freely distribute sanctified vegetarian foods (*prasadam*) for the benefit of the multitudes that attend their worship daily.

Paul Toomey, an anthropologist specializing in India's sacred culture, writes about widespread use of *prasadam* as observed in his field research:

> Food offerings are present in nearly all Vaishnavite worshiping, from the intimacy of the household shrine to the more public setting of the temple. The central transformation in food ritual occurs when food, called *bhoga* (literally, pleasure or sensual enjoyment, anything that can be enjoyed by the senses), is set before Krishna's image and Krishna himself is believed to consume it, usually through . . . his eyes. In this act of consumption *bhoga* is metonymously transformed into more love-laden *prasada* or consecrated food. This is a pan-Indian phenomenon.[19]

One of the most celebrated Vedic sages, Narada Muni, was inspired to embark on the spiritual path by tasting delicious vegetarian foods offered to the Lord. His example in this regard is not uncommon. The entire modern-day Hare Krishna movement might be seen as an institution of Narada Munis, for many of its members were introduced to Vaishnavism by first tasting *prasadam*. Hare Krishnas distribute such sacred vegetarian foodstuffs as a primary religious observance, as an upcoming chapter will reveal in delicious detail.

2

India's Sacred Cows

The blood of the cow is very nutritious, but civilized men utilize it in the form of milk. Milk is nothing but cow's blood transformed. You can make milk into so many things—yogurt, curd, ghee (clarified butter), and so on—and by combining these milk products with grains, fruits and vegetables, you can make hundreds of preparations. This is civilized life—not directly killing an animal and eating its flesh.

—Swami Prabhupada

Cows make milk from grass and blood. Miraculously, their blood carries their digested food into their udders, which manage to change the raw materials into what eventually becomes milk. To make 50 pounds of milk in a day, a cow pumps roughly 10 tons of blood through her udder. She engages in a considerable amount of grazing and cud-chewing, and then, like a magic trick—puff!—we have milk. How can grass and blood produce milk? The transformation that takes place is as mystical as changing ordinary food into *prasadam*; it's as magical as life itself.

"Within your body, by mystic power, you can transform food into blood and tissue," writes Swami Prabhupada. "Similarly, by mystic power, the cow eats grass and produces milk."[1] Modern science expresses the same idea in another way. They say that the chemicals of life vary in proportion and distribution from one species to another, and that a specific biochemical condition accounts for the cow's producing milk. While this sounds more scientific, it still can't explain just how the phenomenon occurs.

Prabhupada asks us to look at the subject more deeply, with a theological lens. "But who produced those chemicals and that arrangement?" He challenges the scientists directly: "You cannot produce milk from grass in your laboratory. But the cow can give you milk by mystic power."[2] Concurring with his spiritual master's vision, Suresvara Dasa (Richard Hall) thinks fondly about the cows of a Hare Krishna farm community in Port Royal, Pennsylvania:

> Twice daily our ruminating mystics enter the barn to let down their milk. Giving milk is a function of motherhood; kindly treatment helps the flow. And so our milkers sing to the cows as they go, handling each mother with care as they draw the sweet liquid from her body. From nature's lab comes miraculous milk.[3]

"So protect the cow," concludes Prabhupada. "Don't be ungrateful. That is Krishna's advice. From infancy, we are drinking the cow's milk, and if in return we cut her throat, that is barbaric, less than animal. Even an animal respects its mother. But the 'civilized' men are doing that—killing mother cow. And yet they want peace."[4]

Despite reserving this special place for the cow, it should be pointed out from the beginning that Hare Krishnas do not revere the cow as a divine being, at least not in the sense of being an *avatara* (Incarnation of God). They acknowledge earlier Vedic tradition, wherein Mother Surabhi—the primeval cow, the original prototype of all bovine entities—was churned at the dawn of creation. Hare Krishnas also have deep regard for the five products of the cow (*pancha-gavya*)—milk, curd (or yogurt), *ghee*, urine, and dung—for these products have objective virtue, as we will soon see. But there is no distinct "cow-goddess," as is generally supposed, nor are temples built in her honor. Rather, devotees of Krishna see an intrinsic value in her as a blessed creature; and her virtue and usefulness are based on common sense, practical concerns—and because she is dear to Krishna.

The Vedic lexicon *Nighantu* offers nine synonyms for "cow," three of which—*aghnya*, or *ahi* (both meaning "not to be killed"), and *aditi* ("not to be cut")—specifically forbid slaughter. These synonyms are found throughout the Vedic literature and are summarized in the epic *Mahabharata* (*Shanti-parva*, 262.47): "The very name of the cows is *aghnya*, indicating that they should never be slaughtered. Who, then, could slay them? Surely, one who kills a cow or a bull commits the most heinous crime." This, in turn, was merely echoing the words of the *Rig Veda* (8.101.15): "The mother of the cosmic powers, the daughter of the beings of light, the sister of the sun gods, the navel center of truth. I speak to those who are aware: do not harm the cow, for, in so doing, you harm the Earth and all of humanity."

Many continue to so glorify cows, especially those who are aware of ancient India's teachings on the subject. David Frawley, Director of the American Institute of Vedic Studies, writes, "The outer care of the cow reflects the inner care of the self: the cultivation of divine awareness, which yields the 'milk' of truth and pure perception."[5] This, of course, is paraphrasing Mahatma Gandhi, who said, "To me, the cow is the embodiment of the whole infra-human world; she enables the believer to grasp his unity with all that lives. . . . To protect her is to protect all the creatures of God's creation."[6]

Why this considerable veneration of the cow, spanning all of Indian tradition from the ancient Vedas to Gandhi and Frawley? Where did it all begin? And why is the cow held as so sacred in India to this day? These are some of the questions we will explore in this chapter. By analyzing the cow as she is perceived in India, past and present, we will shed light on why she holds a special place in the hearts of Krishna devotees worldwide.

Krishna, the Blue Cowherd Boy

Indian tradition's marked reverence and love for the entire bovine species might be traced to the fact that Lord Krishna is Himself a cowherd boy. Indeed, an early Vaishnava prayer, called *Gita-mahatmya* (Verse 7), boldly declares, "The *Bhagavad-gita*, which is the essence of all Upanishads, is just like a cow, and Lord Krishna, who is famous as a cowherd boy, is milking this cow. The hero Arjuna, to whom Krishna explains the *Gita*, is just like a calf, and learned scholars and pure devotees are those who drink the milk of this *Bhagavad-gita*." The "cow, cowherd boy, calf, and milk" imagery is not insignificant, for it serves to stress the wholesomeness and purity with which the *Gita*, Krishna, Arjuna, and "learned scholars and pure devotees" are identified in Indian culture.

This same Indian tradition asserts that the first created being in all the universe is a sage named Brahma, who is held to be the initial teacher of the Hare Krishna lineage. Brahma's very first spiritual instruction, found in the ancient text *Brahma-samhita*, is extremely telling, for it indicates the Supreme Lord's love for cows. The original Sanskrit reads, "*Govindam adi purusham*," meaning that the original person, i.e., God, can be called "Govinda," or "one who pleases the cows." Govinda, of course, is another name for Krishna.

Steeped in the antiquity of Vaishnava tradition, Krishna's popularity was firmly established with the *Srimad Bhagavatam* and the *Bhagavad-gita*, traditionally understood as part of an oral tradition going back well beyond 5,000 years. Lewis G. Regenstein observes bovine prominence in relation to the Krishna tradition:

> Cows are important to Vaishnavas. They figure in an important way in two of the five major Hindu religious holidays. Janmastami, in August, is the birthday of Lord Krishna, who appeared 5,000 years ago as a cow herder in the Indian village of Vrindaban. . . . Krishna demonstrated the necessity of protecting cows, and so is affectionately called Govinda, "One who gives pleasure to the cows."
>
> Today, Govinda is the central figure of renown for the International Society for Krishna Consciousness, popularly known as the Hare Krishnas. They consider it "most sinful to kill and eat the flesh of these noble animals."
>
> Gopastami, falling in mid-November, is the day on which cows and bulls are brought into the temples for worship and to be honored as sacred members of society. Since cows provide milk and bulls plow the fields, these bovines have traditionally been appreciated as important parts of the agricultural society of India.[7]

Here we are introduced to one of India's pragmatic reasons for revering the cow: agricultural necessity. In addition to reverence for Krishna, the people of India focus on the cow for a number of practical reasons, which is why philosopher Jeremy Rifkin has written, "Our relationship to the cow has been both sacred and secular, spiritual and utilitarian."[8] This is a subject to which we will return. For now, let us briefly remark that, while more obvious in India, cow protection and a general back-to-nature sensibility would be a boon to world economy and afford a less stressful way of living throughout our planet. Before we explore this idea more closely, however, let us look at Krishna's relationship with cows, to understand why it leaves such a deep impression on His devotees and on Indian society in general.

Interestingly, Lord Krishna, as God Himself, could have chosen a family of intellectuals (Brahmins) or political leaders (Kshatriyas) in which to enact His childhood pastimes, but He did not. These are, after all, the privileged classes, and one might assume that if God were to take birth at all, He would do so in a higher-echelon family. Still, if it is to be believed that God's appearance in this world is always imbued with special purpose, one must look closely at the choice He did make: to be born in a family of simple cowherds (Vaishyas) and to spend His youthful pastimes in a bucolic setting. Krishna is thus forever identified as the pastoral deity of Vrindaban, a special rural dwelling in India some 90 miles south of present-day Delhi. Here He lovingly tended His cows in the association of His close friends. Naturally, His life as a cow herder includes cows, calves, milk, and stories of nature's wonders. The implicit statement, say the texts, is that life in goodness, close to nature and cows, is preferable for those pursuing spiritual realization.

The stories of Krishna and His cows are famous. They are said to have occurred 5,000 years ago on our planet, to recur repeatedly on other planets, and to go on eternally in the spiritual world. What follows is but a taste of these charming and magical occurrences: Sometimes Krishna would sneak into the houses of the cowherd women, the elderly *gopis*, and steal their yogurt and butter. Then He would run off to a nearby forest to enjoy the goods with some monkeys that frequented His hideout. When the *gopis* would catch Him in the midst of His thievery, He would pretend to be innocent, saying,

"Why do you call Me a thief? Do you think butter and yogurt are scarce in My home?" Did He mean his home with Nanda and Yashoda (His parents) in Vrindaban, or did He mean the universe? Thought-provoking, since the entire cosmos is Krishna's home.

The *gopis*, however, would have none of this, and besides, the evidence—the remains of the stolen butter and yogurt—was all over Krishna's lips, and on the ground right in front of Him. The *gopis* insist that Krishna fess up, but He simply chides them in return: "This butter and yogurt are useless anyway. Even the monkeys won't eat it." (Of course not: Krishna fed them so much that they couldn't eat any more!) In the end, the *gopis* were so charmed by Krishna that they forgave His mischief. More, it endeared Him to them.

Krishna's mother, Yashoda, thought that little Krishna was stealing butter from the *gopis* because He wasn't satisfied with the butter in His own house. So, to improve her butter, Yashoda picked out several of her best cows and had them eat special grass, making their milk incredibly rich, fragrant, and flavorful. After collecting a bucketful of this milk, she began churning butter, with renewed dedication, for her transcendental child. Some might say that Krishna's initial thievery was meant to enhance Mother Yashoda's love as well as to to charm the elderly *gopis*.

As Yashoda busily churned, Krishna woke up from His afternoon nap and felt hungry. He walked over to his mother and caught hold of her churning rod. Yashoda temporarily stopped churning and looked at her divine son with great love. Then she lifted Him tenderly onto her lap and began to nurse Him with her breast milk. At that moment she noticed that the milk on the stove was boiling over. So she quickly put Krishna down and rushed to tend the overflowing milk.

Krishna, angry because his mother had left Him unsatisfied, picked up a stone, broke the container of freshly churned butter, and ran off to a secluded spot to eat it.

Meanwhile, Yashoda, having tended to the overflowing milk on the stove, returned to her churning area. Seeing the broken pot, she immediately understood that Krishna was the culprit and chased Him down by following His butter-smeared footprints. As she finally located Him, she beheld a most endearing sight: He was sitting on an overturned wooden mortar that was used for grinding spices, laughing as He gave butter to the monkeys, just as He'd done after plundering the *gopis'* houses. Recalling, however, that she was disturbed by the recent acts of her naughty child, she bound Him to the mortar to punish Him—but Krishna greatly relished her anger, for it was borne of motherly affection.

What is one to make of such stories?

First and foremost, it should be remembered that Krishna's "mischief" is far from ordinary. His life as an impetuous young boy is a gift to His devotees. True, it can be exhausting while in the midst of it, but Krishna has a way of endearing Himself in the long run—and this is His reason for engaging the devotees in these peculiar ways. Rather than evoking consternation, His rowdy pastimes ultimately serve a soteriological function, purifying, healing, and giving joy to all who take part in them. In short, these stories enable devotees to rise beyond the distance created by awe and reverence and situates them in a loving mood of divine intimacy.

Yashoda had such intense love for Krishna that she thought of Him as her baby boy; she had little concern that He was the Supreme Personality of Godhead, and indeed, contemplating His divinity would only have reduced her affection. In the Gaudiya Vaishnava tradition, one begins with the idea that God is great, as in most religious traditions, where a sense of formality and respect is established toward an almighty Creator. But as one advances in spiritual life, one becomes engulfed in a more intimate relationship. This takes one of five forms: it can be somewhat passive (*shanta*), or active as a servant (*dasya*), a friend (*sakhya*), a parent (*vatsalya*), or a lover (*madhurya*).[9] Such relationships represent an unfolding, if you will, of our eternal relationship with God in the spiritual realm, a relationship that we forget during our millions of years' sojourn in the material world, but that we recall when we become self-realized.

This is the height of Vaishnava mysticism, an extremely accomplished level—not to be imitated or accessed in a cheap way—only achieved by the grace of God and that of His pure devotees. Once attaining this level, the devotee is covered by a phenomenon known as Yoga-maya[10]—a sort of metaphysical curtain that enables one to relish any of the intimate relationships described above.

After all, awareness of Krishna's Lordship evokes a sense of majesty and subservience before the Supreme. To enable His devotees to rise beyond this stage, with the ability to engage in intimate, loving exchange with Him, He masks His divinity. Imagine the *gopis* getting angry at Krishna for stealing their yogurt and butter if they were aware of His supreme position in the cosmic scheme of things. Or consider mother Yashoda: Would she bother to chase after Him or enjoy motherly affection if she were conscious that He is God? Thus, in the higher stages of Krishna consciousness one lets Krishna's divinity fall to the wayside and instead enjoys an intimate relationship with Him, which would be impossible if one were to think of Him as the Supreme Being.

All living beings have an original relationship with God, fitting into one of the categories from *shanta* to *madhurya*, as briefly outlined above. However, from birth to death, we are ensnared by our false bodily identity, having been deeply conditioned by our present life situation. Only by diligently adhering to the process of self-realization can we uncover our true identity and understand ourselves as we truly are.

But Krishna and his inner circle of associates never fall from the spiritual realm. They are eternally engaged in pastimes of love and affection in Goloka—"the world of cows"—which is what Vaishnava cosmological texts call the ultimate spiritual planet.

The scriptures contain numerous stories of Krishna and his cows. After countless early episodes as a precocious young boy, along the lines of the pastime described above, He and His cowherd friends, just a few years old, began taking care of calves. When Krishna turned six, He and the boys were put in charge of some fully-grown cows. Ancient Vaishnava texts tell us that each day they would play together while the cows ate the soft grass in Vrindaban's forests and pasturing grounds. Krishna would warmly hug these docile creatures and play with them; His affectionate relationship with them was the envy of all His cowherd friends. These cows were regarded as the most fortunate beings, associating with Krishna more than most of His human companions. The *Govinda-lilamrita* tells us that sages from the spiritual world and from India's ancient past took birth as cows just to be close to Krishna in His earthly pastimes. The only living beings that received more attention from Him, the *Lilamrita* informs us, were the *gopis*, the cowherd girls who loved Him more than life itself.

These details of loving exchange are elaborated upon in the Vaishnava scriptures, especially in the writings of the six Goswamis of Vrindaban, the intellectual systematizers of Chaitanya's tradition. In the esoteric books of the Goswamis we learn that Krishna's cows had names and distinct personalities, and He would call them with loving affection. This literature explains how Krishna and His cows would communicate by mooing, but that their real language was one of love, which is how Krishna ultimately communicates with all living entities.

The interrelationship between Krishna and His cows is extraordinary, and may be understood on various levels. While Vaishnava texts are clear that the stories should be taken as literal depictions of what actually transpires in the spiritual world, they are equally clear that there are metaphorical and symbolic dimensions to these stories as well. Barbara Powell, in her excellent book *Windows into the Infinite: A Guide to the Hindu Scriptures*, paraphrases Vaishnava commentaries, insightfully expressing these latter ways of perceiving Krishna's mysterious life with the cows:

> More than just a thief of butter, Krishna is the thief of love. The pots of butter represent the hearts of devotees. He breaks through the hard outer shell (ego, desire, ignorance, etc.) and releases the soft, sweet self within, the Atman. This He "devours." . . . It is often a painful process. The women of Vraja and the pots of butter are doubles; Krishna's breaking the pots corresponds to His breaking their hearts by prolonging the agony of the soul's yearning for Him, and the ladies' anger reflects the frustration of the soul struggling for Him. But like the butter inside which He devours, the women soften to Him, are overcome with love for Him, and surrender gladly to this love.[11]

But why this emphasis on cows? As we have seen, the Krishna tradition says that all living beings are equal, i.e., that each bodily form encases the same sort of spirit-soul, part and parcel of Krishna. And yet, a special place is reserved for cows. Why this disparity? In an attempt to answer this question, we will now turn to the distinct qualitative difference of the bovine species and why it is so revered in Indian tradition.

Mother of Mankind

In addition to her Krishna connection, the cow is honored in her own right as a mother of human civilization and as an essential part of the agriculture and economy of India. According to the Vedas, the cow is one of human society's seven mothers—the six others are the biological mother, the wife of the spiritual master, the wives of the Brahmins, the wife of the king, the Earth, and the nurse from early in one's life. But in some ways, the cow is most important. As Gandhi says,

> Mother cow is, in many ways, better than the mother who gave us our birth. Our mother gives us milk for a couple of years, and expects us to serve her when we grow up. Mother cow expects nothing of us but grass and grain. Our mother often falls ill and expects service from us. Mother cow rarely falls ill. Our mother, when she dies, expects expenses of burial and cremation. Mother cow is useful dead as when alive.[12]

Though perhaps overstated, Gandhi's glorification of Mother cow tells us something about the intensity with which Indians regard the bovine species. Indeed, the *Srimad Bhagavatam* (10.8.16) reports that while Krishna loves all living entities equally, He nonetheless has a special place in His heart for both Brahmins and cows. And of the two, says the *Bhagavatam*, Krishna gets more pleasure from serving the cows. This is because He sees Brahmins as those who disseminate knowledge—which is important—but He sees cows as repositories of love, which is more important. He sees them as peaceful and benign, as His dearest friends, and as essential for human society—freely giving their milk to one and all. They feed their own offspring, and, by nature's arrangement, have much milk left over for the nourishment of human society.

According to Ayurveda, the ancient Indian system of natural healing (to be discussed in the next chapter), cow's milk is one of the best foods for human beings, though it should be served hot, not cold, as it usually is in the West. (ISKCON devotees traditionally have a cup of hot milk every evening.) The virtues of milk have long been known, even in the West, though in recent years it has also been associated with a number of health problems. Ayurveda teaches that discolored, odorous, or old milk is toxic and produces diseases. Modern milk is homogenized, changing its molecular structure and turning it into a grayish liquid, which is then bleached or dyed before being sold. In addition, pasteurization causes milk to become odorous, which must be masked with chemicals before it is packaged for its often long journey to local stores. Modern dairy cows, too, are more or less tortured throughout their lives, and are administered numerous drugs for various purposes. By Ayurvedic standards, then, modern milk is problematic and can contribute to disease. Today's Hare Krishna Vaishnavas thus often look for various options, and some even turn to veganism, that is, vegetarianism that eschews the use of dairy products. This is now seen as a legitimate approach to diet, both among nutritionists and within the Krishna movement.[13] In fact, daily Hare Krishna fare—rice, *chapatis* (flat whole grain bread), *dahl* (bean soup), and *sabji* (any of numerous mixed vegetable preparations)— lends itself to a vegan lifestyle. Still, most ISKCON devotees prefer to relish cow's milk and its derivatives with the consciousness that Krishna loves cows and that their milk is as pleasing an offering to Him as any other. That being said, devotees are conscious of the ill-treatment of cows on most dairy farms, and they have established their own rural communities to treat cows properly, so milk may be obtained without exploiting this most vulnerable of all mothers.

Krishna indeed sees cows as true mothers, and His love for them is on a par with His love for Mother Yashoda. Prabhupada, too, forcefully asserts the "cow-as-mother" conception:

So if the cow is your mother, how can you support killing her? You take the milk from her, and when she's old and cannot give you milk, you cut her throat. Is that a very humane proposal? In India those who are meat-eaters are advised to kill some lower animals like goats, pigs, or even buffalo. But cow killing is the greatest sin. In preaching Krishna consciousness we ask people not to eat any kind of meat, and my disciples strictly follow this principle. But if, under certain circumstances, others are obliged to eat meat, then they should eat the flesh of some lower animal. Don't kill cows. It is the greatest sin. And as long as man is sinful, he cannot understand God. The human being's main business is to understand God and to love Him. But if you remain sinful, you will never be able to understand God—what to speak of loving Him.[14]

Elsewhere, expressing the stinging irony of the law of karma, or the idea that every action carries with it an appropriate reaction, Prabhupada says, "If you kill, you must be killed. If you kill the cow, who is your mother, then in some future lifetime your mother will kill you."[15] Prabhupada's allusion to karma is especially poignant here because of its implication of abortion—"kill your mother now and, in a future birth, she will kill you." Prabhupada means it quite literally. In numerous written articles he bemoaned the proliferation of abortion in his time (the 1970s), averring that it, and war, too, were the results of man's inhumanity to animals. He claimed that, metaphysically, a harsh reaction awaited those who supported animal slaughter in any way, and that this subtle reaction would gradually manifest in gross pain and suffering, both on an individual level and in terms of entire countries.

When discussing these matters, Prabhupada often referred to karma; it might thus be useful at this time to take a brief detour and explain exactly what karma means in this context:

One of the earliest principles of justice, emerging from the mists of antiquity and echoed in religions around the world, is the doctrine of karma. This doctrine holds that within the moral universe perfect justice reigns. Just as within the physical universe the law of conservation of energy is inviolate, in the moral universe conservation of *moral* energy is the rule.

As in physics every action produces an equal and opposite reaction, so too in metaphysics the doctrine of karma demands that when a person commits any good or evil action, that person must inevitably enjoy or endure the appropriate reaction to his or her deed. The doctrine of karma extends the pronouncement, "As ye sow, so shall ye reap" into a principle of absolute moral responsibility.

It is easy to understand, therefore, why the multitudes of people who believe in the law of karma as surely as they believe in the law of gravity endeavor to live lives of *ahimsa*—non-injury or nonviolence—since harm done to any other being will certainly result in a commensurate harm to oneself.[16]

Mother of Necessity

How we treat cows and how we treat the Earth—and thus ourselves—are inextricably related. Indeed, the Greek word *Gaia* and the Sanskrit *Gau* refer both to the Earth and to cows, interchangeably, and the words are used as such in common parlance. Western culture and Indian culture thus speak of Mother Gaia and Mother Cow in much the same way. In the *Srimad Bhagavatam* (1.16.18–25), the Earth is in fact personified as a cow. The text tells us that King Pariksit discovered the Earth in a deplorable condition, being tortured by a personification of our evil age, known as Kali. "The personality of religious principles, Dharma, wandered about in the form of a bull," says the *Bhagavatam*, "while the personality of the Earth appeared in the form of a cow. When they saw each other, the cow started to cry like a mother who had lost her child. Her beauty was replaced by remorse." As the text moves on, we see that the tears began to flow because man engages in sinful activities, raping the Earth and slaughtering the cow.

Earth and cow are "mother goddesses" in the sense that they regulate the natural ecosystem of the world and represent an organic intelligence that pervades the biosphere. This sense of natural wisdom associated with Earth and cows is only recently being explored in the West, as in James Lovelock's "Gaia Principle,"[17] but it has been known in India for millennia.

The Gaia hypothesis, first articulated in the West in the 1960s, puts forth the idea that the Earth is in some sense a single organism, defining and maintaining conditions necessary for the survival of all living beings. It argues that Earth's living organisms—as well as "non-living" surroundings, such as air, ocean, and so on—form a complex system that is capable of sustaining life on our planet. Or, when abused, it can turn it into an unfit place. Ideally, though, the environment works in conjunction with living organisms for the ongoing purpose of life and justice. This is in fact a variation on the same idea mentioned earlier, that the mistreatment of cows—who represent the natural world—results in a powerfully destructive karmic reaction. Kill our mother, she kills us. Hurt our world, and we hurt ourselves.

Vaishnavism has for millennia espoused a sort of "ecotheology" that is extremely relevant today. The Rig Vedic Purusha-shukta mantras describe the various parts of the created universe as identical with and yet emanating from the "organs" of the Supreme Being: "The moon was born from His spirit; from His eyes comes the sun; from His navel arose the sky;" and so on. The *Srimad Bhagavatam* continues along these same lines: the mountains are described as His bones, the rivers as His veins, ad infinitum. In this way, in addition to their strong sense of monotheism, Vaishnavas are also pantheists, holding that the visible universe is a manifestation of God. This vision enables Vaishnavas to revere the created world, not only as implied by their vegetarianism and sense of animal rights, but in their deep appreciation of nature. This appreciation is so intrinsic to their worldview, in fact, that it permeates their theology: They cherish, for example, stories about Krishna banishing the demon Kaliya for polluting the Yamuna River—evidence that their Lord protects the environment. Another example: The *Srimad Bhagavatam* contains, among other relevant passages, a segment (11.7) in which Dattatreya, a young ascetic, chooses nature as his guru. The sage reveals in detail what he learns from such representatives of nature as the Earth, fire, wind, spiders, children, and even his own body. The teachings are practical and ecologically significant. Though the moral of Dattatreya's story is not necessarily to seek out nature as one's guru, there is an implicit statement here about the high regard Vaishnavas have for it.

This profound respect for the natural world is crystallized in human interaction with the bovine world. As Gandhi says, "Cow protection to me is one of the most wonderful phenomena in human evolution. It takes the human being beyond his species. The cow to me means the entire subhuman world. Man through the cow is enjoined to realize his identity with all that lives . . . ."[18] In other words, through the cow, humans may learn to have greater regard for all of creation. More, they may become sensitive to the truth that hurting cows, or exploiting nature, means hurting and exploiting ourselves. Though in the West the karmic consequences of harming cows might seem like little more than philosophical abstraction, in India the idea is brought home in day-to-day life. As Barbara Powell writes,

> Cows, of course, are revered in India, being a universal Mother Goddess symbol. This is not strictly a psychological phenomenon; cattle are the mainstay of Indian rural life and, as far as we know, always have been. Milk and milk products are a staple element of the Indian diet, and dung is used as fuel for cooking and heating. Bulls are work animals which pull plows and grindstones. In the Indian economy the cow is literally life itself. Dead cows mean dead humans. The bull is a father who works the land while the cow is a mother who feeds her hungry human children along with her calves.[19]

Thus, we are introduced to the grassroots reasons for "cow worship" in India: Mother cow adds to the longevity and life cycle of the Indian people. Simply put, cattle are more valuable to farmers when grazing than when on their plate. Since the protection of cattle also means protection of the farmer's lifeblood and the nation's economy, the living cow is understandably revered in Indian culture. Mahatma Gandhi confirmed this pragmatic reading of the cow's divinity: "Why the cow was selected for apotheosis is obvious to me. The cow was, in India, the best companion. Not only did she give milk, but she also made agriculture possible."[20]

Products coming from a living cow are thus considered pure and purifying for those who use them. It should be noted that when Indians speak of "cows," they are generally referring to all bovine cattle (though the cow herself, of course, is especially revered). Prabhupada supported this view:

Prabhupada: The duty of the agriculturist is to give very careful protection to the cows especially.

C. Hennis: This doesn't apply to bulls and bullocks and male animals generally, does it?

Prabhupada: No, bullocks also. Cow means bullock also. . . . Cow is feminine, bullock is the masculine, that's all.

C. Hennis: So it's the whole bovine race that's protected, and not just the female cows?

Prabhupada: No, both the male and female. The bullocks are used for so many other purposes. They can till the field. They can be used for transportation, so many other purposes. Or even we are using them to spread Krishna consciousness. During Krishna's time . . . Krishna was born of a very well-to-do father, but at that time the bullocks were engaged for transportation from one village to another. (Conversation in Geneva, May 31, 1974)

In this way, bulls and even buffalo are also important. For people who till the land, the value of the cow is not only in her giving of milk but in her potential to provide male offspring, who then serve as tractors or trucks for farmers. The buffalo provides high-fat milk, more so than the cow herself, which is then converted into *ghee*, clarified butter, and used in cooking. *Ghee* does not raise cholesterol levels, is high in various vitamins, and stores well for long periods of time—one of the many bovine products that has miraculous qualities.

Amazingly, the ancient Vedas mentioned the purity and all-purpose nature of cow products thousands of years ago. But only in the last century has science been able to support these claims. Cow dung, for example, is widely used as a purifying agent when mixed with water. Throughout India it is applied as a wash to the body or to household objects—and, due to modern research, it is now found to have all antiseptic properties, making its use as a cleansing agent understandable.

Cow excrement is also a cost-effective fertilizer. Through a form of organic composting, dung naturally generates methane fuel; cow's manure can be sun-dried into patties, creating a slow-burning cooking and heating fuel that does not require the cutting down of trees. These dung cakes are superior to both coal and wood for cooking, because their slow-burning quality makes them especially useful in the gradual warming of milk—essential in the production of *ghee*. Also, since grain crops can't be digested unless baked or boiled, Indian farmers view this kind of cooking as essential. Narasimha Dasa, an author and scholar of India's sacred traditions, writes:

> Cow manure could transform desert soils, such as those in the Middle East and northern India, into fertile humus-rich soils that would retain moisture and support vegetation even with scarce rainfall. As the ground-cover vegetation became more lush and trees started growing, moisture retention would increase the natural opulence of the land with beneficial microbes and plants and soil-building insects and animals. Manure, in fact, makes cow protection highly profitable even if the milk production is low and the bulls are not fully engaged. Cow protection and bull protection are one and the same, of course, but people usually think the monetary profit is found in milk. Manure can be more profitable, however, because it leads to greater milk and grain production.[21]

Cow urine, in its own way, is equally valuable: It is a natural and fully biodegradable cleanser and proven disinfectant (with an extremely high ammonia content). Cow urine is also useful as an ingredient in any number of Ayurvedic medicines. Rifkin sums up the usefulness of the cow as follows:

> To a great extent, the very survival of the Indian population depends on the contribution of this most useful of animals. The cows provide most of India's dairy requirements. The ox provides traction for 60 million small farmers whose land feeds 80 percent of the Indian population. Indian cattle excrete 700 million tons of manure annually, half of which is used as fertilizer to maintain the soil. The rest is burned to provide heat for cooking. Harris has estimated that cattle

dung provides Indian housewives with the thermal equivalent of "27 million tons of kerosene, 35 million tons of coal, or 68 million tons of wood." Cow dung is even mixed with water and used as a paste to make household flooring. Each day small children all over India follow the family cow around on her daily rounds collecting her valuable excrement for a variety of household uses.[22]

Interestingly, with the exception of lactating cows and working bullocks, the majority of India's bovine population do not feed off fodder crops. Rather, they eat straw, stalk, grass, and other things that have little value to humans.[23] And it will always be this way: If India's wandering bovines were fed fodder crops rather than straw or grass, their dung would be too liquid, rendering it useless as fuel. Consequently, cattle in India do not compete with humans—they exist symbiotically.

Still, a team of experts has concluded that perhaps one-half of India's cattle should be regarded as surplus—useless—and should be eliminated.[24] Though this idea is accepted blindly by some of India's political leaders, it has been challenged by anthropologist Marvin Harris, whom Rifkin mentions in the above quote. Harris notes that "useless" might mean one thing to a farmer, and still another to a price- and market-oriented agronomist.[25] Besides, why should any cows be considered surplus? The roaming half-starved cattle in India have proven that they are in many cases resilient, with remarkable recuperative abilities. As a result, their breeding patterns are erratic. Since an Indian farmer can't know which of his cattle are "useless," i.e., unable to reproduce, it is disadvantageous for him to slaughter any one of them.

In addition, if governmental leaders put into effect their ongoing plans to eliminate their less fortunate, sickly cattle, they would then also need to include plans for an alternative energy source. From the perspective of India's rural population, the development of any other type of fuel, regardless of its quality, could never compete with cow dung, for such dung is available to India's multitudes at no cost. Thus, it is unlikely that tractors, petrochemicals, and even nuclear power will ever replace the simple bull and cow.

It should be mentioned here that devotees of Krishna support organic, free-range farms (if Hare Krishna farms as such, a subject to which we will soon return, are not located near one's home), for at least on some organic farms the cows are treated well and are not fed genetically modified feed or treated with antibiotics or hormones. Devotees want to offer Krishna the best ingredients, too, which are naturally organic and relatively free of modern-day poisons. Unfortunately, the vast majority of all dairy cows in the United States and Europe are tortured and genetically altered in various ways, and their byproducts are irradiated and full of pesticides, hormones, and insecticides. For these reasons many devotees are now looking to alternatives: milk from non-animal sources or from organic, free-range farms. Paying attention to such things is all part of applying Gaudiya Vaishnavism in the present day and age.

In India, such natural approaches to farming and life have been applied for millennia, for their scriptures tell them that a polluted environment grows out of a polluted consciousness. And so Krishna-conscious farmers—whether in India or in the West—take great pains to keep a pure heart, which is naturally reflected in their approach to the environment.

When their bovine friends die of natural causes, farmers traditionally give them to members of lower castes according to their needs. Cattle protection does not prohibit the "untouchables" in India from even eating the flesh of these animals, or from using their horns, hoofs, and skin in countless other ways. Likewise, while Prabhupada clearly taught respect for Mother cow, he was willing to tolerate compromise for those who could not restrain themselves from eating meat, as long as they did not kill the animal, waiting instead for it to die of natural causes. He did not encourage organized slaughterhouses, but he could understand a given individual's attachment to beef-eating. In his teachings to others, therefore, his first principle was no meat-eating at all; then, if that was not possible, he allowed the eating of animals other than cows; and, finally, if one could not refrain from eating beef, then one could do so after the cow had died on its own. Of course, these concessions were for the common people, not for his disciples, whom he expected to live at the highest standards. He was easier on others. In his own words,

manpower and funding to keep such a program going, and so the success of establishing this little glimpse of Vedic India in modern-day Pennsylvania suffered from the economic ups and downs associated with much farming in the United States.

For this reason, in 1985, the devotees in Gita-nagari organized a visionary program that revolutionized cow protection around the world. The "Adopt A Cow" program, as it was called, began as the brainchild of Advata Acharya Das (Arvind Singh), an anesthesiologist from Uttar Pradesh, India, who made his home in Gita-nagari. Confident that his Indian countrymen had a deep-rooted, inborn love for cows—even if they set this love aside as they relocated in the West—he devised a program that would give Indians and others an opportunity to help and protect them. Gaura Hari (Herb Bressack) and Paramananda (Ben Jenkins), two leading devotees at Gita-nagari, immediately recognized the substance of Advaita Acharya's plan and met with the board of directors at Gita-nagari to push the program through. The idea met with some resistance. The question was an obvious if depressing one: "Who will contribute money to a cow protection program in the States, where meat-eating is practically a way of life?"

It became increasingly clear to Advaita Acharya that if he wanted others to make a commitment, he would have to lead the way. He spent $1,500 of his own money to place an advertisement in *India Abroad* (a New York-based Indian newspaper)—a double-page spread that explained the philosophy behind cow protection, listed prices for cow adoption, and included visuals of the beautiful cows themselves. The ad encouraged natives of India to actually follow the tradition of their birth—to "make a stand for world peace" and to fulfill their religious obligation to "protect the cow." Similar ads soon appeared in newspapers and magazines throughout the States; personal letters were sent to 15,000 Hindus—and this was just the initial endeavor. While Indians comprised the first contributors to "Adopt A Cow," animal lovers from around the world, of all different nationalities, began to lend support. As the months turned into years, the program became a huge success.

In fact, the success was almost immediate. CNN filmed a documentary that aired on TV stations nationwide. *The New York Times*, the *Philadelphia Inquirer*, and other major newspapers and magazine sent reporters to cover "Adopt A Cow," and all initial reports were favorable.

All of the people who "adopted" cows received a framed, full-color picture of their adopted bovine, along with a monthly newsletter and a milk-sweet made directly from the assets of their newly chosen family member. In this way, hundreds of thousands of people adopted cows, and millions of dollars were collected on their behalf. The funds enabled devotees to care for their bovine population in style, with the cows and bulls living well, as nature intended.

ISKCON farm projects around the world began to open up and prosper, and numerous such communities thrived for many years, throughout the '90s. These programs, however, were difficult to keep in place. Manpower and enthusiasm tended to fall away, as did youth, and most of these projects are now merely being maintained, rather than growing. Still, there are a number of hard-working cow-related projects in ISKCON today, reminiscent of Gita-nagari in its heyday. Labangalatika Dasi runs a thriving cow protection program in Maharashtra, India, while Shyamasundar works diligently in the movement's *goshala* for cows and agriculture at Bhaktivedanta Manor, in the UK. Rohita is in charge at New Talavan in Mississippi, and Kurmarupa has a "save the cow" project—*pinjrapoli*, a retirement program for cows—in Vrindaban, India. In short, devotees from all quarters are working hard to apply Swami Prabhupada's teachings on cow protection:

> At the present moment in this age of Kali, both the bull and the cow are being slaughtered and eaten up as foodstuff by a class of men who do not know the brahminical culture. The bull and the cow can be protected for the good of all human society simply by spreading brahminical culture as the topmost perfection of all cultural affairs. By advancement of such culture, the morale of society is properly maintained, and so peace and prosperity are also attained without extraneous effort. When brahminical culture deteriorates, the cow and the bull are mistreated . . . .[28]

Though there are numerous devotees taking up the mantle, several of the most prominent should be mentioned. First, there are Suresvara, Vishakha Devi (Jean Griesser), and Hare Krishna Dasi (Noma Petroff)—three outspoken authors in the movement, who write on cows and agriculture from a number of different perspectives. Ranchor Prime, too, is active in the field of cow protection, but from a slightly different angle. Also a published author, with numerous books to his credit, Ranchor tackles the subject from an environmental perspective. He is an advisor on religion and conservation to the Alliance of Religions and Conservation, and he is co-founder and director of Friends of Vrindavan, an environmental charity active in Britain and India.

Nowadays, cow protection in ISKCON is virtually synonymous with the husband-and-wife team of Balabhadra (William Dove) and Chayadevi Dasi (Irene Dove), the managing directors of the International Society for Cow Protection (ISCOWP). Incorporated in Pennsylvania in March 1990, ISCOWP's primary concern is to present alternatives to agricultural practices that support and depend upon the meat industry and industrialized, petroleum-powered machinery. To this end, ISCOWP trains oxen (male cows or steers) to replace farm machinery and thereby show that the slaughter of these animals is not only cruel but a waste of resources. ISCOWP teaches that cow protection and ox-power are universal and nonsectarian, available to all regardless of race, creed, or nationality, and needed by all, whether they know it or not.

ISCOWP seeks to make widely known ISKCON's standards of cow protection, which are based on the teachings of Swami Prabhupada and the earlier Vedic tradition. Under the auspices of ISKCON's Ministry for Cow Protection and Agriculture (the chief minister of whom is Balabhadra himself), devotees concerned about cows have formulated ISKCON's Minimum Standards for Cow Protection. These standards, which are available on the ISCOWP website (www.iscowp.org), are the basis of ISKCON's Law 507, which provides for the protection of cows and oxen. They contain many specific guidelines for proper care of animals, which can be usefully applied even to organizations outside ISKCON.[29]

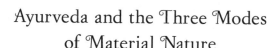

3

Ayurveda and the Three Modes of Material Nature

The *Ayurveda-shastra* recommends, *aushadhi chintayet vishnum:* "Even while taking medicine, one should remember Vishnu [Krishna]," because the medicine is not all and all [sic] and Lord Vishnu is the real protector.

—Swami Prabhupada

From the preceding chapters, it should be clear that ISKCON's diet is lacto-vegetarian, that is, a non-meat diet that includes dairy products. Such a diet is supported by India's ancient system of natural healing, known as Ayurveda (pronounced "I-your-VAY-da"), which distinguishes food in terms of the three modes of material nature—goodness, passion, and ignorance. These three modes and how they apply to food will be explained later in this chapter. What is interesting here is that Krishna devotees also compartmentalize food in this way, though they base their perceptions of the modes more on the *Bhagavad-gita* than on Ayurveda. Still, much like India's ancient medical texts, devotees claim that "we are what we eat," i.e., that various edibles affect the consciousness in various ways. Thus, while only peripherally interested in Ayurveda as such, the Hare Krishna movement is in line with much of what this system teaches, and a close examination of the movement in conjunction with Ayurveda will reveal this quite clearly.

Before coming to America, as a young man Swami Prabhupada

was a chemist, and his knowledge of herbs, spices, food, and healing was considerable. Consequently, in guiding his disciples, he often sprinkled his teachings with small bits of advice on nutrition and healthful living. For example, he encouraged devotees to each drink a small cup of hot milk every evening. Warming the milk, he told them, simulates the way it appears in nature. When it comes from the teats of cows in pasture, it is naturally warm and sweet. In this form it "helps to develop finer brain tissues," he told them, and, unlike cold milk, it would enable them to sleep more peacefully. His words are backed by science: the amino acid *tryptophan*, found in milk, functions as a natural and mild sedative, and it is more easily absorbed in the system when milk is heated.[1]

Prabhupada also encouraged massage, morning walks, and two showers each day—elements of Ayurveda that would be of practical value in devotees' lives. In this way, he offered his young followers advice on diet and holistic approaches to health and well-being. If allopathic medicine was deemed necessary, he encouraged it, urging the devotees to use common sense—"Judge something by its results," he would say. If it worked, then it was all right. Overall, however, Prabhupada favored naturopathic medicine and earthy responses to life and healing.

Prabhupada's faith in Ayurveda came not only from practical experience but from the fact that it is part of the *Atharva Veda*, one of the four revered Vedas of ancient India. Prabhupada thus saw the Ayurvedic system as divinely inspired, if also improperly practiced by the majority of its modern advocates. While he considered it among the best of all prevailing medical systems, he also cautioned devotees about its application—it is a material science, however subtle that science might be, and because of this, he noted, its limitations should be carefully marked.

Regarding food, the basic Ayurvedic paradigm unfolds as follows: When one consumes pure food, the body becomes healthy and the mind becomes pure; when the mind is pure, concentration is steady; when concentration is achieved, one can loosen the knots of the heart that bind us to the world of illusion.[2] This, of course, is a diet that Prabhupada could fully endorse, and he naturally recommended it for the devotees. After all, purity is among their many goals. And if bodily and mental purity lead to freedom from illusion, it is all the more desirable an achievement—for this can lead to Krishna consciousness. ISKCON, then, encourages its followers to eat the purest foods, and to make them even more pure by first offering them to Krishna.

At this point it would be prudent to look more closely at Ayurveda itself, even if this presents a slight detour from our central subject. By so doing, the reader will observe the impressive history and scope of Ayurvedic study and will understand an abiding aspect of ISKCON's heritage. Additionally, the reader will see one of the many reasons why devotees are enamored with early Vedic tradition and why it speaks to them in such unmistakable tones.

A Closer Look at Ayurveda

Ayurveda is perhaps the oldest system of natural healing in the world—predating even the Chinese system of medicine. The word *Ayurveda* is Sanskrit and is generally understood to mean "the knowledge of life" (*veda* = knowledge; *ayu* = life). A more accurate translation, however, would be "the knowledge of longevity." This is so because the sages of ancient India were extremely careful to distinguish between life, a spiritual phenomenon, and longevity, a term that refers to the proper maintenance of the material body. Here, too, resonance with Hare Krishna philosophy is immediately apparent: The distinction between body and self is fundamental to ISKCON thought.

Though death and disease present an ongoing dilemma for all humans, encased as we are in a material body, we nonetheless search for practical and effective methods of bodily maintenance. Of course, people on the spiritual path look for this as well. The difference is that aspiring spiritual seekers want to maintain and care for their bodies in ways that do not compromise or infringe on their spiritual practices. The achievement of these dual and interdependent goals is the purpose of Ayurveda, which makes it more than an ordinary medical science. It not only elucidates the healthiest interaction of body and mind but also prescribes guidelines for realizing the relationship between these two and the eternal spirit within each of us. It is thus totally holistic.

While the science of Ayurveda was put into written form about 50 centuries ago, it has an oral tradition that dates back even further. Modern practitioners of the science, however, are more indebted to latter-day encyclopedias—such as the *Charak Samhita* and the *Shushruta Samhita* (named after their respective authors)—than to the ancient Vedic texts. Still, these works are based on knowledge found in the Vedas, and discuss in detail such subjects as pediatrics, obstetrics, gynecology, internal medicine, otolaryngology and plastic surgery. Modern scientists are still in awe at the depth and clarity of Ayurvedic information; it is a mystery that such a complex system was conceived so long ago.

An understanding of the Tridosha theory is central to an understanding of Ayurveda. The *doshas* are dynamic forces within the body and mind whose interactions produce the psychosomatic entity of a given person. The *doshas* are called Vata, Pitta, and Kapha—Sanskrit words that refer, respectively, to activity and motion, heat and energy, and structure and density. On the most gross platform, Vata, Pitta, and Kapha also refer to air, bile, and mucus. These three interact with the seven *dhatus*, or tissues—those derived from digested food, blood, muscle, fat, bone, bone marrow, and reproductive tissue.

Through our daily activities, the *doshas* and *dhatus*, which are interdependent, are constantly moved into a state of disequilibrium, and this is what causes disease. Proper equilibrium and thus health can only be regained by considerations of diet, climate, season, physical activity and mental discipline. Ayurveda deals with these things as a minute science. Its methods are mainly preventive (rather than waiting for disease to begin and attempting to cure it when it may already be too late). But the system also includes effective approaches to rejuvenation and the healing of established diseases.

Although genuine Ayurveda must be studied within a particular esoteric tradition—and, for this reason, Prabhupada was skeptical of many modern Ayurvedic doctors who showed no evidence of connection to any such lineage—a good facsimile exists today and is actually quite common among the people of the Indian subcontinent. According to estimates made by the World Health Organization, there are over 500,000 practitioners of Ayurveda, a quarter of whom have undergone five and a half years of training in recognized institutions. Of 115 institutions where Ayurveda is taught, 98 offer training exclusively in Ayurveda and most are affiliated with major universities. Two hundred and thirty-nine hospitals and 15,000 dispensaries offer Ayurveda treatment throughout India.[3]

Ayurveda is comprised of eight branches, viz., Kaya (general medicine), (2) Shalya (major surgery), (3) Shalakya (ear, nose, throat, mouth, and eye disease), (4) Bhuta Vidhya (psychiatrics), (5) Kaumara Bhritya (pediatrics), (6) Agada (toxicology), (7) Rasayana (rejuvenation or tonics), and (8) Vajikarana (virilification). The distinguished historian Will Durant, in his famous work *Our Oriental Heritage*, explains the unique nature of Ayurveda, and gives the reader a good idea of his respected opinion on the subject:

> Appended to the Atharva Veda is the Ayurveda (the Science of Longevity). In this system of medicine, illness is attributed to disorder in one of the four humours (air, water, phlegm, and blood) and treatment is recommended with herbs and charms. *Many of its diagnoses and cures are still used in India, with a success that is sometimes the envy of Western physicians.* [italics added for emphasis] The Rig Veda names over a thousand such herbs and advocates water as the best cure for most diseases. Even in Vedic times, physicians and surgeons were being differentiated from magic doctors and were living in houses surrounded by gardens in which they cultivated medicinal plants.[4]

India's ancient art of natural healing has been practiced on the subcontinent for over 2,000 years, and likely even longer than that. It continues on as a living medical tradition, its underlying principles and therapies forming the basis of many modern-day holistic techniques, such as complementary medicine, now used in the West. What is Ayurveda's staying power, and what is the basis of this unique system of healthy living?

How Ayurveda Works: The Personal Approach

According to Ayurveda, the body is made up of five basic components:

Prithvi (earth), Jala (water), Agni (fire), Akash (ether), and Vayu (air). The entire universe is also composed of these elements, and hence the food we eat, the water we drink, the air we breathe—all are combinations of these five, as all share with us the basic constituents of existence. These elements give rise to the three somatic *doshas* previously mentioned, Vayu (or Vata), Pitta, and Kapha, which in turn regulate the *dhatus*, or the tissues of the body. Each individual body is designed to elicit a particular interaction between these elements, and disease occurs when it does not take place. Ayurveda teaches that, according to these variables, persons should be given distinct medical and dietary recommendations, due to their having different types of physical constitutions. This principle is known as Prakriti ("nature"), or the unique genetic code of each individual. The word carries the implication of "one's own intrinsic nature," especially according to Ayurvedic texts. In the West, we might understand this as follows: No two people have the same fingerprints. The underlying teaching of Ayurveda is based on a similar truth.

This view is gaining ground among scientists and nutritionists.[5] In fact, Ayurveda has much in common with the Blood Type Diet (BTD), conceived by Dr. Peter D'Adamo (and popularized in his book, *The Eat Right Diet*)—a theory that is becoming prominent in America and Europe. This theory tells us that people are biologically grouped according to body/mind characteristics and should be prescribed specific lifestyles and diets that are appropriate for their individual blood type. Yolande Manson, a qualified Ayurvedic medicine practitioner and naturopath, notes the correlation between the two systems, but writes that "BTD recommends meat and animal products for all people except [blood type] 'A's. Ayurveda recommends meat and eggs for no one."[6] Manson attributes BTD's pro-meat stance to the fact that the theory is still in its infancy—still experimental—unlike its age-old Ayurvedic counterpart.

Ayurveda's similarity to BTD, however, is significant, for the principle of individual diets for individual people is the hallmark characteristic of India's ancient science. Though each physical constitution, being different, is naturally suited to differing diets and habits, there are other factors, too, such as race, country, seasons, hereditary concerns, environment, and so on, that play a role. In the same way, differing physical constitutions elicit different reactions to particular drugs or remedies, and therefore a conscientious Ayurvedic physician will never prescribe the same drug or medicine to any number of people, but will make necessary changes in prescription according to individuality. Modern medicine, on the other hand, mainly addresses generic bodily problems. Its treatment generally consists of masking the symptoms or, at best, killing the germs, bacteria or virus that may have caused a given infection. The "whole person" and underlying cause of disease are rarely taken into account.

Back to ISKCON

As stated, Ayurveda generally prescribes a lacto-vegetarian diet. However, being based on individual constitution, there are exceptions—and Ayurveda deals with these as well. The three modes of material nature, which we will discuss later, are central to Ayurvedic dietary considerations. For example, if one is in goodness, one will get the most out of a proper combination of healthy vegetarian foods; for those in passion, increased desire for bitter and spicy foods is not uncommon; and, in ignorance, people relish stale foods and even meat products. In certain circumstances, meat is even prescribed, though rarely. Prabhupada wanted the devotees to be Brahminical, in other words priestly, and he therefore recommended a diet that would bring them into goodness—lacto-vegetarianism.

According to Swami Sada Shiva Tirtha, a prominent authority on Ayurveda, "Ayurveda suggests using meat only as a medicine since meat does not actually rebuild and regenerate the cells and tissues. In the case of extreme weakness, such as advanced cases of anemia, red meat (or its substitutes like liver pills) and bone soups are useful to take until the anemia is treated."[7] Shubhra Krishan, author of the book *Essential Ayurveda*, writes, "Meat is considered a tamasic food [in the mode of ignorance]: one that carries with it the toxic chemicals and negative emotions (chiefly terror and helplessness) that sweep through an animal before it is slaughtered. Besides, it is seen as heavy, hard to digest. But if you cannot give up meat, you should eat it at lunchtime, when your *agni* [fire of digestion] is strong enough to digest it well."[8] In short, meat is frowned upon in Ayurveda, and only used in exceptional circumstances. This is implicit in the Hare Krishna movement, whose devotees, again, reject meat in toto. But their conception of food goes further. Already accepting vegetarianism as a given, Vaishnava food choices, based squarely on Ayurvedic principles, revolve around ideal food combinations for individuals in the mode of goodness.

The point is this: Different people require different elements for proper nutrition. Nutrition here refers to the health-giving substances found in food. We are accustomed to hearing about the calories, vitamins, minerals, carbohydrates and proteins contained in a particular food. But Ayurveda bases its nutritional science on a different set of measurements, the most important of these being the effects produced by the six *rasas*—sweet, sour, salty, hot, bitter, and astringent. These *rasas* refer to the food's ultimate response in the body—not necessarily to how the foods taste. And although there are only six *rasas*, the combinations of these *rasas* are extensive. Just how and when one combines these various tastes will affect one's nutrition and overall health as well. Prabhupada was a master at combining these *rasas*, and he incorporated much of this knowledge into the average Hare Krishna diet.

In the last century, modern nutritional therapy developed the use of large doses of vitamins and minerals synthesized from nature. But, for thousands of years, Ayurveda has taught the science of nutritional therapy without the need for expensive laboratories to produce artificial supplements. It recommends various food combinations and simple herbs to compensate for any deficiency in one's constitution. While Prabhupada did not deny the devotees the right to use vitamin supplements if they wanted to, he always encouraged proper eating and healthy behavior as more important.

The Yoga of Balance

The balance of the *doshas* (and the good health that results from their balance) depends on moderation and regulation in eating and sleeping. This is central to both Ayurvedic treatment and the practice of Krishna consciousness. The *Bhagavad-gita* itself (6.16) says that the true practitioner of spiritual life should not eat too much or eat too little, sleep too much or not sleep enough. When eating or sleeping is excessive, deficient, or done at improper times or in an inappropriate way, there is every chance that the body's *doshas* will become disturbed. Excessive eating or sleeping is called Athi-yoga and most people have experienced its disruptive effects. Deficient eating or sleeping is called Hena-yoga. When we artificially decrease our food or minimize our time for rest, we invite a disturbance of the *doshas* that will lead to disease. Improper action in regard to bodily demands is called Mithya-yoga. Eating at the wrong time or in an unsuitable place are examples of this. Ayurveda recommends Sama-yoga—meeting bodily needs in a regulated and proper manner.

Proper eating must create a satisfied mind and a balanced feeling in the body. If after eating the mind becomes agitated or dull, or if the body becomes heavy and tired, the food was inappropriate for the eater's constitution. To adhere to proper eating habits, six factors should be considered: the place, the time of day, the duration of time since the last meal, the kind of foods to be eaten, the order in which the food should be eaten, and the person's state of mind while eating. ISKCON devotees try to take these factors into account, though their overriding concern is that their food is *sattvik*, vegetarian, and offered to Krishna.

In Ayurveda, it is recommended that one drink water before a meal. This will help one avoid obesity and slacken appetite. Water *after* a meal, it is said, leads to obesity and disease.

As far as eating goes, Ayurveda suggests taking sweets at the beginning of one's meal, and in moderation. Aside from the foods we normally taste as sweet, Ayurveda includes legumes and wheat in this category. (Remember, Ayurveda judges by the ultimate reaction in the stomach—not by the way the food tastes.) These foods introduce body-building materials (such as amino acids) into the system. Ayurveda recommends that bitter, hot, or astringent foods be taken at the beginning of a meal as well. Modern science is also finding, after years of research, that such foods prepare the body for eating yet more food, and so they are preferable at the beginning of a meal.[9] The reason that heavy—and especially sweet—foods should be taken at the beginning is that the stomach secretes a large amount of hydrochloric acid at this time, enabling these dense foods to be more easily digested. In the West, we are accustomed to having our desserts last—and for this reason (among others) we have a problem with obesity and indigestion.

After the "sweet" foods are eaten, Ayurveda recommends the sour and salty foods. These consist of juicy, cooked vegetables, bean soup, and dairy (yogurt, perhaps). They are basically liquid in character and increase the fire of digestion. Then, after this, some rice or solid food can be eaten, which will lead to a satisfying meal and will minimize one's chances of becoming ill. Papaya, mango and yogurt may be taken as digestive aids. If a salad is eaten, Ayurveda suggests that it is taken with the sour or salty part of the meal. And the dressing should always have yogurt or lemon juice and salt. This makes the salad easier to digest and removes its tendency to increase the Vata *dosha* (which produces distention of the abdomen, gas, and constipation). Salads should not be eaten at the beginning of one's meals (as many people do) for the same reason. It is also recommended that one be wary of combining cooked and uncooked foods, as this can lead to indigestion. Similarly, fruits, say Ayurvedic texts, should not be eaten with a heavy meal. They should be eaten alone or with milk for a separate, light snack.

There are many variations on these themes, but this is a general overview of dietetics in Ayurveda. Prabhupada's prescribed diet for devotees, offered with tremendous latitude and incorporated loosely in ISKCON temples worldwide, is as follows: The morning meal consists of cereal, fruit and yogurt; midday the devotees eat rice, *dahl* (spiced bean soup), *chapatis* (a yeast-free, whole-grain flat bread), and *subji* (a variety of delicately cooked vegetable preparations, often with curd and *ghee*); before sleep, they usually have a light snack and a warm cup of milk. Alternate meals might include a healthy mix of nuts and raisins, or *kitchari*, which is a tasty blend of *dahl* and rice. Sunday evening and festival days are exceptions, and devotees partake of rich feasts that satisfy body, mind, and soul. They adjust the above diet according to both taste and their perceived individual constitutions, and they enjoy such healthy fare as they practice Krishna consciousness.

The diet recommended by Ayurveda, and adopted by ISKCON, is nutritionally sound, even by today's standards.[10] What's more, Ayurvedic traditions include literally hundreds of delicious, age-old recipes so that an ardent follower doesn't get bored. It offers a great deal to eat, a procedure for eating, and food for thought.

Doctors of the Soul

It must be reiterated here that devotees are more concerned with the soul than with the body, and while embracing Ayurvedic principles for bodily care, they look to the *Bhagavad-gita* and the *Srimad Bhagavatam* for spiritual advancement. According to Atmatattva Dasa, a senior member of ISKCON in Mysore, India, and a noted scholar of Vedic tradition: "[J]ust like the *dasha mulas* made into an 'arishtam' cures the diseases caused by the imbalance of the three *dhatus*, viz., *kapha*, *vayu* and *pitta* (mucus, air and bile), in the same way the *dasha mulas* of *Srimad Bhagavatam* (the 10 root subjects) will cure the diseases of material identification caused by the imbalance of the three modes (*gunas*), viz, *sattva*, *rajas* and *tamas* (goodness, passion and ignorance)."[11] In plain language, Dasa is saying that, in Ayurveda, there is a special medicinal product (*arishtam*) made from 10 herbal roots, and that this product can cure imbalances in the body. Similarly, he says, there are 10 primary subjects in the *Srimad Bhagavatam*, and, like their Ayurvedic counterparts, they have the power to correct the imbalances of the soul.

"Having established this *samya* and *sambandha* (resemblance and relationship) of Ayurveda and Vedanta," Dasa continues, "let us make an analytical study of the subject through the eyes of both Vedantic and Ayurvedic Acharyas. . . ." His idea here, based on traditional texts, is that there is an interrelationship between doctors who tend to our physical and mental woes—Ayurvedic physicians—and Vaishnava devotees of the Lord, who are doctors of the soul.

"In contemporary times," he continues, "it is Lord Chaitanya Mahaprabhu who has elaborately presented this vision, or *darshanam*, of Ayurveda-vedanta. He is the great Kaviraja (physician) of modern times, presenting the perfect medicinal *arishtam* to balance the three *doshas* of *sattva*, *rajas* and *tamas*. . . . The 10 essential subject matters of *Srimad Bhagavatam* are like 'Vedantic observation and prescription' by the (Ayur)Vedic Acharya Vyasadeva based on his own study of the (Ayur)Veda *shastra*, the *Vedanta-sutras*."

The analogy should be clear: Gaudiya Vaishnavism sees itself as a panacea for social ills, and, more, as the ultimate cure for all ontological ills as well. It is the healing herb for our spiritual estrangement from God. Dasa tells us exactly how this spiritual healing takes place: "In Vedanta, the '*guna samya*,' or the equilibrium of the three modes of nature, viz., *sattva*, *rajas* and *tamas*, which can be effected only by transcending them, is the prescription to become free from the disease of material existence, of repeated birth and death."

He elaborates: "Vedanta confirms that by the improper use of the three modes of nature, viz., goodness, passion and ignorance, one aggravates the sickness [known as] *samsara*, the cycle of repeated birth and death; and [when these three modes are in] good balance . . . one becomes unaffected [by them]." He sums up his study with the following six observations:

> From the *gunas* manifest the five material elements, viz., earth, water, fire, air and ether.
> The five elements constitute the physical body.
> From the same *gunas* manifest one's identity, intelligence and mind, which constitute the subtle body.
> Three *dhatus* are direct manifestations of the three *gunas* (*sattva*, *rajas* and *tamas*) and they interact through the predominance of two *gunas* (passion and ignorance).
> The imbalance of the *dhatus* causes diseases. Either excessive, deficient or misuse of the potency of the body causes this imbalance. The purpose of Ayurveda is to prescribe medicine and diet to balance the *dhatus*.
> The imbalance of the *gunas* causes the repetition of material existence and the miseries therein. The transcending of the *gunas* is the solution. Thus one becomes free from the miseries, even while living in the body.

"The body is a symbol of disease," concludes Dasa. "The disease may differ from one variety to another, but disease must be there, just as there is birth and death for everyone. So, by the grace of the Personality of Godhead, disease of body and mind are cured. Not only are diseases of the body and mind cured, but also the soul is relieved of the constant repetition of birth and death—our ultimate disease. . . . By raising the consciousness beyond the limiting influences of passion and ignorance (the [more] grossly influencing modes of matter), one can re-identify with the soul through factual realization of the self beyond the body."[12] To fully understand Dasa's conclusion, let us now more closely look at the three modes of material nature.

The Three Modes of Material Nature

As explained in the *Bhagavad-gita's* thirteenth chapter, the soul is entangled in the material world because of association with the three modes of material nature. The word "mode" is a translation of *guna*, which could more accurately be translated as "rope." In other words, the modes "tie a person up"—they keep him bound to the world of illusion. In the fourteenth chapter, Krishna explains in greater detail what the modes of nature are, how they act, how they bind us to the world of matter, and how one is liberated from their influence.

Krishna first explains that all living beings are born in the world when He personally places us here. He therefore describes Himself as the "seed-giving father" of all the various species of life, and explains that while related to us in this way, He is beyond the modes that engulf us. He is, after all, the source of these modes, and is consequently unaffected by them. Next, He elaborates on just what these modes are: *sattva* (goodness), *rajas* (passion) and *tamas* (ignorance).

Sattva, He tells us, is characterized by such qualities as truthfulness, virtue, purity, cleanliness, happiness, and wisdom. It situates us in gratitude and illumination, allowing us to proceed toward self-realization. *Rajas* is the mode of action; it is characterized by passion (in the sense of energy), emotion, desires, and greed. Ultimately, it leads to misery, for it incites an urgent need for sense gratification, forging a tight bond to the bodily concept of life. The symptoms of *tamas*, the mode of darkness, are illusion, lethargy, madness, and apathy. It serves as a conduit of bondage, immersing one in ever greater depths of ignorance.

These three qualities condition all living entities who take birth in the material world. Each of these qualities accumulates in a particular way in a given person's psyche, formed by activities that stretch back into past lives. If we look at people closely, we see that one mode tends to outweigh the others. In other words, in every person's life, one mode will predominate, governing the ways in which he or she acts, determining his or her inclinations and tastes.

As the *Gita's* fourteenth chapter moves on, Krishna describes the fate of differently conditioned souls after death, but this is too elaborate to address here. Most importantly, Krishna informs us that one can transcend the influence of the three modes and attain perfection by understanding just how these modes work and that Krishna, as their creator, is never conditioned by them. This is all we learn about the modes in the *Gita's* fourteenth chapter.

By the seventeenth chapter, however, the plot thickens considerably. Arjuna inquires about the validity of "making up" one's own process of religion. What is the fate, he asks, of one who concocts a method of worship, ignoring scriptural regulations? His question is pointed: "Is the faith of one engaged in such an imaginary form of piety considered to be in goodness, passion or ignorance?" In response, Krishna explains that there are three types of faith, corresponding to and evolving from the three modes of nature. He then describes the characteristics of four items—food (*ahara*), sacrifice (*yajna*), austerity (*tapasya*) and charity (*dana*)—according to each of the three modes. While his full exposition is theologically elaborate, in relation to our subject, Krishna says:

Foods in the mode of goodness increase the duration of life, purify existence, give strength, and increase health, happiness, and satisfaction. Such foods are juicy and fatty. And they are very conducive to the healthy condition of the body. Food that is too bitter, too sour, too salty, too pungent, too dry, or too hot causes distress, misery, and disease. Such food is very dear to those in the mode of passion. Foods prepared more than three hours before being eaten, which are tasteless, juiceless, decomposed, and have a bad smell, consisting of remnants and untouchable things, are very dear to those in the mode of darkness. (*Bhagavad-gita* 17.8–10)

This much is a translation from the Sanskrit. Swami Prabhupada comments on these verses in the following way:

The purpose of food is to increase the duration of life, purify the mind, and aid bodily strength. This is its only purpose. In the past, great authorities selected those foods that best aid health and increase life's duration, such as milk products, sugar, rice, wheat, fruits, and vegetables. These foods are very dear to those in the mode of goodness. Some other foods, such as baked corn and molasses, while not very palatable in themselves, can be made pleasant when mixed with milk or other foods. They are then in the mode of goodness. All these foods are pure by nature. They are quite distinct from untouchable things like meat and liquor. Fatty food, as mentioned in the eighth verse, has no connection with animal fat obtained by slaughter. Animal fat is available in the form of milk, which is the most wonderful of all foods. Milk, butter, cheese, and similar products give animal fat in a form which rules out any need for the killing of innocent creatures, and it is only through brute mentality that this killing goes on. The civilized method of obtaining needed fat is by milk. Slaughter is the way of sub-humans. And protein is amply available through peanuts, split-peas, *dahl*, whole wheat, etc.

Foods in the mode of passion, which are bitter, too salty or too hot, cause misery by producing mucus in the stomach, leading to disease. Foods in the mode of darkness are essentially those that are not fresh. Any foodstuff cooked more than three hours before it is to be eaten (except *prasadam*, food offered to the Lord), is considered to be in the mode of darkness. Because they are decomposing, foods in the mode of darkness frequently emanate a bad smell, which often attracts people in these modes, but repulses those in the mode of goodness. Remnants of food may be eaten only when they are part of a meal that was first offered to the Supreme Lord, or first eaten by saintly persons, especially the spiritual master.[13]

Thus, we see that Ayurveda, the *Bhagavad-gita*, and the teaching of the three modes loudly sing the praises of the lacto-vegetarian diet. In Prabhupada's commentary, he draws on the insights of great sages from the past. All of the renowned teachers of Gaudiya Vaishnavism support these conclusions, encouraging votaries to imbibe pure foods in the mode of goodness, to minimize foods in passion, and to do away with edibles in the mode of ignorance. Most of all, the Vedanta *acharyas* ask us to offer our food to Krishna as a religious sacrifice, because by so doing we will maintain ourselves not only materially, but spiritually as well.

4

"Thou Shalt Not Kill"

"Thou shalt not kill" does not apply to murder of one's own kind only, but to all living beings; and this Commandment was inscribed in the human breast long before it was proclaimed from Sinai.

—Count Leo Tolstoy

Some people argue that devotees are vegetarians solely because of *prasadam*—i.e., that Krishna only accepts non-meat foods offered to Him in sacrifice—and that if this were not the case, devotees might actually adhere to a carnivorous diet. Indeed, Prabhupada himself has said, "[W]e are not advocates of vegetarianism or non-vegetarianism. Of course, vegetarianism is very good, even for health's sake. But we do not take [i.e., eat] even vegetables if it is not offered to Krishna. That is our principle. If Krishna said that 'You give Me non-vegetarian diet,' then we can eat [that] also. But Krishna does not say."[1] Prabhupada makes this point in several places in his massive literary oeuvre. Such statements have been noted both by academics looking at the movement in terms of vegetarianism and animal sacrifice and by animal rights activists, who naturally view these quotes with some concern.

However, while the *prasadam* factor may be the devotees' main reason for vegetarianism, it is clearly not their only one. We have already explored the ancient mandate for cow protection; the importance of *ahimsa*, or non-aggression; the application of Ayurveda; and the impact of nature's three modes on life and food. These are also prominent factors in the devotees' chosen diet. But a Vaishnava also feels deeply for suffering beings. The *Srimad Bhagavatam* (3.21.31) is clear: "Showing compassion to all living entities, you will attain self-realization. Giving assurance of safety to all, you will perceive your own self as well as all the universe in Me, and Myself in you." In other words, a heart full of compassion for all living creatures holds the key to self-realization, the goal of all Vaishnava devotees of the Lord.

Ancient texts describe the ideal Vaishnava's characteristics. Among other things, he is *para-dukha-dukhi*—"In other words, he has no personal troubles, but he is very unhappy to see others in trouble."[2] This is a form of compassion that extends to all species. A Vaishnava believes that it is wrong to give "trouble" to any living entity, and that the height of giving trouble is to prematurely end that entity's life. Thus, for a Vaishnava, it is wrong to kill any living being. As Prabhupada says,

But when you're actually on the platform of love of God, you understand your relationship with God: "I am part and parcel of God—and this dog is also part and parcel of God. And so is every other living entity." Then you'll extend your love to the animals also. If you actually love God, then your love for insects is also there, because you understand, "This insect has got a different kind of body, but he is also part and parcel of God—he is my brother." *Samah sarveshu bhuteshu:* you look upon all living beings equally. Then you cannot maintain slaughterhouses. If you maintain slaughterhouses and disobey the order of Christ in the Bible—"Thou shall not kill"—and you proclaim yourself a Christian, your so-called religion is simply a waste of time . . . because you have no love for God.[3]

Prabhupada frequently uses the "Thou shalt not kill" motif in his presentation of Krishna consciousness—it is one of the most persistently recurring themes in his books, and the attentive reader can find reference to it in nearly every one of them.[4] His insistence on its importance is clear not only from the number of times he refers to it, but from the force and intensity with which he does so. Some examples:

Animal sacrifice in the name of religion is current practically all over the world in every established religion. It is said that Lord Jesus Christ, when 12 years old, was shocked to see the Jews sacrificing birds and animals in the synagogues and that he therefore rejected the Jewish system of religion and started the religious system of Christianity, adhering to the Old Testament commandment "Thou shalt not kill." At the present day, however, not only are animals killed . . . but the killing of animals has increased enormously because of the increasing number of slaughterhouses. Slaughtering animals, either for religion or for food, is most abominable and is condemned herein. Unless one is merciless, one cannot sacrifice animals, either in the name of religion or for food. (From *Srimad Bhagavatam*, 7.15.11, commentary)

It is not that national leaders should be concerned only with human beings. The definition of native is "one who takes birth in a particular nation." So, the cow is also a native. Then why should the cow be slaughtered? The cow is giving milk and the bull is working for you, and then you slaughter them? What is this philosophy? In the Christian religion it is clearly stated, "Thou shalt not kill." Yet most of the slaughterhouses are in the Christian countries. (From *The Quest for Enlightenment*, "The Mercy of Lord Caitanya")

If Mr. Nixon loves his countrymen, why does he not love his country's cows? They are also born in the same land, and they have the same right to live. Why are they killed? "Thou shalt not kill." But the animals are being killed. That is imperfection. Krishna embraces both the cows and Radharani. That is perfection. (From *Life Comes from Life*, "The Eleventh Morning Walk," May 15, 1973)

If one kills many thousands of animals in a professional way so that other people can purchase the meat to eat, one must be ready to be killed in a similar way in his next life and in life after life. There are many rascals who violate their own religious principles. According to Judeo-Christian scriptures, it is clearly said, "Thou shalt not kill." Nonetheless, giving all kinds of excuses, even the heads of religions indulge in killing animals while trying to pass as saintly persons. (From *Chaitanya-charitamrita, Madhya-lila* 24.251, commentary)

They should have been ashamed: "Lord Jesus Christ suffered for us, but we are continuing the sinful activities." He told everyone, "Thou shalt not kill," but they are indulging in killing, thinking, "Lord Jesus Christ will excuse us and take all the sinful reactions." This is going on. (From *Perfect Questions, Perfect Answers*, Chapter 6)

As far as the Christian religion is concerned, ample opportunity is given to understand God, but no one is taking it. For example, the Bible contains the commandment "Thou shall not kill," but Christians have built the world's best slaughterhouses. How can they become God-conscious if they disobey the commandments of Lord Jesus Christ? And this is going on not just in the Christian religion, but in every religion. The title "Hindu," "Muslim," or "Christian" is simply a rubber stamp. None of them knows who God is and how to love Him. (From *Science of Self-Realization*, "What Is Krsna Consciousness?")

Jesus Christ taught, "Thou shalt not kill." But his followers have now decided, "Let us kill anyway," and they open big, modern, scientific slaughterhouses. "If there is any sin, Christ will suffer for us." This is a most abominable conclusion. (From *Science of Self-Realization*, "Jesus Christ Was a Guru")

If we look at all of Prabhupada's proclamations on the subject, the ones that stand out are found in his now famous conversations with two Christian clerics of some renown: Cardinal Jean Danielou, from Paris, and Father Emmanuel Jungclaussen, a Benedictine monk from West Germany. While there is little space to reproduce these classics in their entirety, the pertinent sections appear below:

Srila Prabhupada: Jesus Christ said, "Thou shalt not kill." So why is it that the Christian people are engaged in animal killing?

Cardinal Danielou: Certainly in Christianity it is forbidden to kill, but we believe that there is a difference between the life of a human being and the life of the beasts. The life of a human being is sacred because man is made in the image of God; therefore, to kill a human being is forbidden.

Srila Prabhupada: But the Bible does not simply say, "Do not kill the human being." It says broadly, "Thou shalt not kill."

Cardinal Danielou: We believe that only human life is sacred.

Srila Prabhupada: That is your interpretation. The commandment is "Thou shalt not kill."

Cardinal Danielou: It is necessary for man to kill animals in order to have food to eat.

Srila Prabhupada: No. Man can eat grains, vegetables, fruits, and milk.

Cardinal Danielou: No flesh?

Srila Prabhupada: No. Human beings are meant to eat vegetarian food. The tiger does not come to eat your fruits. His prescribed food is animal flesh. But man's food is vegetables, fruits, grains, and milk products. So how can you say that animal killing is not a sin?

Cardinal Danielou: We believe it is a question of motivation. If the killing of an animal is for giving food to the hungry, then it is justified.

Srila Prabhupada: But consider the cow: we drink her milk; therefore, she is our mother. Do you agree?

Cardinal Danielou: Yes, surely.

Srila Prabhupada: So if the cow is your mother, how can you support killing her? You take the milk from her, and when she's old and cannot give you milk, you cut her throat. Is that a very humane proposal? In India those who are meat-eaters are advised to kill some lower animals like goats, pigs, or even buffalo. But cow killing is the greatest sin. In preaching Krishna consciousness we ask people not to eat any kind of meat, and my disciples strictly follow this principle. But if, under certain circumstances, others are obliged to eat meat, then they should eat the flesh of some lower animal. Don't kill cows. It is the greatest sin. And as long as a man is sinful, he cannot understand God. The human being's main business is to understand God and to love Him. But if you remain sinful, you will never be able to understand God—what to speak of loving Him.

Cardinal Danielou: I think that perhaps this is not an essential point. The important thing is to love God. The practical commandments can vary from one religion to the next.

Srila Prabhupada: So, in the Bible God's practical commandment is that you cannot kill; therefore killing cows is a sin for you.

Cardinal Danielou: God says to the Indians that killing is not good, and he says to the Jews that . . .

Srila Prabhupada: No, no. Jesus Christ taught, "Thou shalt not kill." Why do you interpret this to suit your own convenience?

Cardinal Danielou: But Jesus allowed the sacrifice of the Paschal Lamb.

Srila Prabhupada: But he never maintained a slaughterhouse.

Cardinal Danielou: [Laughs.] No, but he did eat meat.

Srila Prabhupada: When there is no other food, someone may eat meat in order to keep from starving. That is another thing. But it is most sinful to regularly maintain slaughterhouses just to satisfy your tongue. Actually, you will not even have a human society until this cruel practice of maintaining slaughterhouses is stopped. And although animal killing may sometimes be necessary for survival, at least the mother animal, the cow, should not be killed. That is simply human decency. In the Krishna consciousness movement our practice is that we don't allow the killing of any animals. Krishna says, "Vegetables, fruits, milk, and grains should be offered to Me in devotion." We take only the remnants of Krishna's food (*prasadam*). The trees offer us many varieties of fruits, but the trees are not killed. Of course, one living entity is food for another living entity, but that does not mean you can kill your mother for food. Cows are innocent; they give us milk. You take their milk—and then kill them in the slaughterhouse. This is sinful. (From *Science of Self-Realization*, "Thou Shalt Not Kill")

The exchange with Father Emmanuel is similar:

Srila Prabhupada: The first point is that they violate the commandment "Thou shalt not kill" by maintaining slaughterhouses. Do you agree that this commandment is being violated?

Father Emmanuel: Personally, I agree.

Srila Prabhupada: Good. So if the Christians want to love God, they must stop killing animals.

Father Emmanuel: But isn't the most important point—

Srila Prabhupada: If you miss one point, there is a mistake in your calculation. Regardless of what you add or subtract after that, the mistake is already in the calculation, and everything that follows will also be faulty. We cannot simply accept that part of the scripture we like, and reject what we don't like, and still expect to get the result. For example, a hen lays eggs with its back part and eats with its beak. A farmer may consider, "The front part of the hen is very expensive because I have to feed it. Better to cut it off." But if the head is missing there will be no eggs anymore, because the body is dead. Similarly, if we reject the difficult part of the scriptures and obey the part we like, such an interpretation will not help us. We have to accept all the injunctions of the scripture as they are given, not only those that suit us.[5] If you do not follow the first order, "Thou shalt not kill," then where is the question of love of God?

Visitor: Christians take this commandment to be applicable to human beings, not to animals.

Srila Prabhupada: That would mean that Christ was not intelligent enough to use the right word: murder. There is killing, and there is murder. Murder refers to human beings. Do you think Jesus was not intelligent enough to use the right word—murder—instead of the word killing? Killing means any kind of killing, and especially animal killing. If Jesus had meant simply the killing of humans, he would have used the word murder.

Father Emmanuel: But in the Old Testament the commandment "Thou shalt not kill" *does* refer to murder. And when Jesus said, "Thou shalt not kill," he extended this commandment to mean that a human being should not only refrain from killing another human being, but should also treat him with love. He never spoke about man's relationship with other living entities, but only about his relationship with other human beings. When he said, "Thou shalt not kill," he also meant in the mental and emotional sense—that you should not insult anyone or hurt him, treat him badly, and so on.

Srila Prabhupada: We are not concerned with this or that testament but only with the words used in the commandments. If you want to interpret these words, that is something else. We understand the direct meaning. "Thou shalt not kill" means, "The Christians should not kill." You may put forth interpretations in order to continue the present way of action, but we understand very clearly that there is no need for interpretation. Interpretation is necessary if things are not clear. But here the meaning is clear. "Thou shalt not kill" is a clear instruction. Why should we interpret it?

Father Emmanuel: Isn't the eating of plants also killing?

Srila Prabhupada: The Vaishnava philosophy teaches that we should not even kill plants unnecessarily. In the *Bhagavad-gita*

(9.26) Krishna says: "If someone offers Me with love and devotion a leaf, a flower, a fruit, or a little water, I will accept it." We offer Krishna only the kind of food He demands, and then we eat the remnants. If offering vegetarian food to Krishna were sinful, then it would be Krishna's sin, not ours. But God is *apapa-viddha*—sinful reactions are not applicable to Him. He is like the sun, which is so powerful that it can purify even urine—something impossible for us to do. Krishna is also like a king, who may order a murderer to be hanged but who himself is beyond punishment because he is very powerful. Eating food first offered to the Lord is also something like a soldier's killing during wartime. In a war, when the commander orders a man to attack, the obedient soldier who kills the enemy will get a medal. But if the same soldier kills someone on his own, he will be punished. Similarly, when we eat only *praaāda* [the remnants of food offered to Krishna], we do not commit any sin. This is confirmed in the *Bhagavad-gita* (3.13).

Father Emmanuel: Krishna cannot give permission to eat animals?

Srila Prabhupada: Yes—in the animal kingdom. But the civilized human being, the religious human being, is not meant to kill and eat animals. If you stop killing animals and chant the holy name Christ, everything will be perfect. I have not come to teach you, but only to request you to please chant the name of God. The Bible also demands this of you. So let's kindly cooperate and chant, and if you have a prejudice against chanting the name Krishna, then chant "Christos" or "Krishta"—there is no difference. Sri Chaitanya said: "God has millions and millions of names, and because there is no difference between God's name and Himself, each one of these names has the same potency as God." Therefore, even if you accept designations like "Hindu," "Christian," or "Muhammadan," if you simply chant the name of God found in your own scriptures, you will attain the spiritual platform. Human life is meant for self-realization—to learn how to love

God. That is the actual beauty of man. Whether you discharge this duty as a Hindu, a Christian, or a Muhammadan, it doesn't matter—but discharge it!

Father Emmanuel: I agree. (From *Science of Self-Realization*, "Krsna or Christ: The Name is the Same")

Interestingly, Prabhupada rarely allows conversations with religionists (of other persuasions) to move beyond these fundamental points of animal welfare, vegetarianism, and the horrors of killing. He deemed it impossible for a person to understand higher subjects while still involved in animal slaughter. This is based on a principle found in the *Srimad Bhagavatam* (10.1.4). Here we learn that a person who acts as "a butcher" (*pashu-ghna*)—a phrase that includes not only the one who actually kills the animal but also the one who eats it or is otherwise a party to its harm—cannot understand the absolute truth. For this reason, explain Vaishnava texts, the Buddha also emphasized the teaching of compassion and the rights of animals.

Prabhupada's emphasis on this subject has a long history in Gaudiya Vaishnavism, stretching back to the example of Chaitanya Mahaprabhu himself. In his meeting with Chand Kazi, a Muslim magistrate of his time, Mahaprabhu refused to speak about the deep theological subjects for which he was so well known. Instead, he spoke to the Kazi about the foolishness of harming the cow and about meat-eating's adverse effects. Prabhupada follows in this same line, never moving to more advanced subjects until these basic points are understood.

Analysis of the Sixth Commandment

Though this book is not a study of the Bible or its related traditions, if we want to understand Prabhupada's insistence on biblical vegetarianism, it is imperative to look at his usage of the Sixth Commandment (Exodus 20.13), "Thou shalt not kill," more closely. As a side note, given the variety of interpretations to which this commandment is open—and we will briefly discuss these below—it is far from the strongest biblical support for the doctrines of vegetarianism and animal rights. Scholars such as Richard Schwartz (in Judaism) and Andrew Linzey (in Christianity) have written volumes on the more compelling biblical evidences. But since Prabhupada focused on the Sixth Commandment, it behooves us, given the subject of this work, to look at his reasons for doing so.

There are only several studies on the significance of "Thou shalt not kill" from a vegetarian point of view. The most noted work from this perspective would be Aaron Frankel's much-referred-to book, *"Thou Shalt Not Kill"—The Torah of Vegetarianism*, which was published, interestingly, in the year of Prabhupada's birth (1896). Since then, only a handful of outspoken vegetarian advocates have explained the commandment in terms of their dietary preference. In 1903, J. Todd Ferrier, a founding father of the Order of the Cross, released a little book called *Concerning Human Carnivorism*, later reprinted in 1968 as *On Behalf of the Creatures*. Some years later, The Reverend V. A. Holmes-Gore wrote a similar volume entitled *These We Have Not Loved*, which was followed by Geoffrey L. Rudd's *Why Kill for Food?* Such books are few and far between, but they do allow us to see the Sixth Commandment from a broader perspective.

In Prabhupada's conversations with Danielou and Emmanuel, several important questions come to the fore. They talk about interpretive problems associated with the commandment—are we being told not to *kill*, or not to *murder*? They also discuss the difference between human life and animal life, and whether or not animals have a soul. These are some of the points we will now discuss using easy-to-understand biblical exegesis and common sense, along with quotes from prominent authorities on the subject.

Briefly, Prabhupada's main argument is that the commandment should be taken at face value—it is wrong to kill, plain and simple. When seen in this light, there are few who would argue. But when we get into particulars, the commandment gets more complicated. What about self-defense and capital punishment? Or when killing occurs by accident? The Bible makes allowances for these things and thus excludes them from the demands of this commandment.[6] According to the Bible, enemies of Israel can also be killed.[7] So where do we draw the line? If the command does not even include all humans, what hope is there to include animals in its scope?

Given the culture and context in which the commandment was revealed, in all probability it originally meant, "You shall not kill 'unnecessarily,' " for, as noted, the Bible clearly permits certain forms of killing. And it probably focused on human concerns rather than those of animals. However, given the ideals of peace and compassion espoused by the Judeo-Christian tradition, it would not be unnatural to extend this command to include the lesser creatures, for modern science—especially the nutritional sciences—indeed teaches that *we don't have to kill animals, even for food*. Such foods are no longer deemed necessary for humans to maintain proper health.

Mark Mathew Braunstein is among those who see in the command a clear ordinance against harming any living beings. He writes, "Moses the messenger brought down the decree 'Thou shalt not kill.' Period. While coveting refers specifically to a neighbor's spouse, or honoring to one's parents, prohibition against killing is not specific: it says simply and purely not to kill."[8] This is an important point—the other commandments tell us exactly who falls within their jurisdiction, or who might be deemed their beneficiaries. But, here, we are simply told not to kill, without any such qualifying considerations. This, too, is Prabhupada's argument: "If the commandment doesn't specify whether it is referring to both humans and animals or merely to humans, then why should we interpret it? Why not just understand it in its most simple and direct way?" But people do insist on interpreting, and for this reason we will look at the words in question and to see if we can find some reasonable resolution to the dilemma.

Meat-eating interpreters of the Bible would have us believe that theirs is the only way to view the Sixth Commandment. But their position is simply not true. For example, Philip L. Pick (1910–1992), the Founder of the Jewish Vegetarian Society, after researching the subject for nearly 30 years, concludes as follows:

The Ten Commandments are the basis of the Jewish Faith, and in the Fourth Commandment domestic animals along with the family are commanded to observe the Sabbath Day. The Talmud discourses on this subject . . . [saying] they must be allowed freedom to roam the fields and enjoy the sunshine, air and grass, generally to enjoy the work of the Creation in the same way as man. A far cry from the present practice of permanent incarceration in darkened factory farms.

Again the Sixth Commandment "Thou shalt not kill," seals the general teachings relating to carnivorous habits. The implication is that one shall not kill unnecessarily and the oft-used translation "thou shalt not commit murder" wrongfully restricts the original meaning of the word. Certainly today, the abundance of non-flesh, health giving foods unquestionably means that every time a creature is killed for food a sin against God has been committed.[9]

According to Reuben Alcalay, one of the twentieth century's great linguistic scholars and author of *The Complete Hebrew-English Dictionary*, the commandment refers to "any kind of killing whatsoever." The original Hebrew, he says, is *Lo tirtzakh*, which asks us to refrain from killing in toto.[10] If what he says is true, we can analyze the commandment as follows: "Thou shalt not" needs no interpretation. The controversial word is "kill," commonly defined as (1) to deprive of life; (2) to put an end to; (3) to destroy the vital or essential quality of. If anything that has life can be killed, an animal can be killed as well; according to this commandment, then, the killing of animals is forbidden.

"Kill" Versus "Murder"

The problem is that all manuscripts of the Bible are not the same. Further, there are numerous references to this same command in the Old and New Testaments, some of which are nuanced in slightly different ways.[11] Modern scholarship now leans toward "Thou shalt not murder" as opposed to "Thou shalt not kill." How do scholars come to this conclusion, and what really is the distinction between the two? First, let us examine what the Bible actually says. The Hebrew word for "murder" is *ratzakh*, whereas the word for "kill" is *haroq*. The commandment, in the original Hebrew, indeed states: "*Lo tirtzakh*" (a form of *ratzakh*), not "*Lo Taharoq*." In other words, it is "Thou shalt not murder," as opposed to "Thou shalt not kill." Why, then, does

Reuben Alcalay say that *tirtzakh* refers to "any kind of killing whatsoever"?

The difference between these two words—"kill" and "murder"—has more to do with modern usage than original texts: the demarcation between these words may have been different in biblical times. Indeed, the Bible appears conflicted in this regard, as do Bible translators. *The HarperCollins Study Bible*, which is the New Revised Standard Version and the rendition used by the Society of Biblical Literature, interprets the commandment as "Thou shalt not murder," but it then includes a footnote saying "or kill." *The New Oxford Annotated Bible* does the same.

The King James Version of the Bible, and others too numerous to mention here, translate the verse as "Thou shalt not kill," while others keep going back and forth, changing from "kill" to "murder" and, every few years, back again. Perhaps the most important version to use the word "kill" instead of "murder" is *The Holy Bible: From Ancient Eastern Manuscripts*.[12] This work is based on the earliest editions of the text, making use of rare Aramaic fragments. Here we find that the Exodus verse is unequivocally rendered as "Thou shalt not kill," though a lengthy Introduction explains why well-meaning translators might choose otherwise.

Rabbi Joseph Telushkin writes about one of the many dangers of interpreting the word as "kill":

> If the commandment had read "You shall not kill," it would have suggested that all killing is illegal, including that in self-defense. Indeed, certain religious groups such as the Jehovah's Witnesses take this position, and insist that their members refuse army service (during World War II in Germany Jehovah's Witnesses refused to fight for the Nazis while their American co-religionists refused to fight against them).[13]

These are very real concerns for biblical translators and commentators, and while they may have diverse opinions on whether to use "kill" or "murder" while addressing any number of complex issues, one thing is certain: In current usage, the two words carry very different meanings. According to *Webster's New Universal Unabridged Dictionary*, "killing" is straightforward, and its definition is given above. But "murder" is more complicated. Webster defines it in legal terms. Its first definition as a noun is "the unlawful and malicious or premeditated killing of one human being by another"; as a verb, it is defined as "to kill (a person) unlawfully and with malice." These are first entry definitions. If we look at secondary ones, we find "to kill inhumanly and barbarously, as in warfare" or "to destroy; to put an end to."

Prabhupada admits in his conversation with Father Emmanuel that "murder" refers to humans, and this is borne out by the primary definitions given above. But who defines these words? Because animals do not have the same rights as humans, at least in contemporary Western society, they are omitted from the definition of murder—and so it is not considered unlawful to take their lives. But if we look at murder practically—at what it really is, beyond mere legalistic formulas—we are confronted with the secondary definitions of "murder" given above, both of which can certainly be applied to animals.

Literalists may tightly cling to the primary definitions, saying that murder refers only to humans, and that this is where the argument should end. But, as if anticipating this response, the Bible tells us, "He that killeth an ox is as if he slew a man" (Isaiah 66.3). Perhaps this suggests a closer link between "kill" and "murder." Food for thought.

Moreover, traditional biblical commentators viewed "murder" in a way that expands on the formal definitions of today, with subtle nuances infused with heartfelt compassion. In commenting on Exodus 20.13, early Jewish scholars write as follows: "Sages understood 'bloodshed' to include embarrassing a fellow human being in public so that the blood drains from his or her face, not providing safety for travelers, and causing anyone the loss of his or her livelihood. One may murder by the hand or with the tongue, by talebearing or by character assassination. One may murder by carelessness, by indifference. . . ."[14] Thus, rabbinical interpretation of the commandment includes more than just the literal taking of life. Worded another way, accepted Jewish definitions of murder stretch the envelope, as it were. It would not be unreasonable, then, to include the killing of animals—which necessitates the actual taking of life—under the general rubric of murder, for this would in some ways be less of a stretch than that which is traditionally found in normative Jewish definitions of the word.

But there is more. When Prabhupada refers to the "Thou shalt not kill" commandment, he generally refers to it as "the commandment of Jesus Christ," or he will preface it by saying, "Jesus says." This is quite telling. In fact, the New Testament reading of this commandment seeks to expand on its original definition: Luke (18.20), Mark (10.19), and Matthew (5.21) all exhort followers to go beyond conventional understandings of this command. To give but one example, let us look at the verse from Matthew as translated from the Aramaic fragments mentioned above (though similar versions exist in nearly every version of the Bible): "You have heard that it was said to those in ancient times, 'You shall not murder'; and 'whoever murders shall be liable to judgement.' But I say to you that if you are angry with a brother or sister, you will be liable to judgement; and if you insult a brother or sister . . ." In other words, we are no longer talking about "murder" but of inappropriate treatment. True, these statements are addressing human interaction, first and foremost. But given biblical ideals about the original diet of man, which was vegetarian (see Genesis 1.29), and the ultimate vision of Isaiah (11.6–9)—that all creatures will one day live together in peace—it is clearly desirable that man begin to treat his co-inhabitors of the planet with dignity and respect. He can begin by not killing them.

This is Prabhupada's main point: In whatever way the original Jewish prophets and their modern representatives interpret the word "murder," a religionist should be able to invoke common sense and inborn human compassion—it is wrong to unnecessarily kill any living being. Prabhupada believes that a practicing religionist, especially, should have the good sense, character, and purity of purpose to know that taking life is not in our charge: We cannot create the life of an animal, and so we have no right to take it away. Prabhupada's understanding of "Thou shalt not kill" can thus be considered legitimate—especially in light of the commandment's restructuring as found in the New Testament. This is so because modern slaughter-

1. His Divine Grace A. C. Bhaktivedanta Swami Prabhupada (1896–1977), the founder and spiritual preceptor of the International Society for Krishna Consciousness (ISKCON).

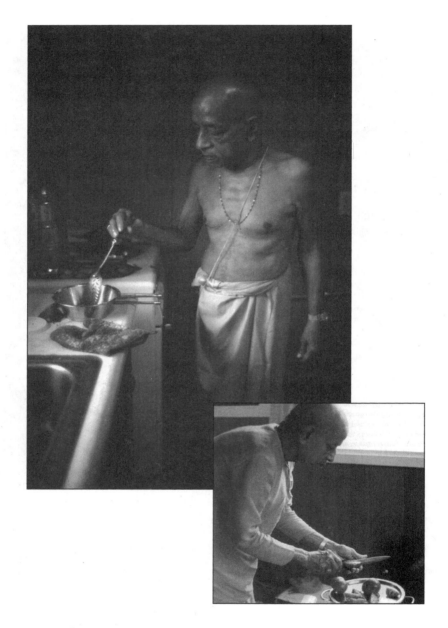

2. Swami Prabhupada in the kitchen, cutting vegetables and cooking *prasadam*.

3. Lord Krishna, loving cowherd and Supreme Personality of Godhead.

LORD KRISHNA'S CUISINE

The Art of Indian
Vegetarian Cooking

YAMUNA DEVI

More than 500 Recipes with Illustrations from India's
Great Culinary Tradition

4. Yamuna Devi, ISKCON's legendary chef, and the cover of her award-winning cookbook.

5. Yamuna enjoying lunch *prasadam* (spiritual vegetarian cuisine) with George Harrison and wife Patty at John Lennon's Tittenhurst Estate in Ascot, 1969.

6. Kurma, following in Yamuna's footsteps, is now the preeminent ISKCON cook.

7. The Hare Krishna movement is primarily known for chanting and dancing through the major cities of the world. They enthusiastically glorify Krishna, God, with heartfelt song and rhythmic movement.

8. Lord Chaitanya, Krishna Himself, incarnated as His own devotee, circa 500 years ago, in Bengal, India. He is depicted here in loving association with the animals of Braj. Lord Chaitanya popularized singing and dancing in glorification of God as the modern era's most effective yoga technique. He is seen here singing and dancing with the animals of the forest.

9. Devotees distribute *prasadam* around the world. Regular festivals are held in various strategic locations, such as the yearly one in Poland (as depicted here).

10. Massive *prasadam* distribution initiatives are underway in India, Africa, Australia, and Eastern Europe.

11. Millions of plates of sacred vegetarian food have been distributed thus far.

12. Devotees have opened restaurants in all parts of the globe. Here we find two happy customers at Chez Govinda in Montreal, Canada.

13. Swami Prabhupada's motto was "simple living and high thinking." To implement this ideal, many devotees went back to a more agrarian lifestyle, establishing farm communities around the world.

14. Devotees of the Lord love not only Krishna but His world, His nature, His people, and His animals, particularly the cow.

15. The Deities of Radha-Govinda. It was this manifestation of Krishna who inspired the name "Govinda's" for ISKCON restaurants around the world.

16. Lord Krishna the cowherd, lovingly embracing a calf.

houses go against the very spirit of the entire Judeo-Christian tradition—of religion in general—which seeks to abolish wrongful killing and to establish universal harmony and love throughout the creation.

Do Animals Have Souls?

In Prabhupada's conversation with Cardinal Danielou, we are introduced to the idea that human life and animal life are distinct, and later in their conversation we are told by Danielou that animals do not have souls. What follows is part of that exchange, but first we offer snippets of similar conversations that Prabhupada had had with other close friends and disciples at the time:

> Srila Prabhupada: The soul is always the same.
> Bob: In each person? In each person is it the same?
> Srila Prabhupada: Yes.
> Bob: [pointing to two devotees] If these two are Krishna conscious, are their souls the same?
> Srila Prabhupada: The soul is the same but always individual, even if one is not Krishna conscious. For instance, you are a human being, and I am a human being. Even if I am not a Christian, even if you are not a Hindu, still we are human beings. Similarly, the soul may not be Krishna-conscious, or he may be Krishna-conscious—it doesn't matter. But the soul is the soul.
> Bob: Can you tell me more about this?
> Srila Prabhupada: Soul—as pure spirit, all souls are equal. Even in an animal. Therefore it is said, *pandita sama-darshinah* [*Bhagavad-gita* 5.18]: "Those who are actually learned do not see the outward covering, either in a human being or in an animal." (From *Perfect Questions, Perfect Answers*, Chapter 3)

> Student: Srila Prabhupada, Christianity's sanction of meat-eating is based on the view that lower species of life do not have a soul like the human being's.
> Srila Prabhupada: That is foolishness. First of all, we have to understand the evidence of the soul's presence within the

body. Then we can see whether the human being has a soul and the cow does not. What are the different characteristics of the cow and the man? If we find a difference in characteristics, then we can say that in the animal there is no soul. But if we see that the animal and the human being have the same characteristics, then how can you say that the animal has no soul? The general symptoms are that the animal eats, you eat; the animal sleeps, you sleep; the animal mates, you mate; the animal defends, and you defend. Where is the difference?

Cardinal Danielou: We admit that in the animal there may be the same type of biological existence as in men, but there is no soul. We believe that the soul is a human soul.

Srila Prabhupada: Our *Bhagavad-gita* says *sarva-yonishu,* "In all species of life the soul exists." The body is like a suit of clothes. You have black clothes; I am dressed in saffron clothes. But within the dress you are a human being, and I am also a human being. Similarly, the bodies of the different species are just like different types of dress. There is a soul, a part and parcel of God. Suppose a man has two sons, not equally meritorious. One may be a Supreme Court judge and the other may be a common laborer, but the father claims both as his sons. He does not make the distinction that the son who is a judge is very important and the worker-son is not important. And if the judge-son says, "My dear father, your other son is useless; let me cut him up and eat him," will the father allow this?

Cardinal Danielou: Certainly not, but the idea that all life is part of the life of God is difficult for us to admit. There is a great difference between human life and animal life.

Srila Prabhupada: That difference is due to the development of consciousness. In the human body there is developed consciousness. Even a tree has a soul, but a tree's consciousness is not very developed. If you cut a tree it does not resist. Actually, it does resist, but only to a very small degree. There is a scientist named Jagadish Chandra Bose who has made a machine that shows that trees and plants are able to feel pain when they are cut. And we can see directly that when someone comes to kill an animal, it resists, it cries, it makes a horrible sound. So it is a matter of the development of consciousness. But the soul is there within all living beings.

Cardinal Danielou: But metaphysically, the life of man is sacred. Human beings think on a higher platform than the animals do.

Srila Prabhupada: What is that higher platform? The animal eats to maintain his body, and you also eat in order to maintain your body. The cow eats grass in the field, and the human being eats meat from a huge slaughterhouse full of modern machines. But just because you have big machines and a ghastly scene, while the animal simply eats grass, this does not mean that you are so advanced that only within your body is there a soul and that there is not a soul within the body of the animal. That is illogical. We can see that the basic characteristics are the same in the animal and the human being.

Cardinal Danielou: But only in human beings do we find a metaphysical search for the meaning of life.

Srila Prabhupada: Yes. So metaphysically search out why you believe that there is no soul within the animal—that is metaphysics. If you are thinking metaphysically, that's all right. But if you are thinking like an animal, then what is the use of your metaphysical study? Metaphysical means "above the physical" or, in other words, "spiritual." In the *Bhagavad-gita* [14.4] Krishna says, *sarva-yonishu kaunteya*: "In every living being there is a spirit-soul." That is metaphysical understanding. Now either you accept Krishna's teachings as metaphysical, or you'll have to take a third-class fool's opinion as metaphysical. Which do you accept? (From *Science of Self-Realization*, "Thou Shalt Not Kill")

Dr. Singh: Srila Prabhupada, what is the difference between the transmigration of souls in animal bodies and the transmigration of human souls?

Srila Prabhupada: Animals transmigrate in only one direction—upward—but human beings can transmigrate to either a higher or a lower form of life. The body is awarded according to the living entity's desire. The lower animals have one kind of desire, but the human being has thousands and millions of desires—animal desires as well as human desires. By nature's law, the lower species are coming up from animal forms to the higher, human forms. But once you come to the human form, if you don't cultivate Krishna consciousness, you may return to the body of a cat or dog. (From *Life Comes From Life*, The Ninth Morning Walk: May 13, 1973)

Every major religious tradition teaches that there is a soul, or life-force, in every animated being, both moving and nonmoving. While Church authorities from medieval times to the present day say that a living soul is peculiar to the human species, this idea finds no substantiation within the Bible itself. Indeed, before the time of St. Thomas Aquinas (thirteenth century) it was a non-question: The very word *animal* comes from *animale*, which in turn comes from the Latin *anima*, or "soul." Animals were souls. Period. *That's what the word means*. But all this was forgotten with the onslaught of the scientific age. Insult was added to injury with René Descartes (seventeenth century), who found use for animals in science, and, referring to them as "soulless automata," argued that they were merely machines. After he convinced others of his case, animals were then treated like scrap metal, merely created to be used for human purposes. This correlated well with Thomistic ideas about "dominion" and human centrality in God's creation.

If we look at the Bible itself, however, a different story unfolds. Job (12.10) speaks of the soul of every living thing, while Genesis (1.30) declares that "every beast of the earth, every fowl of the air, as well as everything that creepeth, has a living soul." The exact Hebrew words used here are *nephesh* ("soul") and *chayah* ("living"). Many have translated this as "life," but according to Dr. Reuben Alcalay (author of *The Complete Hebrew-English Dictionary*, previously mentioned), the exact Hebrew translates as "living soul." Some, like Aquinas, have argued that there are various kinds of souls, like vegetative, animal, and human ones, but these are later ideas with little biblical support.

Particularly noteworthy in this connection is the fact that exactly the same words used in the Bible to describe the animal soul are also used to describe the human soul. Thus, one should not give credence to the claim that animal and human souls are of a different quality. While we may want to establish our superiority out of a sense of ego, we can also admit that we are all God's children—and that a parent loves all his children equally. If humans are superior in terms of their ability to appreciate their Creator and to understand matters of the spirit, this is simply a difference in bodily facility, not a statement on the quality of the soul. An underlying spiritual unity between humans and animals—indeed, between humanity and all of creation—was recognized by important philosophers and Christian leaders. For example, Plato and St. Francis, among others, counter Aquinas and Descartes by putting forward a creation-centered spirituality, one that honors the animals and the natural world and allows for a vegetarian sensibility.

Different spirit-souls inhabit different kinds of bodies just as different human beings inhabit different homes, according to their means. The ancient Upanishads tell us that there are 8.4 million species of life, and each is equipped with a particular sensory skill or trait. The reason for this is that living entities inhabit various bodies according to their desire to enjoy in a particular way—and God facilitates these desires by awarding an appropriate body. Once encased in a particular animal form, say the Upanishads, the living entity naturally evolves to the human form, in which he or she is once again given the opportunity to break free from the cycle of birth and death and develop love for God. This is what Prabhupada says, too, in his conversation with Dr. Singh.

Given this understanding of the soul and the material body (that different bodies are vehicles and nothing more), vegetarianism follows logically. Why? Because if one sees all living beings equally, and recognizes the body as a vehicle for the soul and as one stage in the soul's evolution to human consciousness (which may in turn lead to liberation from the cycle of reincarnation), then one would be no more anxious to eat a cow than to eat one's own son. Whether or not one finds this argument convincing, the underlying principle is compelling: If on the spiritual platform all living entities are equal, who could justify killing of any kind?

Even if one does not believe that animals have a soul, it does not follow that one should kill and eat them. As Bernard E. Rollin, Professor of Philosophy at Colorado State University, writes:

> It is instructive to examine one of the most pervasive reasons usually offered for excluding animals from being direct objects of moral consideration—the claim that whereas man possesses an immortal soul, animals are not so blessed. Though such a claim is invariably met with raised eyebrows among intellectuals in our age of skepticism, it permeates the popular mind and has certainly dominated Catholic thought for centuries. (It is still, in fact, official Catholic dogma.) Laying aside positivistic doubts about the grounds for such a claim, let us explore its logic. Even if we suppose that animals do not have a soul while humans do, the key question is this: what does the possession of a soul have to do with being an object of moral concern? Why does the lack of a soul exclude animals from moral consideration? In fact, even some Catholic theologians who did deny souls to animals drew an opposite conclusion from that fact. Since, argued Cardinal Bellarmine, animals do not have immortal souls, wrongs perpetrated upon them will not be redressed in an afterlife in the way human wrongs will be rectified. For this reason, animals most certainly ought to be objects of moral concern for us and even ought to be treated better than we treat one another![15]

The Golden Rule—"Do unto others as you would have others do unto you"—is often considered the very basis of morals and ethics in the Western world, and it includes an implicit argument against eating meat, unless, that is, we would ourselves like to be eaten by those who are more powerful than we are. Accordingly, this golden rule has parallels in each of the world's major religious traditions: in Judaism, it is taught, "What is hateful to you, do not to your fellow men"

(*Talmud, Shabbat,* 31a); Christianity teaches, "Whatever ye would that men should do to you, do ye even so to them" (Matthew, 7.12); Islam declares, "No one of you is a believer until he desires for his brother that which he desires for himself" (*Sunnah, Hadith*); Buddhism teaches, "Hurt not others in ways that you yourself would find hurtful" (*Udana-Varga,* 5.13); and in Hinduism we find, "This is the sum of duty: Do naught unto others which would cause you pain if done to you" (*Mahabharata,* 5.1.517). This rule speaks directly to our quality of mercy. How can we pray to God for mercy and then not extend that same sense of mercy to others?

"Killing Plants Is Still Killing!"

So what do we eat? Even a vegetarian is guilty of killing the vegetables and various other foods that he or she consumes. This was one of the arguments that Father Emmanuel brought up in his conversation with Swami Prabhupada. Let us look at this argument a little more closely.

We learn from the Vedic literature as well as from practical experience that in this world there is danger at every step. Death is a part of life. Even when we breathe, we necessarily kill hundreds if not thousands of microorganisms. Life in this world is a fight with material nature, which imposes death upon all. A moral and ethical person thus tries to do the least possible amount of harm to sentient creatures. When it comes to our diet, the question is not *if* we have to kill, but whom and how much. A vegetarian actually kills less than a meat-eater, both in terms of killing animals and plants. This is so because vegetarians eat plant food directly, as opposed to eating plant food *as well as* feeding animals an abundance of plants and then killing the animals for meat. Because animals have to eat about 10 times as much vegetarian food to return a single unit of food value as meat, a vegetarian diet means less destruction of the plant kingdom. In other words, only about 10 percent of the protein and calories we feed to livestock is returned in the meat those animals provide. In addition, hundreds of thousands of acres of arable land are occupied in raising livestock for food. One acre used to raise a steer provides only about one pound of protein. That same one acre planted with soybeans will provide 17 pounds of protein. In short, raising animals for food is a tremendous waste of the world's resources.[16]

This important point is augmented by the fact that most vegetarian food can be obtained without any killing at all, through the gathering of ripe fruits and nuts, berries, melons, seeds, legumes, tomatoes, squash, cucumbers, pumpkins, and assorted other vegetarian foods. As Keith Akers writes in *The Vegetarian Sourcebook*, "Finding an ethically significant line between plants and animals . . . is not particularly difficult. Plants have no evolutionary need to feel pain, and completely lack a central nervous system. Nature does not create pain gratuitously, but only when it enables the organism to survive. Animals, being mobile, would benefit from having a sense of pain; plants would not."[17] Animals suffer horribly when they are killed for the sake of our palate, whereas plants do not suffer in the same way. Since we require plants to survive, and they do not suffer a horrible fate by contributing to our survival, they constitute our natural source for food. Hence, it is morally superior to live by eating a healthful vegetarian diet. This is not to encourage a "holier than thou" attitude among vegetarians, but rather to establish a demonstrably appropriate diet for human beings. Indeed, one can be a vegetarian and still fall short in terms of character and integrity—there are many factors that contribute to the wholeness of an individual, and there have been many books written on this subject. But, for now, let us admit that, based on what we have determined thus far, a vegetarian diet is objectively superior to one that involves the needless killing of animals.

The Ethical Implications of Vegetarianism

Because animals are mobile, sentient organisms, moralists and philosophers throughout history, under the principle of utilitarianism—an ideology stating that a truly moral person wants to contribute to the greatest happiness for the greatest number of living beings—have argued that animals have rights and should be treated equitably.[18] Though there were notable exceptions, such as Descartes and Thomas Aquinas, history has given us a plethora of deep thinkers who support kindness to animals on ethical grounds. Kant, for one, believed that cruelty to animals should be abjured if for no other reason than that "such brutality leads to a violent mentality that is then likely to be directed at one's fellow man."[19] And there were others: Ovid, Pythagoras, Empedocles, Plutarch, Porphyry, Plato, Leonardo da Vinci, Mahatma Gandhi, Albert Einstein, Ralph Waldo Emerson, Henry David Thoreau, Isaac B. Singer, and many more—some of the greatest minds of all time spoke out about the virtues of the meatless diet. While many of these luminaries may not have been vegetarian for their entire lives, they clearly appreciated the vegetarian ideal. Their statements and that of others like them can be found in *The Extended Circle*,[20] a virtual encyclopedia of humane thought. The book contains numerous quotes by prominent historical personalities, listing original sources and documentation for further research.

One final thought: The argument that animals do not feel pain (Descartes) and are thus not privy to moral concerns can hardly be taken seriously. It is clear that animals do indeed feel pain: their nervous systems are much akin to our own, and they yelp and make various noises signaling distress. Whether or not they can reason or intelligently verbalize their dislike for pain is irrelevant. If we omit animals from our moral conscience because they cannot verbally express their pain, or because they do not have higher intelligence, we might also disregard mute, feeble or mentally challenged humans. British philosopher Jeremy Bentham articulated the simple truth: "The question is not, Can they talk? nor, Can they reason? but, Can they suffer?"[21] Clearly, any being who can feel pain should come under our moral umbrella. According to the principle of moral utilitarianism, then, if we contribute to animal suffering—not to speak of human suffering—we are behaving in an unethical way. Eating meat, without doubt, contributes to the suffering of animals worldwide. Thus, to be truly moral, we should adhere to the biblical command, "Thou shalt not kill," and we should embrace it while considering its widest application.

5

Food for Life

Here [in Grozny, Chechnya] they [the devotees of Krishna] have a reputation like the one Mother Teresa has in Calcutta: it's not hard finding people to swear they are saints. In a city full of lies, greed, and corruption, the Krishnas deliver the goods. Each day they serve more than 1,000 hot meals, as many as any organization in the city.

—*The New York Times*, Tuesday, December 12, 1995

In the previous chapter, it was shown that ISKCON devotees take compassion and empathy as religious imperatives, central to the practice of genuine spirituality, and that they extend this sense of selfless love to all living beings. We explained that their adherence to the Sixth Commandment, which they understand to include both humans and animals, manifests in their vegetarian diet and in the gentle way they treat all of God's creatures. In this chapter, we will look at yet another manifestation of this compassion, one that again performs the dual function of serving humans as well as animals. It is called *prasadam* distribution. By offering food first to Krishna and then to both needy and non-needy, the devotees perform a valuable service. Because they use only vegetarian ingredients, they avoid exploitation of animals; and because they feed people, they help humans. But more than merely serving those with whom we share the planet, *prasadam* distribution is unique—for it also serves God, or Krishna, both by offering the food to Him and by distributing it to His children. The "Food for Life" (FFL) program was established for just this purpose.

Of course, *prasadam* distribution predates FFL. The Vedic literature sets the precedent with stories of pious individuals who gave donations of food to learned Brahmins and pure Vaishnavas. These texts also provide examples of saints who help the needy, irrespective of social status or spiritual realization: In the *Srimad Bhagavatam*, for example, we find the story of King Rantideva, who, at the point of breaking a 48-day fast, fed two beggars the very food he was about to eat. Prabhupada explains this selfless act in the following way:

> A Vaishnava is therefore described as being . . . very much aggrieved by the suffering of others. As such, a Vaishnava engages in activities for the real welfare of human society.[1]

In medieval Vaishnava works, such as the *Chaitanya-charitamrita*, there are descriptions of huge festivals, in which sumptuous feasts are freely offered to everyone for miles around. Such generosity is framed by the larger understanding of spiritual service, but it is also suffused with concern for all of God's creatures. Bhaktivinode Thakur, a great saint in the same lineage, explains the importance of this compassion: "Those who think that devotion to God and kindness to living entities are different from each other and act accordingly in their life will not be able to follow devotional culture. Their attempt only looks like devotion. All types of beneficence to others, like kindness, friendliness, forgiveness, charity and respect, are included in devotion to God. Giving shelter during adversity; offering academic and spiritual education; giving charity of medicine, clothes, food, and water are activities included in devotional culture" (*Sri Tattva-sutram*, 35, circa 1893).

Swami Prabhupada, in the mood of Sri Chaitanya and Bhaktivinode Thakur, underlined the importance of helping others in a spiritual way, particularly by feeding them with Krishna *prasadam*. In ISKCON's earliest days, he instituted "the Sunday Love feast," where people were invited to exotic Hare Krishna centers for large, multi-course meals—free of charge! He also made a similar arrangement to get his food to people on the streets. Devotees marched outside their sacred temples armed with literally thousands of little *prasadam* "bullets"—sweet balls, a Hare Krishna confection—and other delectable foods, for free distribution. But Prabhupada sent devotees beyond the streets as well. He encouraged them to seek out speaking engagements and to vigorously attend other social venues, all with the purpose of facilitating people in the spiritual goals of life—giving people an opportunity to "taste Krishna," both figuratively and literally. Such practices still go on today, with FFL leading the way in terms of success and public support.

The Distinguishing Quality

ISKCON goes to great pains to distinguish FFL, and its other food distribution programs, from ordinary welfare activity—again, its food programs are based on the spiritual principle of *prasadam* and are thus unique among free food initiatives worldwide. After all, there are many tireless social workers endeavoring with heart and soul to help the needy. Even in India, Mother Teresa's mission, the Ramakrishna Mission, Sai Baba's people, the Salvation Army, the Red Cross—all work hard to help the masses by providing food and shelter. This is admirable, but it is not *prasadam* distribution. As Prabhupada says,

> This Krishna consciousness movement means to become Vaishnava and feel for the suffering humanity. So to feel for the suffering humanity, there are different angles of vision. Somebody is thinking of humanity's suffering from the bodily conception of life. Somebody is trying to open [a] hospital and give relief to the diseased condition. Somebody is trying to deliver foodstuff in poverty-stricken countries or places. These things are certainly very nice, but [the] actual suffering of humanity is due to lack of Krishna consciousness.[2]

He further says,

> When there is an epidemic disease, an antiseptic vaccine protects a person from the attack of such an epidemic. Similarly, food offered to Lord Vishnu [Krishna] and then taken by us

makes us sufficiently resistant to material infection, and one who is accustomed to this practice is called a devotee of the Lord. . . . The material world is full of contaminations, and one who is immunized by accepting *prasadam* of the Lord is saved from the attack, whereas one who does not do so becomes subjected to contamination.[3]

Prabhupada concludes, "[T]o distribute *prasada[m]* to millions of hungry people hankering for spiritual emancipation. This is the mission of the Krishna consciousness movement" [*Srimad Bhagavatam*, 1.13.9 commentary]. And further, "Everyone should be given a chance to take *prasada[m]* and thus be induced to chant the holy names Hare Krishna and also dance in ecstasy" [*Chaitanya-charitamrita, Antya Lila*]. In other words, Prabhupada's compassion, while intense, was not one-dimensional—it took into account the whole person, the material *and* spiritual dimensions of reality. Rather than merely focusing on relative, perceptible concerns—as most altruistic welfare workers do—Prabhupada's interests went beyond the body. His compassion always engendered a sense of the ultimate. That is to say, it was grounded in spiritual truth, never limiting itself to physical and psychological concerns. In the words of Satsvarupa Dasa Goswami (Stephen Guarino), one of Prabhupada's earliest and most dedicated disciples,

Prabhupada's compassion was not ruled by emotion but by intelligence. He didn't just feel sorry for the conditioned souls but thought carefully how to uplift them. Then he worked to do so. If he saw that something he was doing was not effective, he changed his tactics. He never lost sight of his goal to bring the people he met (or met through his followers) to spiritual awakening. He was flexible in his approach, concentrating on education but using other means to attract people to receive it. Although he often decried mundane welfare work, he encouraged the devotees to use food distribution to attract both good publicity and the public. However, it should not be *food* distribution but *prasadam* distribution.[4]

Emphasis on *spiritual* food is what separates ISKCON's efforts from all others.[5] As noted, the distribution of such food began long before Food for Life, but with the inauguration of this specific outreach program it received a new boost, garnering accolades both within ISKCON and beyond its borders. Consequently, FFL devotees are enthusiastic to feed the hungry and to feed everyone else as well. Why are they equally anxious to feed those who are not needy? Because when it comes to *prasadam*, we are all "needy"—for even those of us fortunate enough to be well fed may very well be starving when it comes to spiritual realization. *Prasadam* thus helps the world materially, by feeding all who will give it a try, and also spiritually, by making sure the food is power-packed with a good dose of love for Krishna.

ISKCON Food Relief Origins

In March 1974, Swami Prabhupada summoned his leading disciples to his room. At the time, he was staying at ISKCON's international headquarters in Mayapur, West Bengal. When the devotees entered, they were shocked to see him standing with tears in his eyes, staring intently out the window at what was evidently a ghastly sight. They immediately rushed to his side, hoping to understand the intense emotions emanating from his face. As they gazed upon the scene below, they saw, a short distance away, a group of small children and several dogs rummaging through piles of garbage in search of food.

"How hungry they must be," said Prabhupada. "We must arrange for *prasadam*." He looked at the temple walls surrounding them: "If you want to make this a temple, a house of Lord Krishna, you must see that within a 10-mile radius no one goes hungry. God is everyone's father. How can the child go hungry in the presence of the father?"

As a result of Prabhupada's compassion as articulated on that day, the devotees began to distribute sacred food to the needy. This was the birth of the FFL project. Australian-born Priyavrata Dasa (Paul Turner), who has for many years been the project's global coordinator, writes about the early days:

Regarding . . . the origin of FFL, it really came from the
ISKCON Food Relief Program of Mayapur back in the mid-
1970s. However, the first "FFL program" as we know it today
was actually started by Ramai Swami at the ISKCON temple
in Sydney, Australia. It too was called ISKCON Food Relief
and was operated through the back entrance of the Sydney
temple. It attracted a lot of media attention, especially because
the area was so notorious for drug addicts, and the devotees
were getting some great results by so helping people. Many
were getting off drugs and joining the movement, or at least
supporting us in our mission. Mukunda Goswami visited the
temple and was so impressed that he wanted to expand the
program around the world. He got together with
Nrsimhananda of ISKCON Television (ITV) and
Yashomatinandan (an early Australian devotee) to brainstorm
ways that they might accomplish this. As I understand it, it
was Yashomatinandan who came up with the name "Food for
Life." Very soon the program took on a much slicker image
and began spreading around Australia and then around much
of the USA. There was a big FFL boom in the early to mid-
1980s. However, with success came greed, and soon there
were people exploiting the program. Because of this, some
FFL programs closed down. Then in the late '80s and early
'90s I got involved and, under Mukunda Goswami's able guidance, and with his support, I revitalized the program and
spread it to several Eastern European countries. I also revived
the older ones in the West and traveled to more than 50 countries, establishing new FFL programs.[6]

Mukunda Goswami (Michael Grant), mentioned above, was one
of the great champions of FFL in the early '80s. Indeed, it was he,
through his reports in *Back to Godhead* magazine and *ISKCON World
Review* (now *Hare Krishna World*) who popularized the program, winning the support of the devotees and finding helping hands in the
Krishna community worldwide. He was adept at communications
technology and used his abilities to broadcast FFL goals and activities,

not only in ISKCON but in the popular media as well. Soon, newspapers, magazines, and television programs sang the glories of FFL, and the project grew to previously unexpected heights. Mukunda remembers his early days with FFL:

> We began in 1982 with a small booth from which devotees fed 150 hungry and homeless people free *prasadam* three days a week in downtown San Diego's Horton Plaza. Within five years the program had spanned the globe and is now active in dozens of cities worldwide. Substantial government and private donations of food, money, and other items for the program were significant signs of approval by the establishment.[7]

Once started, FFL took off like wildfire—a fire that cooked *prasadam* down to its essence. Devotees volunteered to distribute *prasadam* with renewed enthusiasm, and sacred vegetarian food was now given out in unprecedented proportions. Devotees around the world started FFL affiliates, accepting government funding for purchasing and preparing food—and then giving out *prasadam* freely, or, in some cases, with nominal charge. Many of these projects fell short of the ideal, but just as many accomplished miraculous feats. In a promotional article co-authored with Priyavrata, Mukunda cites several examples of FFL campaigns that were, in his view, exemplary:

> A few very good models for Food for Life can be found in Australia. In Perth, Australia, there is a "budget-style" restaurant named "Hare Krishna Food for Life," which serves students, seniors, welfare recipients and others with low incomes. Mellow *kirtana* [Hare Krishna chanting] accompanies the serve out and there is Krishna consciousness literature on display for reading. Crossways Food for Life in Melbourne and the Food for Life center in Newtown (Sydney) are other examples of successful, *prasadam* distribution "budget-style" restaurants. Here the fare is limited to three or four preparations, but the taste is excellent and large numbers of customers come by every day!

Another fine example of an ideal Food for Life service is in Durban, South Africa, conducted by Kapiladeva Das. The free *prasadam* distribution is mostly done in townships and sometimes even in prisons. This daily distribution to thousands always includes live *kirtana*. In Riga, Latvia, up to one thousand government-referred elderly come to the Hare Krishna center for *prasadam* every day and accept it in an atmosphere where soft *kirtanas* and *bhajans* [meditative chanting sessions] are played on a cassette player. All these programs are unique—conducted according to time, place and circumstance. However, all of them center on the common principle of all successful Food for Life services—liberal *prasadam* distribution, *harinam* [singing God's names] and distribution of transcendental knowledge.

FFL Success Stories

Over the past 25 years, ISKCON's "Hare Krishna Food for Life" has served more than 85 million hot, nutritious vegetarian meals throughout America, Asia, Africa, Australia and Europe. "ISKCON is trying to benefit people of the world who are less fortunate than ourselves," said Priyavrata, international director of the Food for Life program. "Too much grief and despair in the world is caused by hunger. Therefore, Krishna devotees are dedicated to preparing healthy, sanctified, vegetarian foods knowing that it will bring people hope."[8] A brief look at the Global Food for Life website (www.ffl.org) reveals the magnitude and breadth of the project, with major affiliates in the United States, India, Chile, the United Kingdom, Ukraine, Argentina, Australia, Peru, Brazil, South Africa, Canada, Italy, New Zealand, and many others.

The success stories in each of these places are too numerous to mention here. A few examples should suffice: Even before FFL officially existed, the devotees in Gainesville, Florida, took it upon themselves to feed the college students of that area. Since 1971, they have been distributing *prasadam* on campus at the University of Florida—with more than one million free meals distributed thus far. From this endeavor, among others, it becomes clear that *prasadam* distribution is not just for the needy, and any number of hungry college students will vouch for that. The Gainesville initiative is the longest-running public *prasadam* program in ISKCON, and has served as an example for other such programs established in the intervening years.

In 1985, a French Food for Life program started by distributing 1,000 meals daily, seven days a week. Registered under the name Nourriture Sans Frontieres ("Food Without Borders"), the endeavor was spearheaded by Adiraja (whose work we will explore more closely in the next chapter) and Vishvakuru. The program began in response to "the New Poor," a social phenomenon in France that shocked the government and the middle class in the mid-'80s: More than six million French people, they found, were below the poverty level. The central government, anxious to remedy the situation, decided to integrate the devotees into a master plan. As part of that plan, NSF received top priority in procuring vast amounts of surplus food, and subsidized discounts on the purchase of milk products. All of this was to go to the French FFL program, which has since reduced the problem in France.

In 1986, under the leadership of Bhakti-Tirtha Swami (John Favors), FFL took its rain of mercy to developing African nations. In Lagos, Nigeria, for example, 20,000 plates of *prasadam* were distributed in especially needy areas. The same was done in Ghana. "One might think this was the second coming of Jesus," announced a major Nigerian radio station, "because just as he fed the masses, so the Hare Krishnas were feeding thousands of people."

In 1988, devotees traveled deep into Kwazulu, the homeland of the Zulu nation in South Africa. Headed by Giriraja Swami (Glenn Teton) and Indradyumna Swami (Brian Tibbitts), two ISKCON leaders of substantial renown, FFL devotees brought trucks of tasty *prasadam* into an area where tens of thousands die every day. They set up emergency stations for the welfare of the local people, saving lives and feeding the hungry. FFL's work is especially significant in these African nations, since of the 31 counties declared underdeveloped, 22 are found here, where 300 million people suffer from anemia and millions of children are at risk of dying due to malnutrition and vitamin deficiency.

A couple of years ago in Durban, South Africa, Food for Life hosted the world's largest gathering of school children for a free picnic—that day, more than 40,000 picnic lunches were served. President Mandela was the special guest of honor. He later told reporters that it was "his happiest day," attributing his glee to the devotees and their life-saving activities. Said Mandela, "Hare Krishna Food for Life has set an example for all South Africans of a caring and community spirit. . . ."[9]

Many Food for Life volunteers have risked their lives working in war zones. For example, ISKCON devotees in Sarajevo, Bosnia, visited orphanages, homes for the elderly, hospitals, institutes for handicapped children, and basement shelters daily throughout the three-year conflict. Moreover, an estimated 20 tons of food have been distributed in Sarajevo since 1992. As *Vegetarian Times* reported in 1996 (August): "Though it may not get top mention on the nightly news, Food for Life is among the world's most intrepid relief organizations, in at least one case delivering food to a war-torn region after the Red Cross and other agencies gave up."

ISKCON members also implement food relief programs in times of natural disasters. For instance, in 1993 an earthquake devastated Latur, India. Krishna devotees from ISKCON's Bombay temple drove more than 100 miles to be on the scene within hours, supplying 52,000 meals, as well as clothing and medical supplies, to distressed villagers.

Or consider the massive cyclone that crashed through coastal Orissa in 1999, bringing with it 30-foot tidal waves and wind speeds of up to 300 kmph. Local reporters claimed that the whirlwind conditions caused coconuts to fly as fast as bullets. The aftermath killed more than 20,000 villagers, and destroyed hundreds of thousands of acres of cropland and cattle. More than one million were left homeless, as well as hungry and bewildered. Enter FFL. Devotee volunteers filled four trucks and just as many boats with delectable vegetarian stew and bottles of clean drinking water, and traveled throughout the region delivering the goods to as many survivors as possible. They then sent for more supplies, as necessary. In all, FFL, in response to this particular calamity, distributed more than one million vegetarian meals and 40,000 bottles of water, blankets, clothes, and first aid treatment to the needy.

More examples of FFL selflessness took place in Mozambique, Africa, in 2000, when the largest floods in that country's history covered entire villages, destroyed precious crops, and rendered arable land unusable. And in Gujarat, India, in 2001, the largest earthquake in 50 years killed up to 30,000 people. FFL teams set up temporary hospital and food relief services to provide tens of thousands of survivors with a hot vegetarian meal, as well as clothing, fuel, water, and survival kits for the homeless.

The establishment of living facilities for the homeless, and tending to the basic needs of ex-drug addicts (and others in the process of rehabilitation), represents a new direction for FFL, and many feel that this will be a growing area of FFL concern. In Philadelphia, Pennsylvania, for instance, there have been remarkable inroads as far as helping the needy in the above-mentioned ways. FFL was established in this region by Chandrika Devi (Charlotte Sorlien) in 1983, and it developed into a massive outreach program through the determined efforts of Devi Deva (David Dobson) soon thereafter. It started as a *prasadam* soup kitchen of sorts, and gradually morphed into an important housing facility for people with health or drug problems. Recently, it has further developed into housing for homeless veterans. But the main focus is still feeding *prasadam* to all who need it, and then some. FFL Philly is exemplary in its ability to interface with the Department of Public Welfare, the Department of Housing and Urban Development, the Federal Emergency Management Agency, and the City of Philadelphia. Accordingly, it garners enough funds—through city-sponsored grants—for its many *prasadam* distribution programs, and serves as a beacon for FFL endeavors elsewhere as well.

Grants at federal, state, and local levels rush in to help ISKCON's noble endeavor in much of the known world. The United States Department of Agriculture regularly donates surplus foodstuffs in huge quantities, and leaders of FFL now have access to private food banks from countries around the globe. An in-depth article on FFL summarizes its accomplishments as follows: "Besides ISKCON's ongoing work in India (over 12 million meals served to date), Food for Life now reaches the needy in Peru, Bolivia, Spain, France, the Philippines, Australia, Nigeria, Kenya, and remote villages in South Africa. The program seems to grow with the hunger. As one Australian clergyman put it: 'Hare Krishna, I think, will be the Salvation Army of the twenty-first century.' "[10]

Victory in Chechnya

Without doubt, Food for Life's most valiant efforts were realized during the conflict in Grozny, the capital of the Russian republic of Chechnya, where a war for independence has been raging for a decade. Since March 1995, Food for Life has been at work in Chechnya. A *New York Times* article, entitled "Krishnas Cast Bread on Roiling Waters in Russia" (December 12, 1995), was quoted at the onset of this chapter. It bears repeating: "Here, they have a reputation like the one that Mother Teresa has in Calcutta: it's not hard finding people to swear they are saints." These sentiments were echoed by *The Moscow Tribune* (August 30, 1995): "The Hare Krishna cooks have established themselves as the chief emergency feeding program in war-torn Chechnya."

In fact, Salambek Hadjiev, the former Prime Minister of Chechnya, observing ISKCON's selfless service there, said, "I pray that your Food for Life program will expand to bring about a peaceful world." The (London) *Financial Times* (June 8, 1996) may have said it best: "[W]hile the Kremlin has been willing to spend trillions of rubles on its soldiers, only one Russian civic organization has come to Chechnya to provide emergency aid for its often homeless and sometimes starving compatriots—the Russian branch of the Hare Krishna [movement]."

A detailed report was submitted to the worldwide community of devotees about the work of their dedicated brothers and sisters in Grozny. Priyavrata submitted it to the author of this book for publication, and while the English is poor, the message is clear:

16 May 1996

Please accept my humble obeisances. All glories to Srila Prabhupada.

This is to submit to your kind attention a more or less detailed report on the Food for Life program carried out by a handful of devotees for the last 15 months in Grozny. The program is receiving attention from the devotees and general public from all over the world; therefore it seems necessary to give more insight to what exactly is going on over there.

During April–May, I happened to visit Grozny twice. Each of the visits was full of impressions, events worth reporting on, but I hope you'll excuse my making them into one summary report....

The program is now being run by 10 devotees who volunteered to come there from different places—two from Arkhangelsk (Rasaraj Das and Gunagrahi Das), five from St. Petersburg (Kamsanasa Das, Vanipati Das, Balidvamsi Das, Sergey, and Ilya) and two from Moscow (Vrsakapi Das and Kalikrt Das). It started on March 16, 1995, and was not ever interrupted during the whole period, giving out from 1,500 to 3,000 hot meals a day to the needy of the city. It has been managed by Sukhananda Das. He is a very dedicated devotee and manager, expert in explaining our mission to the government. The program could not have been such a success without his selfless and fearless (here is a lot of things to be afraid of) service.

The devotees are still living in an abandoned canteen in Zavodskoy district of the city. They repaired the premises and furnished and equipped it to suit *ashrama* life and FFL kitchen demands. The surrounding is quite calm and peaceful, save for incessant machine gun fire at night. The devotees have become so accustomed to it that they say they now cannot even sleep without it. Each and every night is marked with several flurries of violent fights in close-by neighborhoods, as it is all over the city.

Once, in March 1996, there was even a battle between Russian soldiers located just 10 meters away from our center on its one side and Chechen fighters who climbed atop a burnt three-story building situated in our courtyard. Bullets were flying over our roof for one and a half hours, but, surprisingly enough, both sides seemed to deliberately spare us, avoiding to shoot at our compound. Devotees were lying on the floor and praying, but only a few bullets (from the Russian side) flew inside the compound. Lord Nrsimhadeva [Krishna] never forgets His servants!

In the FFL center in Grozny the devotees gorgeously (according to Grozny standards) worship Sri Sri Gaura-Nitai Deities. They have a well-organized morning program, adjusted to fit into the requirements of the demanding work here. Devotees chant all the prayers in one session starting at 6:30 A.M., and before the program begins they chant all or most of their rounds [rosary].

For the *prasadam* distribution the devotees cook 350 liters of milk porridge, bean soup or *kichri*. This goes on every day using huge gas-heated pots. They also prepare the same quantity of vitamin drink made of special "dog-rose bush" berries, and bake bread—of this bread, the *New York Times* reported it to be the most tasty in the whole city. After the food is offered to the Deities, devotees put it in special metal and plastic containers with tight lids and drive them in a rented car or in our own ambulance van around the city to seven different locations, where recipients come by at a certain time to receive their meals. When the FFL team arrive to the next point, the people, mostly old Russian men and women, surround the van and line up with their jars and plastic bags to fill them with hot and delicious *prasadam*. Sometimes they quarrel among themselves to get closer to the van outlet, and devotees have to assure them that there is enough for all. Devotees also serve *prasadam* to the patients of the Republican TB hospital and to children of three local schools including a boarding school for mentally disturbed children.

By this time devotees managed to distribute over 750,000 meals to the needy of Grozny. This is no doubt the biggest and most effective food relief program in the city. Besides, Hare Krishna Food for Life (HKFFL) seems to be the only Russian non-government charity program in the whole Chechnya region! This puts Krishna Consciousness in a unique position in the region, vividly showing our tremendous social contribution.

Now devotees are planning to make the program a long-termed one, establishing strong relations with Chechen and Russian government welfare departments and local authorities. As the war gradually calms down, the problems in social field are also going to decrease, therefore there will be on the one hand less need in emergency food relief programs, but on the other hand there will be more need in thorough and systematic welfare help and care of the veterans, invalids, orphans and incomplete families. We are now trying to find ways of joint program with the government social services in this area.

To be continued . . .

Your unworthy servant,

Maxim

What the Future Holds

Other significant FFL programs, growing rapidly, include the one in Bangalore, India. Known as Akshaya Patra ("inexhaustible pot") to the locals, FFL activity here was formally inaugurated on November 11, 2000 and currently feeds 43,000 rural children in 210 schools on a daily basis. The Akshaya Patra Foundation, which, like many FFL branches, is a not-for-profit organization, focuses on providing free meals to poverty-stricken school children in and around Bangalore city in southern India. Akshaya Patra has demonstrated how it is indeed possible to care for poor children in India: by alleviating hunger and offering free education. The institution's goal is to serve over 250,000 children per day by the year 2005. Says Atal Bihari Vajpayee, India's Prime Minister: "I am confident that ISKCON's 'Akshaya Patra' program will serve both as an inspiration and a practical logistical guide to other institutions interested in taking up such activities. I wish the program all success."[11]

The United Kingdom's FFL institution, founded in 1980, is also one to watch in upcoming years: Free meals are distributed by rickshaw and van in the Camden area of London. Meals are also provided at the Camden resource center, which operates from 8 A.M. to 4 P.M. The meals are cooked from the Food for Life kitchen in Camden, and distributed to 500 people daily. The project is geared toward the homeless, drug abusers, single parents, the unemployed, as well as others who have fallen on hard times.

So, too, is FFL Vrindavan, India, doing significant work. Hundreds of poor children at schools in Vrindavan and nearby villages receive assistance from FFL by way of a freshly cooked vegetable stew, bread, *halava*, and fruits delivered daily. More than 1,000 other needy children, holy men, widows, and pilgrims receive a hot meal from the local ISKCON temple. Food for Life Vrindavan also provides educational aids, clothing, and free medical care. They recently opened a day school offering free education to 100 local children.

These are just a few of the burgeoning FFL programs with a potentially bright future. One reason that FFL does so well is that it has a policy of cooperation and respect—it is willing to work with others who share their goals of feeding the hungry and helping the needy. But FFL is also always insistent on emphasizing its unique contribution: *prasadam*.

Currently, Hare Krishna Food for Life works in cooperation with animal rights groups and vegetarian organizations throughout the world. People for the Ethical Treatment of Animals (PETA) and the Farm Animal Reform Movement (FARM) are but two such organizations to have helped ISKCON over the years, and there is hope for more cooperative efforts in the future. FFL regularly participates in such annual events as the Great American Meatout in the United States and the protest staged against Italy's hunting law on the first day of that country's hunting season. These are the kinds of activities with which FFL aligns itself. Its main focus, of course, continues to be hunger-relief—by way of *prasadam*—though it is increasingly interested in working with housing and shelter groups around the world, as in its relief work in Philadelphia, and launching culinary and nutritional instruction programs for the homeless, especially in developing countries.

FFL's most ambitious project to date is "Hare Krishna Feed the World Day." On November 23, 1996, this program was launched with great enthusiasm: four million plates of sacred vegetarian food were distributed to those in need. The plan was to reenact this every year, and ISKCON has done so to the present day. Praised as the largest free food event in the history of the Western world, it is but a precursor to more massive events to come. ISKCON plans to increase yearly, eventually feeding all who need it. A lofty goal? Certainly. But it is clearly a worthy one. And, if events up until now are any indication, it is achievable as well.

6

Restaurants and Cookbooks

I think it's great. It's a pity you don't have restaurants or temples
on all the main streets of every little town and village like those
hamburger and fried chicken places. You should put them out of
business.

—George Harrison

With the success of "Food for Life," or *prasadam* distribution in general, devotees continued to find new and inventive ways to get their message to the masses. More than just their message—they came up with fresh means to get *prasadam*, something tangible, to just about every man, woman, and child in the world. Naturally, delicious vegetarian food lends itself well to the opening of gorgeous restaurants and the publishing of award-winning cookbooks, and these in fact greatly helped devotees in the mass distribution of *prasadam*. Indeed, ISKCON was a forerunner in the popularization of vegetarianism in the West, using restaurants and cookbooks as vehicles to accomplish this end. This is not to say that the Western world did not already have strong supporters of the meatless diet and compassion for animals. But Western harmlessness was an esoteric heritage, little known by the mainstream.

Pythagoras (582–500 BCE) is often hailed as "the father of Western vegetarianism," and many Greco-Roman intellectuals followed his lead. Biblical vegetarianism was also in vogue from time to time. In the modern era, it was poet-philosopher Percy Bysshe Shelley (1792–1822) who revived interest in compassion for animals in the West, and through him the Vegetarian Movement in Great Britain took firm root. Soon after, the American Vegetarian Society was born.

As the nineteenth century changed to the twentieth, Henry Salt (1851–1939) wrote prodigiously on the subject, and the movement found important representatives in playwright George Bernard Shaw (1856–1950) and novelist Leo Tolstoy (1828–1910). John Harvey Kellogg (1852–1943), too—though known primarily as the originator of cornflakes—was a strong supporter of the vegetarian way of life. Organizations with an Eastern bent, such as the Theosophists and the Vedanta Society, also popularized the harmless diet and other forms of *ahimsa* in the Occidental world, as did the writings of Mahatma Gandhi (1869–1948). The Seventh-Day Adventists contributed to this awareness of vegetarianism and its virtues as well.

But it was not until the rise of Krishna Consciousness in the '60s, and the large-scale *prasadam* distribution of the '70s and '80s, that vegetarianism and animal rights became well known on Western shores. The vegetarian movement, especially, enjoyed a pronounced resurgence at this time. Sparked by the initial endeavors of Krishna devotees, an increasing number of detailed studies found their way into bookstores. Some were influenced directly by the Hare Krishna movement. Others evolved independently. Prominent examples of this latter category include Francis Moore Lappé's *Diet for a Small Planet* (1971) and Peter Singer's *Animal Liberation* (1975), and many others followed soon thereafter. These books led to special interest groups that eventually made vegetarianism part of the mainstream. With the People for the Ethical Treatment of Animals (PETA), founded in 1980, the harmless diet and its underpinning of compassion for animals were established once and for all. And ISKCON played a prominent role in all this, for unlike movements like the Seventh-Day Adventists, for example, who merely praised vegetarianism as "an ideal diet" but never made it a requirement for its members, Swami Prabhupada saw vegetarianism as mandatory, at least for his serious followers. Historian Jon Gregerson notes the Hare Krishna contribution in this area:

With the coming of the so-called Counterculture of the '60s, a number of small Hindu-oriented groups and movements, headed by various swamis and "spiritual masters," came to enjoy a certain popularity throughout North America. Most of these advocated a vegetarian diet either as a required practice or at least as a preferable ideal. Chief among such religious groups was the "Krishna Consciousness Movement," the importance of which for vegetarianism in general is undeniable. Not only does this spiritual organization require a vegetarian diet of its followers, but it has popularized vegetarian cuisine through dispensing free vegetarian meals to the public at its ashrams and at public festivals. Its adherents have also produced a number of excellent vegetarian cookbooks.[1]

Gregerson here writes that ISKCON's "importance for vegetarianism in general is undeniable." He is referring, no doubt, to the fact that Hare Krishna devotees were pioneers in this area. As psychologists Paul Amato and Sonia Partridge write,

Many people at the time *had their first taste of vegetarian food courtesy of the International Society for Krishna Consciousness (ISKCON)*—one of the most successful and conspicuous of the Hindu sects operating in the West. ISKCON not only operates a chain of low-cost lacto-vegetarian restaurants, but also puts on regular free feasts for the public at local temples.[2] (Italics added.)

With some of the earliest vegetarian restaurants in North America and Europe to its credit, and popular *prasadam* cookbooks dating back to the Counterculture and eventually receiving praise from connoisseurs of fine cuisine, ISKCON's place is secure in the history of vegetarianism in the West. Gregerson's remarks—and those of the two psychologist-historians—are in no way an exaggeration, as this chapter will soon prove. True, the Seventh-Day Adventists had already opened vegetarian restaurants, and others, such as Cranks in England, predated ISKCON by some years. But it was only *after* ISKCON opened such restaurants *en masse* that vegetarianism as a lifestyle became widespread—giving birth to a cornucopia of meat-free restaurants and cookbooks that catered to the desires of an ever-increasing market.

The Next Phase

From ISKCON's earliest days, Swami Prabhupada made clear his desire for *prasadam* restaurants. Although he had written numerous letters on this subject, in 1968 he wrote to one disciple in particular, Dayananda (Michael Wright), saying, "Regarding the idea of a *prasadam* restaurant, I am advocating it from the very beginning."[3] And indeed he did: In 1965, before officially founding ISKCON, Prabhupada wrote letters to Sally Agarwal, wife of Gopal Agarwal, who sponsored the Swami's initial journey to the West, about the opening of such restaurants. Prabhupada stayed as a guest in the Agarwals' home in Butler, Pennsylvania, when he first arrived in the United States. After leaving for New York, in his letters to them, he urged Sally to open "an Indian *prasadam* restaurant," telling her that she could easily make a good living in this way, since there were few vegetarian establishments at that time, and none that served *prasadam*. It would be unique, he told her, and it would enable people to "forget meat-eating." He wrote her two letters to this effect, one on November 13, 1965, and again the following week. Unfortunately, she was never able to realize his vision.

The reality of these restaurants manifested several years later, not through Sally but by the grace of Prabhupada's initiated followers. In the late '60s and early '70s, the devotees opened small-scale juice bars and portable *prasadam* carts, and some even managed one or two short-lived restaurants, projects with minimal manpower and lacking the professionalism needed to sustain them. For this reason, Prabhupada was hesitant about starting restaurants in the movement's earliest days, and he wrote several letters discouraging devotees from taking on this monumental task. But in 1974, he reiterated with renewed force his desire for full-scale *prasadam* restaurants. A letter written by Satsvarupa Dasa Goswami, Prabhupada's secretary at the time, went out to all Hare Krishna centers:

June 18, 1974

Please accept my humble obeisances. All glories to Srila Prabhupada.

The other day, His Divine Grace [Prabhupada] revealed in detail his plans for Hare Krishna Restaurants, which can be opened anywhere in the world. I know this subject has been discussed somewhat over the years, but after his talk most recently he told me to see that this information be disseminated to all the devotees. He described it as "the next phase of our movement." Please therefore make a newsletter of the information that follows for all-ISKCON distribution.

Our Krishna Conscious farms, like New Vrindaban, are producing much *ghee*. This *ghee* should be distributed at a fee to the different centers, and once restaurants begin opening, the *ghee* will be one of their prime materials. Other supplies, such as vegetables, grains, etc., can be obtained locally.

The restaurants should be cafeteria style. The food is to be kept out on counters and people can approach on a line with a tray and take what they want. Prabhupada proposed that there should be one [monetary] charge and if a person takes more than another person, he is not charged more. "As much as you like for a certain fee." But there should be no waste. A person should take what he can eat. One devotee, hearing this, said, "Prabhupada, I think people will be carrying *samosas* home in their pockets."

"No," he said, "it is a business. Only what they can eat. But they don't get charged more for eating more, like in a hotel—immediately there is a bill if you eat more." We can also make home deliveries. The food is cooked fresh, and as it is taken [i.e., eaten], more fresh batches are put on the counter; always fresh. There will be about 20 sweet preparations, and 20 salty preparations, like *samosas* (made with potatoes, peas, cauliflower, white flour and *ghee*) and *kachories*, etc. The vegetable preps must be served hot. Everything should be so clean that not a single fly will be seen. After the first batch of *prasadam* is made, it will be offered to Lord Chaitanya with *arotik* [a traditional ceremony], and then the *prasadam* for the rest of the day will be considered offered. Smoking is of course prohibited in the restaurant. Tapes can play of our *kirtans*. The idea is that people who will not come to our temples will come and eat at our restaurants and be engaged in eating *prasadam* and hearing [about Krishna]. Also it will engage men, our devotees, in new varieties of pursuits, not that without engagement men should sleep and eat in our temples in the name of devotional service. "Hare Krishna Restaurants!" The name, Srila Prabhupada said, should also be legally registered so that others may not imitate.

Foods cooked in *ghee*, foods cooked in water, all the standard varieties will be there. Foods cooked in *ghee* are especially wonderful and healthful. People should come and be relaxed, eat and talk relaxed, and see how nice Krishna Consciousness is. There will be a small book and record store in the restaurant.

Devotees will do all the work in the restaurant. We can even import an expert Indian cook if necessary. At the end of the day everything must be thoroughly washed down and no leftovers. No *prasadam* will be given away free. At a certain hour at the end of the day the leftovers can be sold half price or some even given away. But the venture has to be an economically profitable business.

Start out the business small and train up men in one restaurant; then you can expand gradually. You can give them nice drinks. *Masala* milk made with small quantities of ginger, saffron, pepper and cinnamon can be served hot, and cold juices. No tea is served. Yogurt can be made from hot milk and then drunk as whey; this is very good for digestion.

So here is the idea. Now our business-inclined devotees should plan and organize this into a reality, by starting one restaurant that can be a model for others. It is not a pipe dream or vague suggestion but a new plan that Srila Prabhupada wants implemented. If in time he can visit the first Hare Krishna Restaurant and see it running as he has outlined it, he will be very pleased.

Your servant,
Satsvarupa Dasa Goswami

Govinda's Restaurants, et al.

Though it was slow going at first, with Satsvarupa's letter came a barrage of restaurants. Vatsal and his wife Shashikala (Peter and Deborah Corbett), for example, opened The Hare Krishna Restaurant—

Prabhupada's preferred name for his proposed eating establishments—in Palo Alto, California, in 1974. The enterprising Toshan Krishna (Tom Allin), to cite another early example, began his spiritual sojourn in New York in the late '60s, but 1974 found him in Honolulu, Hawaii, negotiating for property on behalf of his spiritual master. This real estate venture was initially meant for purchasing a temple, but Toshan found an additional property that would be perfect for a restaurant. Aware of Prabhupada's clearly stated desire as conveyed in Satsvarupa's letter, he secured both properties and began what became one of ISKCON's first successful restaurants. Feeling separation from and warm feelings for New York's deity form of Lord Krishna (who goes by the name Govinda), Toshan named the restaurant "Govinda's."

Soon businessmen and hippies alike lined the streets to sample Krishna *prasadam*, and they became regulars at Govinda's in Hawaii. The delectable and nutritious Hare Krishna fare was habit-forming, and the restaurant grew into a financial and spiritual success. Before long, Toshan was called to help in yet another new temple project— this time, back in his old stomping grounds, New York. He excitedly arranged for ISKCON's newly purchased high-rise apartment building on West 55th Street in Manhattan to include a restaurant in the basement. By 1976, it was completely redone and elegantly decorated; the basement restaurant transported visitors to the spiritual world. Beautiful paintings and sculptures of Krishna adorned the hallways, while the charming decor and lighting worked in tandem with exotic incense and the aromas of *prasadam* to transform the atmosphere into something wonderful. No longer were guests in some basement space in the City; they were instead in Krishna's own transcendental playground.

Experienced devotees came from other temples to help. Karuna Purna (Carl Haynes), Prahladapriya (Phillip Gallelli), Bhaktivinode (Ben McLeod), Vishnu-Gada (James Evans), Mathuresh (Andrew Day), Hansarupa (Jeffrey Moy), Achyuta Priya (Julie Bennedetto), and many others—all talented in various ways—worked together to make this restaurant successful, exceeding the now legendary status of Govinda's in Hawaii. Naturally, they called the New York restaurant

Govinda's as well. After this, nearly all ISKCON restaurants used the same name.

Meanwhile, Govinda's in New York was flourishing. Although no formal advertisements went out, early morning would see lines form by the restaurant doors, up the stairs, through the temple entrance and down the block, with multitudes waiting for a taste of "Govinda's cuisine." There was a buzz in the neighborhood that extended throughout much of Manhattan and even into the neighboring boroughs. "We had no idea at the time," says Hansarupa, the restaurant's manager, "but Gary Null, a popular nutritionist, author, and vitamin specialist of some renown, used to promote us on his radio show. He told his listeners that the best-kept secret in New York was hidden in the basement of the Hare Krishna temple. And he would rave about the delicious food and transcendental atmosphere." This might explain the lines around the block.

The restaurant included its own baking department, and so fresh whole-grain bread and delicious vegan cakes were a special feature of Govinda's in New York. The devotees also imported milk from Gitanagari, their own farm in Port Royal, Pennsylvania, for use in the restaurant. This allowed them to at least partially implement Prabhupada's recommendation of self-sufficiency, and made good use of the rich by-products of happy and healthy cows. Govinda's menu changed regularly, but commonly offered two sumptuous vegetable preps, one an elaborate stew of mixed vegetables drenched in *ghee*, or clarified butter, and the other a vegetable, cheese-curd blitz that satisfied every urge of the senses. There was often a succulent sweet-and-sour preparation as well, made with pineapple, plantains, eggplant, tamarind water, and spices. Restaurant specialties included banana and sometimes date *halava*, various kinds of pizza, eggplant and cauliflower *pakoras*—which are bite-sized chunks of vegetable dipped in spicy batter and then deep-fried in *ghee*—and a medley of tasty soups. Diverse chutneys and rice preparations were also available, as were desserts galore. These also might explain those lines around the block.

The restaurant quickly sprouted into *prasadam* carts. Prahladapriya and his wife began to sell Govinda's goodies on the streets, offering New

Yorkers mock-tuna sandwiches made from chick-peas and soy, along with hot soup, farina *halava*, and other Hare Krishna favorites. "We sold tons of *samosas*," Prahlada says, "which are like subtly spiced vegetable-filled turnovers, deep-fried in clear butter, and also *lassi*, a whipped yogurt drink, made with fruit juice and berries, over ice." The cart did so well that it quickly expanded to four, six, and then eight venues. At its height, Govinda's boasted a fleet of 18 food carts in New York City. This enabled devotees to frequent various strategic locations, where they found new customers for the restaurant at the temple. Prabhupada himself finally came to New York to inspect Govinda's success, and the devotees happily guided him through their first flourishing Hare Krishna restaurant.

Other ISKCON centers followed suit, and restaurants became "the next phase," as Prabhupada had predicted. By 1980, the movement's magazine, *Back to Godhead*, started listing the restaurants along with their usual list of temples and farm communities.[4] As of that listing, there were only restaurants in Toronto, Canada; Austin, Texas; Columbus, Ohio; Washington, D.C.; and St. Louis, Missouri. Elsewhere in the world, Hare Krishna eateries could be found in India, naturally; and in Adelaide, Melbourne, and Sydney, in Australia. But soon virtually every temple opened a restaurant, either within the temple facility itself (as in the example set by New York's basement restaurant), which Prabhupada preferred, or else by establishing a separate building specifically for their restaurant business.

Govinda's became a trendy hangout for celebrities, particularly musicians, such as Alice Coltrane, John McLaughlin, Carlos Santana, John Lennon, George Harrison, Paul McCartney, Mick Jagger, Jerry Garcia, and Stevie Wonder. As time went on, Bob Marley, Sting, Boy George, Annie Lennox, Chrissie Hynde, Ray Davies, Todd Rundgren, Erykah Badu, and others too numerous to mention showed up as well. Some of these people frequented the Govinda's in New York; others came later, and learned of Krishna's varied tastes at the many other Hare Krishna restaurants around the world. Particularly famous for feeding the in-crowd was Healthy, Wealthy, and Wise, which opened in London in 1979; the Govinda's on Venice Blvd., in Los Angeles, California, opening at roughly the same time; and Kalachandji's, the restaurant in Dallas, Texas, that took the Lone Star state by storm in 1982.

Kalachandji's (which means "the beautiful moon-faced one," a name for Krishna) was especially singled out for accolades, though similar praise could apply to all Hare Krishna restaurants. Beautifully conceived by Tamal Krishna Goswami (Thomas Herzig), the elegant eatery was initially managed by Sunanda (Saul Porecki), who also served as its one-of-a-kind cook. His expertise was quickly acknowledged by connoisseurs of fine food. *The Dallas Times Herald* dubbed the restaurant "a gift from the gods," while *Vegetarian Times* said it was among the best vegetarian restaurants in the country. "The ambience of Kalachandji's is magical," the March, 1987, article states. "As you enter, you are greeted by the aroma of incense and a host dressed in traditional Indian garb. You can dine either indoors or on the outdoor patio. Soothing Indian music plays as sari-clad women serve your meal."[5] *The Dallas Observer* awarded the restaurant first place in the category of "unique dining experiences" and second place in "natural foods / vegetarian restaurants."

Such high-quality restaurants were Prabhupada's dream come true. And he enjoyed similar successes again and again. The devotees in Philadelphia, Pennsylvania, for example, opened a much-loved restaurant right next door to one of the largest and most popular New Age bookstores in the eastern United States. As a result, people would come from the bookstore to the restaurant, and, often, from there to the temple. Another example: A Govinda's opened in Tehran, Iran, and received high praise in the *Tehran Times*, Iran's leading English-language newspaper. When another devotee restaurant opened in Mauritius, R. Chedumbarum Pillay, the Minister of Industry and an important political figure there, gave a speech, saying, "We should be grateful to the devotees of ISKCON for opening this restaurant. Association with devotees engaged in spiritual life will bring bliss, and eating at Govinda's restaurant will be a spiritual experience. It is beyond doubt that the natural ingredients and fine cooking of Lord Krishna's cuisine will be relished by the Mauritians and by foreign visitors as well. I'm sure the restaurant will be in high demand."[6]

This kind of praise became usual as restaurants began to spring up everywhere, from Italy's low-key, meditative Govinda's in Milan and Rome to the colorful and wildly expressive devotional food fiesta in San Juan, Puerto Rico; from the perfectly structured and expensive-looking establishment in Detroit, Michigan, to the more humble and sweet atmosphere of the restaurant in Almaty, Kazakhstan. ISKCON restaurants are now in Hong Kong; Vancouver, B.C.; Tucson, Arizona; Dublin, Ireland; Heidelberg, Germany; Barcelona, Spain; Gothenburg, Sweden; Zurich, Switzerland; Oslo, Norway; Prague, in the Czech Republic; St. Petersburg, Russia; Auckland, New Zealand; Suva, Fiji; Durban, South Africa—and this just scratches the surface. If you have a town, devotees have a restaurant nearby. At one point, there were three ISKCON restaurants in San Francisco, California, alone—The Higher Taste, Seven Mothers, and Jagannatha's Cart. Prabhupada's vision was thus fully realized, producing many smiling faces and stuffed bellies in the process.

Jerry Abrams' *Prasadam* Cart

In addition to restaurants, devotees always found unique ways to distribute *prasadam*, including catering services, such as Magic Lotus, begun by Nrisimhananda (David Shapiro) in Los Angeles, California, in 1980, and developed by Sunanda of Kalachandji's several years later. Extravaganzas like Paul McCartney concerts, Lollapalooza tours, and Earth Day festivals became regular events for devotee catering services. Hare Krishna culinary experts also became well known for their cooking classes and videos, such as those conducted by Kurma, to be discussed later. The most unique of these alternative *prasadam* venues, perhaps, was a series of lavishly designed restaurants on wheels, like the ones initiated by Prahladapriya. These traveling eateries are found in all parts of the globe; most are short-lived endeavors. But Jerry Abrams—with determined enthusiasm—has been dedicated to giving New Yorkers a taste of Krishna for some 20 years.

"Dishes Make Merchant a Taste Treat on Broadway," reads the headline of Warren Woodberry Jr.'s front-page story in *New York Newsday*.[7] "Dozens of people wait patiently in line to be served from the busiest food cart during lunch time." Woodberry describes

Abrams as a phenomenon, and praises his work in superlatives. And that's just one of many major articles—the *New York Times* and *New York* magazine also ran feature stories, acknowledging this distinct cart's culinary specialness. "It's not just because it's vegetarian," says Abrams. "It's because it's *prasadam*."

Jerry Abrams was born in 1955 in northern New Jersey. When he met devotees in 1973 at Port Authority in New York, he listened with great interest as they extolled the virtues of *prasadam*, and after trying a few sweet balls himself, he knew he would eventually dedicate himself to *prasadam* distribution. But it was a long, hard road. For 10 years he sold dried fruit and nuts, then fresh fruit, then frozen fruit drinks or hot herbal tea on the streets of New York, even through cold winters. Then, in the summer of 1982, he founded Nimai's, which became a popular *prasadam* restaurant in the East Village.

But Abrams wasn't satisfied. After all, most of the young people who happened into his restaurant were already familiar with Krishna consciousness and could get *prasadam* down at the temple. He wanted to reach a more mainstream crowd, people who might otherwise never taste the mercy of Krishna's nectar. So, in the mid-1980s, he started to investigate other venues for *prasadam* distribution, until finally he found the perfect set-up: He noticed that outdoor carts and concession stands on Wall Street were cleaning up, as it were. Yuppies and workaday people—by the tens of thousands—were spending huge sums on junk food for their lunch breaks. After interviewing quite a number of residents and employees in his targeted area, he realized that a full-scale outdoor restaurant, a *prasadam* cart—combining his acquired culinary skills from years at Nimai's and his down-to-earth know-how from selling fruit on the street—would allow him to reach a class of people who wanted a healthy alternative to their meat-centered fast-food fare. And it would bring in a good deal of money, too.

So he set up shop, first down in the Wall Street area and then slightly further uptown, right near the World Trade Center. Sandwiched between greasy hot-dog and shish-kebab venders, he often relied on his considerable sense of humor to get him through the day. At first, people were suspicious, "Why vegetarian?" His answers were always quick and to the point: "If it runs away from you," he said with a smile, "then you probably shouldn't be eating it." When some of his early meat-eating customers conceded that food animals are treated poorly, he quipped, "Well, we can probably make amends by not serving them for lunch."

His charming personality was surpassed only by his excellent menu, which gradually won him regulars who, to this day, are faithful to his cart. He served giant potatoes or yams overstuffed with grilled vegetables, a special veggie burger made from a unique recipe of his own, along with whole-wheat pita bread and delicious *tahini* dressing. His regular fare also included subtly seasoned brown rice, a mouth-watering vegetarian chili, freshly squeezed orange-kiwi-banana juice, assorted sautéed vegetables in olive oil, and rich mashed potatoes with delectable carrot and tomato sauces that, as he says, are to die for. "But don't die before reading Swami Prabhupada's books," Abrams warns us. For this reason his cart is always accompanied by a book table—so his customers can drink in Krishna's nectarine words with their eyes even as they taste His *prasadam* with their tongues.

After more than a decade of serving people beneath the twin towers of the World Trade Center in this way, winning literally hundreds of regular customers, his world exploded, literally. September 11, 2001 left him without a business and with serious health problems. But from calamity, it is said, opportunity often arises, and after a brief respite Abrams re-opened, with renewed vigor, at a new uptown location.

"Chez Pascale," the weekly dining column in the *Daily News*, written by Pascale Le Draoulec, recently told Abrams' story: "Abrams owns the Govinda Vegetarian Buffet Cart, which recently re-sprouted at the corner of 52nd and Park [midtown Manhattan], a tofu toss from the Four Seasons restaurant.

"For years," writes Pascale, "Abrams' popular cart was a fixture at the intersection of Church and Cedar Streets, downtown. In a city where hot-dog carts crown every corner, his colorful stand was a little oasis for the meat-free minded.

"Then the calendar turned to September 11. Debris from the first plane's impact crushed his cart; the tumbling towers buried it, along with Abrams and his crew, in powder. A piece of glass wedged itself in one of Abrams' lungs, which explains the gravel in his voice. Doctors can't remove it and if he doesn't take a daily dose of steroids, he could die."[8]

But he persists with the spirit of one possessed. In addition to the cart's old favorites, he now serves soy "chicken," a tofu scramble with a bright lemon carrot sauce, and a specially prepared oatmeal breakfast that is quickly winning over his new customers at his midtown location. And now he tells his story. While anxious consumers wait in line for their enticing meal at Govinda's, Abrams himself is always there, with tales of tragedy and opportunity.

Books That Cook

Before any *prasadam* restaurants came into being, the devotees released a cookbook that included "recipes for the satisfaction of the Supreme Personality of Godhead." It was 1973, and two entrepreneurial young Hare Krishna women, Krishna Devi and Shama Devi, decided the world was ready for *The Hare Krishna Cookbook*, a simple presentation laying bare the basics of Lord Krishna's cuisine. They had been planning the book for years, and, as early as 1969, had even received encouragement from Prabhupada himself. In a letter to Krishna Devi, he wrote:

> I am pleased to learn that you are thinking of putting together a cookbook of our Krishna *prasadam* recipes. I understand that in London, Yamuna Dasi has already done some work on this same project, so you may correspond with her in this connection. I know that at our feasts especially many persons become interested in preparing foodstuffs in this way, so this cookbook is a nice thing to instruct such persons in preparing and offering nice *prasadam* for the Lord. So when there is some tangible book ready for publication, please inform me, and we shall try to arrange for its publication. I am pleased to note your description of the increasing interest in [the] vegetarian diet in this country. Actually, the practice of meat-eating is very detrimental to spiritual life, because in spiritual life the goal is to become free from all sinful reactions, and meat-eating means simply to force oneself to suffer the sinful reactions of killing our fellow living entities. So as many people will be taking to prac-

ticing spiritual life through the influence of our Sankirtana Movement, this cookbook will be very important, and you should work for this as you are able. Please convey my blessings to your husband, Dinesh, and to your child, Visnu Arati. I hope this will find you all well.

> Your ever well-wisher,
> A. C. Bhaktivedanta Swami[9]

When finally published, *The Hare Krishna Cookbook* was a simple, 71-page softbound book, with both Foreword and Introduction by Kirtanananda Swami, one of Prabhupada's earliest followers, and sections on the basic cooking ingredients, such as spices and *ghee;* rice; *dahl;* breads; vegetables; savories; chutneys, *raitas,* and curries; sweets and milk sweets; and beverages. The back cover said it all:

> The recipes in this book are so good that they can carry one a step beyond ordinary sense pleasure . . . into the realm of supreme enjoyment. Handed down for thousands of years by a chain of spiritual masters for whom cooking and eating in Krishna consciousness were holy and joyful celebrations in spiritual life, these vegetarian recipes offer the perfection in purity, nutrition, and taste. Scientifically developed by ancient sages to nourish the body, the mind, and the spirit itself, these palatable dishes, pure by nature, will increase one's life, purify one's existence and give strength, health, happiness and satisfaction.[10]

In all, the book was good promotion for the movement and contained as much *prasadam* philosophy as it did recipes. Most of all, it was a harbinger of what was yet to come.

Adiraja and *The Higher Taste*
The 1980s witnessed a great surge forward as far as Hare Krishna cookbooks are concerned. In 1983, two books revolutionized the vegetarian market: *The Higher Taste,* which was initially published by the American arm of the Bhaktivedanta Book Trust, and the French book *Un Gout Superieur* ("a higher taste"), an entirely different work com-

piled by master chef Adiraja Dasa. The first of these books, whose full title is *The Higher Taste: A Guide to Gourmet Vegetarian Cooking and a Karma-Free Diet*, was the brainchild of Mukunda Goswami. Mukunda worked cooperatively with ISKCON writer Drutakarma (Michael Cremo) to produce this accessible and easy-to-read book on the basics of vegetarianism and its relation to *prasadam*. Though it included recipes, this was more a philosophical work, with sections that explored the health benefits of vegetarianism; the economic problems of a meat-centered diet; a brief history of compassionate living, with details of famous people who adopted the meatless way of life; the ethical and moral contradictions of eating meat; and the spiritual aspects of an *ahimsa* worldview.

Amazingly, the book sold over 20 million copies in English alone, and it also sells significant numbers in Spanish, French, German, and in several other languages. Its success may partly be because of the writing style—it was designed to have international appeal and was written with mass distribution in mind. But, more to the point perhaps, the world was finally ready for its message. After years of receiving *prasadam* from Hare Krishna devotees on streets and in other venues—after going to ISKCON restaurants around the world—people could now hear what devotees had to say. Moreover, the media had by then started to extol the virtues of vegetarianism, and the average person was aware that meat-eating was simply not healthy. The book continues to do well.

The second work mentioned above, Adiraja's *Un Gout Superier*, was more of a conventional cookbook. With only several short chapters on the philosophy behind the diet, Adiraja, born Tom Milano in 1948, decided to let the recipes speak for themselves. And speak they did. The French edition of the book did so well that, by popular demand, it was updated and translated into English by the Bhaktivedanta Book Trust. First published in 1984 as *The Hare Krishna Book of Vegetarian Cooking*, its initial incarnation appeared in England and soon manifested in America. By 1989, it was selling in the millions worldwide, in many different languages. It is particularly popular in Australia, France, the United States, and England.

"This is no ordinary cookbook. You could say it's more a way of life," writes actress Hayley Mills in her preface to the book, whose deluxe edition is now called *The Hare Krishna Gourmet Guide to Vegetarian Cooking*. The hardbound 300-page book includes 30 full-color photos of perfectly prepared *prasadam* as well as 120 tempting recipes by some of ISKCON's most renowned cooks, such as Mukhya Devi, Kishori Devi, Kanti Devi, and, of course, Adiraja himself. In addition to this, the book offers a taste of that special fusion of wisdom and beauty first found in ancient India and now characteristic of the Hare Krishna movement.

Yamuna Makes Waves

Yamuna Devi was born Joan Campanella in 1942, an American of Italian extraction. She spent much of her youth in Oregon, in the Rocky Mountains, attended Reed College in Portland, and opened a ceramics shop in San Francisco as the Hippie movement was gathering strength. One day in 1966, she received a call from her sister, who was soon to be married in New York. So Campanella packed her bags and left the West Coast to journey east—further east than she could have ever imagined at the time. True, her first stop was New York. But even here, the "eastern" dimension of her trip exceeded her wildest expectations. Trish Hall, writing for *The New York Times*, tells the story:

> When Joan Campanella was in her early 20s, she went to New York for her sister's wedding, expecting a traditional ceremony in line with their upper-middle-class upbringing in Oregon. Instead, she found that an Indian swami was to perform the wedding and oversee all the cooking—and he wanted her to help.[11]

The "swami" was A. C. Bhaktivedanta Swami Prabhupada, and he eventually accepted Campanella as his disciple. He gave her the name "Yamuna Devi"—" 'Yamuna,' " she says, "is Krishna's favorite river in India, and 'Devi' means 'goddess.' " It was as if Prabhupada foresaw her future—he immediately engaged her to assist him in cooking for the wedding, and encouraged her from then on to develop her culinary abilities. What she learned from him on that first day about food and spirituality began a lifetime's study that goes on even today.

"The wedding was my Waterloo," Yamuna says. "I became deeply interested in what he [Prabhupada] was saying."[12] And she resolved to be his disciple forever. From New York, she traveled with her teacher to San Francisco, then to Canada and on to England, where the Beatles, spurred by George Harrison, joined the devotees in Krishna consciousness. Yamuna, a gifted singer, was invited to share her talents on several of Harrison's devotional records, and she remembers, shyly, their appearance on U.K. television's *Top of the Pops* show, followed by an Apple Records tour of Europe. This is when her relationship with George, John and Yoko began. She became a friend, taught them cooking, and, for a time, was their personal chef at their country estates.

A more important part of the story, however, is that for several years she served as Prabhupada's personal cook. This provided her with untold opportunities—Prabhupada would give her cooking demonstrations, share culinary wisdom, and direct her to knowledgeable teachers in the field. Further, on Prabhupada's advice, she traveled throughout India for eight years, cooking not only in home kitchens but also in those of sacred Vaishnava temples. This latter aspect is something few Westerners ever get to do. She knew well that it was because she was Prabhupada's protégée that she was given special privilege. And so, knowing she might never get this opportunity again, she diligently took notes on all aspects of her experience—from the arrangement and ambiance of every kitchen she visited to the philosophy behind the eating.

Where did all of this take her? In Vrindavan, India, in the fall of 1976, she went into Prabhupada's quarters and laid before him her plan, which had been brewing since the day she initially met him, almost a decade earlier. "The devotees have asked me to write a cookbook," she said. "I would like to present cooking as you've taught it to me."[13] Prabhupada was visibly pleased. With minimal words and a smile known best only by his disciples, he affirmed her plan. The next few days they met regularly in his room, where he helped her develop ideas for the book. After these meetings, she spent four weeks on a cooking tour of India to increase the knowledge she'd already gained through years of recipe research. As her close friend Vishakha writes, "She met cooks in the famous sweet shops of Calcutta, in the gourmet restaurants of Bombay, and in the homes of connoisseurs. She explored the back rooms of musty bookstores to find old cookbooks, and she observed the techniques of the ubiquitous street venders."[14]

For each recipe, she agonized over what, if any, Western ingredients to use and how to create a legitimate fusion of authentic Indian cuisine and modern technique. In the end, she developed a style of her own, one that took the best of the original Indian versions and joined them with up-to-date, health-oriented Western preferences. "I wanted to dispel the myths about the world's oldest vegetarian cuisine," she later told *The Chicago Tribune*, when her book achieved monumental success. "[I wanted to undo] the myths that Indian cooking is spicy, complicated, overcooked, exotic, and excessively sweet. Most of these myths are derived from the food served at Indian restaurants in this country [America]. The [original] principles of this ancient cuisine are in vogue with today's nutrition focus. The Indians have always combined foods for better nutrition and used a profusion of health-giving natural ingredients."[15]

"By 1978," writes Vishakha, "she'd written 675 recipes, about 85 percent of which were dishes that Srila Prabhupada had either taught to his disciples himself or had instructed his cooks to learn from Indian experts."[16] She was ready to put her initial cookbook—her life's work—into finished form. For more than 15 years, she had been conceiving this exhaustive tome, wading through countless recipes, compiling interesting anecdotes and a lexicon covering just about everything an aspiring cook would need to know. All of this eventually worked its way into her cookbook. And no one knew the material better than she did.

But the difficult part of her journey was just beginning. Working with her chosen publisher, the Bhaktivedanta Book Trust (BBT) in England, had proven difficult. For every step forward, a few more were taken in the opposite direction; the BBT was reconsidering its editorial and managerial policies at the time, and Yamuna's project was temporarily put on hold. In the several years she worked with the

BBT, however, she did make some progress—their editors helped her with the book and, overall, the company financed her while she finessed the manuscript. They also hired David Baird—a shepherd by trade, and a master illustrator—since Yamuna felt that his exquisite style of line drawing would be perfect for her book. She worked with Baird for nine months to get the illustrations just right. But the BBT's vision for the project differed from her own, and she wanted to approach an outside market with which the BBT was unfamiliar. With this in mind, she began to explore alternative presses.

As time went on, she found that the manuscript was just collecting dust; cookbook specialists discouraged her by saying that her manuscript committed the three blunders of cookbook writing—it was too big, too Indian, and too vegetarian. Mostly, it was too many pages, now 1,500 and counting, and so no publisher wanted to take a chance with it. Enter Yogeshvar (Joshua Greene), who was at that time the director and senior editor of Bala Books, an ISKCON-related publisher of children's classics from India, and Prahladapriya, who had been one of the managers of Govinda's restaurant in New York. At last, Yamuna found two devotees who shared her vision and had some substantial experience in publishing. Though it was still slow going—the manuscript had to be edited down, and certain logistics had to be worked out—the project could now move forward.

Yamuna continued to fine-tune her writing with lifelong friend Dina-Tarine (Dina Sugg) as Yogeshvar and Prahlad assembled a team to tend to pre-publication work, including design and layout. After more than two years of hard work, the book was ready for publication.

A book such as Yamuna's, however, is expensive to produce, and Bala Books was a small-budget enterprise. What to do? Prahlad had raised a substantial amount of money, and the small press conceivably could have pulled off the publishing end of things. But what about distribution? Was Bala prepared to get this book out to major chain bookstores, to give the book its due? Yogeshvar doubted it. In addition, they wanted people to take the book seriously, and Bala, while respected within its limited domain, was only a small publisher—a larger, well-known company would get the book where it needed to go. And so Yogeshvar and Prahlad sent the manuscript to some 300 major presses with a special proposal: Bala had put all the work into the project, finishing the manuscript and packaging it in terms of design and layout, and would deliver camera-ready copy. For the other publisher's part, they would simply have to see to the book's promotion and mass distribution. Three out of 300 accepted the offer, and, of the three, Bala chose E. P. Dutton. The two publishers agreed on a split imprint and a unique trade distribution deal. Bala could handle direct mail, along with yoga ashrams, health food stores, and so on, while Dutton would get the major chain bookstores and other large orders.

Finally, in 1987, the book was released: *Lord Krishna's Cuisine: The Art of Indian Vegetarian Cooking*. It was complete with 520 kitchen-tested recipes, 330 helpful illustrations, a 200-page A–Z of complete general information, easy step-by-step cooking instructions, a practical guide to menu planning and serving, and an extensive index. With prose that flowed like the Yamuna River in India, the book, while huge, was an easy read and visually attractive, too. Its wide-scale acceptance exceeded everyone's expectations, with *Vogue* calling it "monumental" and *Kirkus Reviews* claiming it to be "one of the most important cookbooks published in years."

Publishers Weekly, the world's most significant reviewer of newly published books, may have said it best:

A prodigious 800-page labor of love illustrated with delicate line drawings, the meticulous encyclopedic cookbook faithfully reflects the philosophy that cooking is "a spiritual experience . . . a means of expressing love and devotion to the Supreme Lord, Krishna."[17]

Soon, telling comparisons worked their way into positive reviews, establishing Yamuna as a staple ingredient in the realm of world-class cookery: Leo Lerman, writing for *Gourmet*, said, "Yamuna Devi is as explicit about Indian vegetarian cooking as Barbara Kafka is about the uses of the microwave oven."[18] In a similar vein, Elaine Tait, a columnist for *The Philadelphia Inquirer*, wrote, "I'm among those early reviewers who think she [Yamuna] did so well that *The Art of*

Vegetarian Cooking may be to vegetarians of the '80s what *Mastering the Art of French Cooking* was to omnivores in the '60s and '70s."[19] With her name repeatedly turning up in the popular media, the first Hare Krishna pop-diet icon was born. Apropos of this, in the late '80s, Yamuna was called upon to write her own vegetarian cooking column in the *Washington Post;* in the early '90s, she had a similar column in *Vegetarian Times.*

Yamuna's greatest coup was the unexpected series of awards that immediately followed the publication of *Lord Krishna's Cuisine,* particularly when it was named Cookbook of the Year by the International Association of Culinary Professionals (IACP) in 1987. This was major. The event was briefly mentioned by *Vegetarian Times,* who gave Yamuna a "carrot"—their symbol for "high praise"—soon after her victory was announced:

> A carrot—delicately seasoned with a touch of curry—goes to Yamuna Devi, whose book *Lord Krishna's Cuisine: The Art of Indian Vegetarian Cooking* took first place in this year's prestigious International Association of Cooking Professionals / Seagram Food and Beverage Book Awards. This was the first time in its 12-year history that the top award was given to a cookbook devoted to non-Western cuisine.[20]

The significance of this award cannot be overstated. The year's top books were selected by a panel of 36 judges, under the supervision of an independent nominating board of nine food writers, editors of newspapers, and magazine cookbook editors. Nearly 200 entries were received, a record since the program originated as the Tastemaker Awards more than 20 years before. The program of awards is co-sponsored by the 1,200-member International Association of Cooking Professionals and Joseph E. Seagram & Sons, Inc., which include perhaps the most important people in the industry. Moreover, this is the *only* award program for cookbooks worldwide.

Yamuna's book won first place in the Asian Cooking category, one of 13 categories, and then as best cookbook of the year for all categories. As the "surprise winner" of this honor, she beat out the likes of food writers Craig Claiborne, Jacques Pepin, and Barbara Kafka. Donald Schrader, chairman of the awards committee, called Yamuna's cookbook "a breakthrough that will make American people sit up and take notice," and compared it to the work of Julia Child and other significant cookbook writers. It was the first time that this coveted award had gone to a book whose focus was non-Western cuisine, as noted by *Vegetarian Times*, above. But it was also the first time that a new author had won on an initial entry, and the first time that a vegetarian cookbook had even been considered. This is a victory, says Yamuna, not only for vegetarian cooking, but for Swami Prabhupada and the entire Vaishnava tradition.

Seeing the initial success of the book, Bala Books and Dutton made an agreement with Angus and Robertson, Limited, for worldwide distribution, particularly in Australia and England. Gradually, the book was abbreviated into a smaller volume, *The Best of Lord Krishna's Cuisine*, which was more manageable and eventually translated into German, Russian, Italian, and several other languages. The book has sold nearly one million copies, a formidable statistic considering its size and limited market.

Yamuna continues to share her wealth of information: In the 1990s she released *Yamuna's Table: Healthful Vegetarian Cuisine Inspired by the Flavors of India*. Here she concentrates more on fusion—combining the cuisines of many world traditions with those of India. Favorite Indian dishes, including chutneys, yogurt soups, curries, and spicy sauces are adapted to crepes, salads, appetizers, and other more Western recipes. The book won the 1992 James Beard / Faberware first-place award for cookbooks in the "international" category. Several other drops from Yamuna's considerable reservoir have appeared as well, such as *India: The Vegetarian Table*, a colorful book with 80 of her most beloved recipes, all culled from her masterwork, *Lord Krishna's Cuisine*. And, certainly, more is yet to come.

Kurma's Culinary Conquests

Kurma might be dubbed Yamuna's godchild. He carries on in her tradition of culinary excellence and displays an energy and fortitude that would make her proud. Born Phillip David Gordon on December 26,

1952, he relocated to Australia with his family from their native England when he was 12. Looking for God in his early teens, he reached adulthood with more questions than answers. Temporarily leaving aside many of these questions, as people generally do, he briefly studied at the University of New South Wales. A chance meeting with a devotee, however, brought him to the Hare Krishna movement in 1971. With the devotees, his questions again came to the fore, but now he felt he was on the road to getting some real answers. Immediately attracted to the idea of *prasadam* distribution, he started his cooking career in ISKCON's Sydney kitchen, where he began by cutting vegetables, grinding fresh herbs and spices, and assisting in the preparation of their famous Sunday Feasts.

He took to cooking like soft butter takes to warm bread. Developing his culinary abilities with an indescribable passion, he started to experiment by combining age-old Vedic recipes with regional cuisine from around the world. He worked as head chef at Melbourne's most popular vegetarian restaurant, Gopal's, for 10 years, from 1980 to 1990, and there he brought to life his international approach to cooking. Rave reviews came from local newspapers and critics in the know.

Since those humble beginnings, Kurma has gone on to teach his special brand of eclectic vegetarian cuisine throughout Australia, his central base of operations, and around the world—in cooking schools in London, Zurich, Warsaw, Jakarta, Buenos Aires, Delhi, La Paz, Moscow, Stockholm, Milan, Santiago de Chile, Sao Paolo, Beijing, and Frankfurt. Encouraged to further share his know-how with the world, Kurma decided to author vegetarian cookbooks that would convey his unique techniques while appealing to the eye as well. His first, *Great Vegetarian Dishes* (1990), which is currently in its eighth printing, is still widely considered his best. To date, it has sold almost half a million copies.

This work includes over 240 recipes from around the world, with rice dishes, soups, breads, vegetable dishes, salads, chutneys, jams, pickles, savories, pasta and grain dishes, bean and legume dishes, dips, sauces, dressings, sweets, desserts, drinks, special ingredients, and much more. This is as complete as a cookbook gets, barring none save, perhaps, Yamuna's.

His second major work, *Cooking with Kurma* (1998), was an invitation to embark on an exciting journey of culinary exploration. Each lucidly explained recipe is an adventure into new lands of international culture, taste and nutrition. Whether one's preference is to prepare a quick lunch or a 12-course dinner, *Cooking with Kurma* will serve one well. The chapters are full of enticing soups, breads, condiments, drinks, main courses and desserts. A special feature of this handsome book is its extensive glossary, with full-color photographs accompanying most of the ingredients.

By 2000, when his third book, *Quick Vegetarian Dishes*, was published, Kurma was considered *the* cooking guru, the absolute master of elegant *prasadam* preparation. Variegated and multicultural, *Quick Vegetarian Dishes* carries on where the others leave off, with the added feature of focusing on recipes that can be made in a hurry. This work is fast, stylish, and definitely needed in our modern "rush-around" world. The message of *Quick Vegetarian Dishes* is simple: Life in the fast lane doesn't necessarily mean life in the fast food line. Even if one's life is moving at computer speed, one can, with Kurma's expert guidance, quickly prepare something hot and fresh, original and tasty—almost as quickly as one can order out.

In 2003, Kurma published *Vegetarian World Food*, which combined his most delicious recipes from the Middle East, the Mediterranean, Europe, Southeast Asia, the Americas, and, of course, India. He has also created *Quick Vegetarian Cards*, a full-color recipe card deck. These cards offer the culinary equivalent of sound bites— taste bites, essential gourmet vegetarian delights that deliver the most palatable results with the least amount of time and effort. The deck includes 52 laminated cards in all, full-color photos, and quick recipes that are out of this world—Kurma style.

His second recipe card deck is equally practical and eye-catching. *Cooking with Kurma Vegi Cards* allow you to conserve space in your kitchen by having individual recipes on easy-to-read, full-color, laminated cards that you can pin up on a board or stick to your refrigerator. Their tiny size allows you to carry them anywhere. This deck, in particular, includes an enticing selection of the best soups, breads, condiments, drinks, desserts, and main courses from Kurma's classic book *Cooking with Kurma*.

But beyond cookbooks and innovative approaches to cookbooks, Kurma is a personality that shines most brightly when personally teaching his craft. He has hosted three internationally broadcast television series seen in over 46 countries. His cooking shows have been broadcast on 178 PBS stations across the U.S., BBC2 and The Learning Channel in the U.K., STAR satellite TV from Hong Kong to Turkey, Russia, the Middle East, Indonesia, Malaysia, India, and China, and most recently in Australia on SBS and Foxtel's Lifestyle Channel. Nrsimhananda Dasa, the producer and director of the series, tells the story:

> When Kurma, a renowned vegetarian chef in the Hare Krishna Movement, was writing his first cookbook, I contacted him to explore his interest in doing a television series of vegetarian cooking shows for the Public Broadcasting Network (PBS). His enthusiasm for sharing his knowledge and experience was brought to a full boil when he arrived a short time later to begin the arduous task of organizing the production. ITV, aka ISKCON Television, fronted the money to produce and direct the shows without any guarantee that PBS stations would pick them up for broadcast. Previously, they had not aired any vegetarian cooking shows at all and rejected a few comers. In 1989 we completed the editing of the initial 13 of what was to become 39 in the series. I personally arranged for the trailer to be shown at the annual convention of the broadcasters, and the Kalachandji's restaurant in Dallas, the site of the gathering, catered a special dinner to all the administrators. The dishes were based on Kurma's recipes, and, consequently, the demand for the shows was overwhelming. We were in business that next season, and the stations demanded more. BBC, The Learning Channel, Kuwaiti TV (broadcast during Ramadan), SBC (South Africa), SBS (Australia), and finally STAR-TV (China, Malaysia, India) all purchased licensing rights. Kurma and Hare Krishna cooking became world famous.

His books were selling out. By 1992, when the last broadcasts took place, Kurma was seen in every continent, including South America, where his videotapes are becoming increasingly popular. By that time, most of Europe had licensed the series through Agicorp. To this day, Kurma is invited to tour and teach on every continent, and his name is synonymous with haute vegetarian cuisine. His cookbooks have been consistent best-sellers, and each one includes an invocation to His Divine Grace A. C. Bhaktivedanta Swami Prabhupada, who taught his disciples how to cook with sensible nutritional know-how, first-rate ingredients, exquisite spicing, and, most importantly, loving devotion. *Bhakti*, or devotion, is the key ingredient in Hare Krishna cooking, and the spiritual movement based on *bhakti*, ISKCON, has become known as the "kitchen religion." Much of the popularity of Krishna cooking is due in no small part to the television series, "Cooking with Kurma—Great Vegetarian Dishes."[21]

Clearly, Kurma's video series is a huge success, and the praise that continues to pour in is reminiscent of that for the earlier ISKCON restaurants and Yamuna's award winning cookbooks:

"Kurma has a gentle style that is a happy contrast to the frantic and frenzied style of most television cooks. His subtle wit and enthusiasm, combined with his fabulous-looking dishes, can renew your culinary excitement and creativity."
—*Vegetarian Times*

"Meat-eaters and vegetarians alike will certainly find something to fit the bill in *More Great Vegetarian Dishes of the World* on SBS with Kurma Dasa."
—*Screen Watch, The Australian*, May 2000

"Kurma's likeable personality makes it a totally fun experience."
—*Hinduism Today*

"Cooking With Kurma . . . is an excellent and welcomed addition to our cooking program line-up."

—Jeff Clarke, Houston PBS

"We really enjoy Kurma's no-frills, no-gimmicks television show. His enthusiasm for vegetarian food is infectious. . . . Highly recommended."

—*Brisbane Courier Mail*, December 2000

"While Kurma may be the high priest of vegetarian cuisine, you don't have to be a vegetarian to enjoy his cooking. It's fresh, original and delicious!"

—*The Canberra Chronicle*, December 2000

Kurma's light-hearted presentation of healthy, delicious, attractive, and innovative cuisine continues to shake off the outdated notion that vegetarian food is dull and lackluster. Currently, he is presenting gourmet vegetarian cooking classes throughout the world and writing columns for various magazines. He teaches at the Vital Ingredient Cooking School in Melbourne, Accoutrement and AGL Cooking Schools in Sydney, Canberra's Cooking Co-ordinates, Rosa Mato Cooking School in Adelaide, and Drysdale TAFE in Hobart. He is also busily working on more cookbooks.

The Hare Krishna contribution to vegetarianism and animal rights is nowhere as pronounced as in the many restaurants, cookbooks, and general *prasadam* distribution found throughout the movement worldwide. While this short chapter introduces readers to some of these endeavors, it should be pointed out that there are many others as well—thousands of devotees go out regularly with bake tables, have published cookbooks of their own, are involved with catering businesses, and so on. The examples outlined in this chapter are simply meant to offer a taste of the wide-ranging phenomenon known as Krishna consciousness.

7

Recipes for the Soul

Prasadam was your special weapon, no one could resist;
Once the Sunday Feast had started, no one could desist.
Halva, sweet rice, crisp pakoras, subjis, puris, rice—
With these and other preps you did our tongues and hearts entice.

—Dravida Dasa, "Song to Prabhupada," circa 1997

Some important things to know about Hare Krishna cooking: In general, it's actually a blend of western Indian (Maharashtrian and Marwari), eastern Indian (Bengali), southern (Madrasi), northwest central (Gujarati), and northern (Punjabi) cuisine, along with American and various other regional tastes from around the world. The multicultural membership of ISKCON accounts for much of this diversity, as does the movement's nonsectarian philosophy. Devotees are lacto-vegetarian, which means that they refrain from meat, chicken, fish, and eggs, and they also avoid onions and garlic, for these foods are said to be in the mode of ignorance and, in the case of the latter two, make the breath offensive. Caffeine-laden products, too, are taboo, for they are mildly intoxicating, and, by purchasing them, one contributes to the nonnutritive crop industry, which plays a major role in causing starvation for untold millions. Beyond this, any food is fair game, and what follows is a brief example of an average Hare Krishna feast, which readers can now prepare in their own home.

The Taste of Krishna

Kurma Dasa, ISKCON's premier chef whose work was briefly described in the previous chapter, shares with us the following 10 recipes. Though he generally prepares these recipes with organic milk products, he has graciously offered vegan alternatives for those who want to avoid dairy. He wishes all readers of this book happy cooking and an enjoyable feast.

1. Basmati Rice with Cashews, Peas and Fresh Coriander

Basmati rice is the famously light-textured, long-grained aromatic rice from North India and Pakistan. It has a wonderful fragrance and flavor, even when served plain. Basmati rice is easy to cook and, although more costly than other long-grained rice, is well worth the extra expense. This rice dish, studded with crisp toasted cashews, green peas, and fresh coriander leaves, is an ideal dish to make for a party or a special luncheon. Serves four to six.

Ingredients
2 3/4 cups water
1 1/2 teaspoons salt
1/2 teaspoon turmeric
2 tablespoons ghee or olive oil
1/2 teaspoon yellow asafetida powder
1 1/2 cups basmati rice
1 cup peas
1 cup toasted cashews
1/4 cup chopped coriander leaves
extra coriander leaves for garnish

Instructions
Bring to a boil the water, salt and turmeric in a small saucepan over moderate heat. Cover tightly and reduce to a simmer.
Heat the ghee or oil in another, larger saucepan over moderate heat. Sprinkle in the yellow asafetida powder, stir briefly, add the rice, and sauté for about two minutes, or until the rice turns a little whitish in color.
Pour the simmering water into the rice, stir briefly, and, if using fresh

peas, add them now. Increase the heat, return the rice to a full boil, reduce the heat to very low, and cover with a tight-fitting lid.

Simmer the rice for 15 to 20 minutes or until all the water is absorbed and the rice is tender and flaky. If using thawed frozen peas, lift the lid five minutes before the end and toss the peas in, quickly replacing the lid.

Remove from the heat and leave covered and undisturbed for five minutes to allow the tender grains to firm up.

Fold in the cashews and chopped coriander leaves.

Serve hot, garnished with the remaining herbs.

2. Mixed Vegetables in Creamy, Gujarati-Style Karhi Sauce

We all know that protein is an essential substance. It's required for building and repairing tissues, for synthesizing enzymes that start the body's many chemical reactions, for serving as building blocks for hormones and antibodies, for supplying energy, and many other things.

Karhis are smooth, yogurt-based dishes served with rice. Either yogurt or buttermilk is whisked with chick-pea flour and then simmered into a creamy sauce. *Karhi* is an excellent source of vegetarian protein—combining yogurt, a complete protein, with the chick-pea flour, an incomplete protein that becomes complete in conjunction with yogurt. *Karhi* is delicious, light and easy to digest, and good for you—what more could you ask? Serves six.

Ingredients

1 1/4 cups carrots, peeled and cut into half-inch chunks
1 1/4 cups green beans, cut into half-inch lengths
1 1/4 cups small cauliflower florets
1 1/4 cups green peas
2 cups plain yogurt (thick coconut milk is a non-dairy alternative, or soy yogurt)
1/2 cup chick-pea flour (*besan*)
1 pint water
1 teaspoon chili powder
1/2 teaspoon turmeric powder

1 teaspoon coriander powder
2 tablespoons ghee or oil
1 teaspoon brown mustard seeds
1 1/2 teaspoons cumin seeds
1 teaspoon yellow asafetida powder
1 1/2 teaspoons salt
2 tablespoons chopped fresh coriander leaves

Instructions

Steam all the vegetables until just tender, drain, cover and set aside.
Whisk together the yogurt with the chick-pea flour until smooth and creamy. Add the water, chili powder, turmeric powder, and coriander powder, and whisk again.
Heat the ghee or oil in a medium saucepan over moderate heat. When the ghee is fairly hot, sprinkle in the mustard seeds, and fry them until they crackle. Add the cumin, fry until it darkens a few shades, then drop in the yellow asafetida powder and sauté momentarily.
Pour in the yogurt (or coconut milk) mixture, and, stirring, bring to a boil. Reduce the heat, and simmer for 10 minutes, stirring occasionally.
Fold in the steamed vegetables, the salt and fresh coriander.
Serve hot with rice.

3. Succulent Eggplant and Panir Cheese in Rich and Spicy Tomato Sauce

An opulent dish that showcases the incredible meatiness of fried *panir* cheese. Serve with plenty of rice or bread to mop up the rich juices. Serves six.

Ingredients

ghee or oil for deep-frying
1 1/2 teaspoons black mustard seeds
2 teaspoons minced fresh ginger
1/2 teaspoon minced fresh green chili
1/2 teaspoon yellow asafetida powder

2 cups tomato puree

1/4 teaspoon turmeric powder

1 teaspoon ground coriander

panir cheese from 2 1/2 quarts milk, pressed and cut into half-inch cubes (recipe follows) or use 500g firm tofu

1 large eggplant, cut into half-inch cubes

1 teaspoon *garam masala*

2 teaspoon brown sugar

1 1/2 teaspoons salt

Instructions

Heat one tablespoon of ghee or oil in a large frying pan over moderate heat. When the ghee is hot, sprinkle in the mustard seeds and fry them until they crackle. Add the minced ginger and chilies, and fry them until aromatic. Sprinkle in the yellow asafetida powder, sauté briefly, and pour in the tomato purée. Stir in the turmeric powder and ground coriander.

Cook the sauce, stirring occasionally, for 10 minutes, or until a little reduced.

Heat ghee or oil for deep-frying in a wok or pan over moderate heat. When fairly hot, deep-fry the cubes of *panir* cheese or tofu in batches until they are a light golden brown. Remove the fried panir from the ghee, and set it aside to drain.

Deep-fry the cubes of eggplant in batches in the hot ghee until golden brown and tender, and set them aside to drain in a colander lined with paper towels.

Fold the *garam masala*, sugar and salt, the fried *panir* cubes and eggplant into the tomato sauce.

Serve hot, with fluffy rice or crusty bread.

Homemade Curd Cheese (Panir)

Ingredients

2 1/2 quarts fresh (preferrably organic) milk

1–2 cups yogurt or 2–4 tablespoons lemon juice

Instructions

Heat the milk to boiling point in a heavy-based saucepan.

Gradually stir in three quarters of the yogurt or lemon juice. The milk should separate into chunky curds, leaving a greenish liquid residue called whey. If not completely separated, add a little more yogurt or lemon juice.

Drape a double thickness of cheesecloth over a colander sitting in the sink.

Scoop out the curds with a slotted spoon and place them in the cheesecloth. Pour the whey and whatever curds that remain in the saucepan into the cheesecloth. Gather the ends of the cloth together and hold the bag of curd cheese under cold running water for 30 seconds. Twist the bag tightly to squeeze out extra whey, and return it to the colander.

Press under a heavy weight for 10 to 15 minutes. Carefully remove the curd cheese from the cloth. Your panir is ready. Again, 500g of firm tofu replaces this as a non-dairy alternative.

4. Crispy Batter-Fried Cauliflower (*Pakoras*)

The tradition of frying vegetables in batter is popular throughout the culinary world. In Italy, there are delicious Neapolitan fritters known as pasta cresciuta, comprised of things like sun-dried tomato halves, zucchini flowers, and sage leaves dipped in a yeast batter and fried in olive oil. The Japanese dip all sorts of things, including zucchini, eggplant, and carrot, into a light, thin batter and serve the tempura with dipping sauce.

In India, *pakoras* are almost a national passion. Cooked on bustling street corners, in snack houses, and at home, the fritters are always served piping hot, usually with an accompanying sauce or chutney. The vegetables can be cut into rounds, sticks, fan shapes, or slices. The varieties are endless. This recipe makes about 30 *pakoras*.

Ingredients

3/4 cup chick-pea flour
1/4 cup cornstarch
1/2 teaspoon baking powder

1 teaspoon cayenne pepper
1 teaspoon yellow asafetida powder
1/2 teaspoon turmeric
1 1/2 teaspoons salt
1 tablespoon olive oil
up to 1/2 cup water
ghee or oil for deep-frying
1/2 large cauliflower cut into approximately 30 small florets

Instructions

Whisk together the chick-pea flour and cornstarch, baking powder, cayenne, asafetida, turmeric, and salt. Pour in the tablespoon of olive oil and whisk in sufficient water to form a smooth batter, the consistency of medium-thin cream.

Heat the ghee or oil for deep-frying in a wok or deep frying pan. When the oil is hot, dip six or eight cauliflower pieces in the batter, and lower into the hot oil.

Deep-fry the cauliflower pieces for three or four minutes, or until they are crisp and golden brown. Remove, drain on paper towels, and repeat for the rest of the cauliflower pieces.

Serve the *pakoras* hot accompanied by sauce or chutney.

5. Puffed Fried Bread (Poori)

Popular over all of India, *pooris* are ideal to cook for both small dinner parties and festivals with hundreds of guests. On a number of occasions, I've cooked 500 or more pooris in a few hours for big feasts. Once you get the rhythm down, it's effortless and rewarding. *Pooris* are traditionally made with whole-wheat flour, but you can vary the ingredients. One-half whole-wheat flour, or *atta*, and one-half unbleached plain flour makes lighter *pooris*. If you're expert at rolling, try using just plain flour for translucent, gossamer-thin *pooris*.

You can add yeast to your *pooris* for light, bread-like results; you can add spices to your *poori* dough; you can sprinkle sugar on top of *pooris* for a sweet snack; or you can stuff them with various sweet and savory fillings.

The dough for this *poori* recipe differs from *chapati* dough in that butter or ghee is rubbed into the flour and less water is added to form a drier dough. No flour is used on the rolling surface.

Pooris are traditionally eaten hot, straight out of the ghee or oil, but cold pooris are great for picnics or snacks when traveling. Serve pooris with practically any menu at any time. Makes about 16 medium-sized pooris.

Ingredients
2 cups sifted chapati flour or half whole-wheat and half unbleached plain
1/2 teaspoon salt
2 tablespoons melted butter or ghee (or oil)
2/3 cup warm water, or as needed
ghee or oil for deep-frying

Instructions
Combine the flour and salt in a mixing bowl. Rub in the butter, ghee, or oil until the mixture resembles coarse meal. Add up to two thirds of a cup of water, slowly pouring in just enough to form a medium-soft kneadable dough. Turn the dough onto a clean working surface.
Knead the dough for five to eight minutes or until silky smooth. Cover with an overturned bowl and leave for two to three hours.
Re-knead the dough again for one minute. Divide the dough into 16 portions, roll them into smooth balls, and cover them with a damp cloth.
Preheat the ghee or oil in a wok or deep pan over low heat. Meanwhile, with a rolling pin roll all your balls of dough into smooth disks about 4 1/2 inches wide. Increase the ghee or oil temperature until it reaches about 365°F.
Lift up a rolled poori and slip it into the hot oil, making sure it doesn't fold over. It will sink to the bottom, then immediately rise to the surface. Hold it under the surface with a slotted spoon until it puffs up into a balloon. After a few seconds, when it is browned to a light golden color, turn it over and cook the other side to an even golden color. Lift out the poori with the slotted spoon and carefully drain it in a large colander.

Repeat for all the *pooris*. Serve immediately, if possible, or leave in a preheated, slightly warm oven for up to two hours.

6. Hot and Sweet Pineapple Chutney

Pineapple chutney should be "too hot to bear, but too sweet to resist." Makes about two cups.

Ingredients

3 tablespoons ghee or oil
2 teaspoons cumin seeds
4 broken dried red chilies, or as desired
1 large ripe pineapple, peeled, cored, and cubed
1/2 teaspoon ground cinnamon
1/2 teaspoon ground cloves
2/3 cup brown sugar
1/3 cup raisins

Instructions

Heat the ghee in a two-quart, heavy-based saucepan over moderate heat until it is hot but not smoking. Fry the cumin seeds in the hot ghee until they darken slightly. Add the chilies and cook until golden brown. Add the pineapple pieces, ground cinnamon, and cloves.

Gently boil the chutney, stirring occasionally, over moderate heat for about 45 minutes, or until the pineapple becomes soft and the juice evaporates. Stir constantly, as the saucepan dries and the pineapple starts to stick on the bottom.

Add the sugar and raisins and cook for another 10 to 15 minutes, or until the chutney is thick and jam-like. Remove from the heat and allow the chutney to cool.

Serve at room temperature.

7. Cauliflower and Pea Samosas

These triangular, deep-fried, stuffed savory vegetarian pastries have become world famous. Mixed vegetables or cauliflower-and-potato fillings can be substituted for cauliflower and peas. Fresh curd cheese can also be successfully added to *samosa* filling.

When you bite into a warm *samosa*, you'll notice its wonderfully tender, thin pastry crust, golden brown from deep-frying in ghee, and the harmony of flavors of the vegetable filling. *Samosas* should be served warm or at room temperature with a chutney, and make a great traveling snack food. Makes 20 *samosas*.

Filling
2 tablespoons ghee or oil
1 tablespoon cumin seeds
2 teaspoons minced fresh ginger
2 or 3 hot green chilies, seeded and minced
1 teaspoon yellow asafetida powder
1 very small cauliflower, cored, trimmed, diced, and lightly steamed until tender
1 1/3 cups peas, steamed
1/2 teaspoon turmeric
1/4 teaspoon cinnamon powder
1 1/2 teaspoons salt
1 tablespoon minced fresh coriander leaves or parsley
1/2 teaspoon lemon juice
ghee or oil for deep frying

Pastry
1 3/4 cups unbleached plain flour
1 teaspoon salt
4 tablespoons melted butter or ghee (or oil)
between 1/2 and 3/4 cup warm water

Instructions
Make the filling
Heat two tablespoons ghee or oil in a large frying pan over moderate heat.
Sauté the cumin seeds in the hot oil until they turn golden brown. Add the ginger and chilies and stir-fry for one minute. Add the asafetida and stir momentarily; then add the cauliflower and peas. Add the turmeric, cinnamon, and salt.

Reduce the heat to low, stir all the ingredients, and partially cover. Cook, stirring occasionally, for about five minutes or until the vegetables are tender and quite dry. Add the fresh coriander leaves and lemon juice. Remove from the heat and coarsely mash the vegetables. Allow the mixture to cool to room temperature. Divide the filling into 20 even portions.

Instructions
Make the pastry
Mix the flour and salt in a large mixing bowl. Add the melted butter, ghee, or oil and rub it between your fingertips until it resembles coarse meal.

Make a depression in the center of the mixture, add most of the water, and quickly mix and gather it into a ball. If the dough is too dry to cohere, add warm water to make a medium-soft pastry dough.

Knead the dough on a smooth surface for eight to 10 minutes or until smooth and elastic. Cover with a cloth until the filling is cool.

Instructions
Assemble and cook the *samosas:*
Roll the dough into a rope about 10 inches long and cut the rope into 10 equal-sized pieces. Cover with a moist cloth.

Press one piece of dough into a smooth patty. Lightly oil a smooth working surface. With a rolling pin, flatten the patty into a round, thin disk about 6 1/2 inches across. Cut the disk in half with a sharp knife.

Dip your finger into a bowl of water and moisten the straight edge of one semicircle of pastry. Pick up the semicircle and fold it in half, forming a cone. Gently but firmly press the moistened edges together, slightly overlapping them to ensure the seal.

Carefully spoon one portion of the vegetable stuffing into the pastry cone, leaving a small border on top. Dip your finger into the bowl of water and moisten the inside edge of the cone. Firmly press the moistened edges together, thoroughly sealing the filling inside the triangular pastry casing. The top edge can be left plain, crimped with a fork or plaited with your fingers. Place the *samosa* on a tray.

Continue rolling, filling, and shaping the remaining *samosas*.
Heat ghee or oil to a level of 2 1/2 to 3 inches in a wok or deep-frying pan over moderate heat until the temperature reaches about 290°F.
Slowly fry eight to 10 *samosas* at a time for about 10 minutes or until they're flaky and pale golden brown. Remove with a slotted spoon and drain on paper towels. Continue frying the remaining *samosas*.
Serve warm or at room temperature.

8. Walnut and Raisin Semolina Halava

Semolina *halava* is the most popular dessert from the Gopal's Restaurant chain worldwide. This version of the famous hot, fluffy pudding with juicy raisins, raw sugar, and walnut pieces rates high in the "*halava*-top-ten." I have cooked *halava* for four or five persons and for 1,500 persons; either way, following the same basic steps yields equally stunning results.

The secret of good *halava* is to roast the semolina very slowly for at least 20 minutes, with enough butter so as not to scorch the grains. Steam the finished *halava* over very low heat with a tight-fitting lid for five minutes to fully plump the semolina grains; then allow it to sit covered for another five minutes. Fluffy, plump-grained *halava* is best served hot, with a spoonful of cream or custard. Serves six to eight persons.

Ingredients
3 cups water
1 1/4 cups raw sugar
1/2 cup raisins
5 ounces unsalted butter or non-dairy Nuttelex margarine
1 1/4 cups coarse-grained semolina
1/3 cup walnut pieces

Instructions
Combine the water, sugar, and raisins in a two-quart saucepan. Place over moderate heat, stirring to dissolve the sugar.
Bring to a boil, then cover with a tight-fitting lid and remove from the heat.

Melt the butter or margarine in a two- or three-quart non-stick saucepan and over fairly low heat without scorching. Add the semolina.

Slowly and rhythmically stir-fry the grains until they darken to a tan color and become aromatic (about 20 minutes). Add the walnut pieces about halfway through the roasting. Stirring more carefully, raise the heat under the grains.

Turn on the heat under the sugar water and bring it to a rolling boil. Remove the saucepan of semolina and butter from the heat and slowly pour the hot syrup into the semolina, stirring steadily. The grains may splutter at first, but will quickly cease as the liquid is absorbed.

Return the pan to the stove and stir steadily over low heat until the grains fully absorb the liquid, start to form into a pudding-like consistency, and pull away from the sides of the pan.

Place a tight-fitting lid on the saucepan and cook over the lowest possible heat for five minutes. Turn off the heat and allow the *halava* to steam, covered, for an additional five minutes.

Serve hot in dessert bowls as it is, or with the toppings suggested above.

9. Saffron-Scented Rice Pudding (Chaval Kshira)

Kshira is a Sanskrit word for condensed milk. It is commonly known as *kheer* in North India, and regional variations are known as *payasa*, *payesh*, etc. When milk is slowly condensed with rice, the result is this creamy dessert known as *chaval kshira*, sometimes just referred to as "sweet-rice." Serves four or five persons.

Ingredients
1/2 cup short-grain rice
big pinch pure saffron threads
7 cups fresh whole milk (or soy milk)
3/4 cup sugar

Instructions
Clean, wash, and drain the short-grain rice.
Pour the milk into a heavy-based five- or six-quart saucepan. Sprinkle

in the saffron threads. Stirring constantly with a wooden spoon, bring the milk to a boil over moderately high heat. Reduce the heat, add the rice, and, still stirring attentively, boil gently for 25 to 30 minutes.

Reduce the heat to moderately low and boil the milk for another 10 to 15 minutes, still stirring constantly with a smooth, sweeping action. When the sweet-rice becomes creamy and slightly thick, remove the pan from the heat. Stir in the sugar, mix well, and allow the sweet-rice to cool slightly and serve warm. Alternatively, refrigerate for at least three hours and serve chilled.

Note: If the sweet-rice thickens too much after it cools, add a little cold milk or light cream to thin it out.

10. Classic Rose Lassi

My first taste of *lassi* was in New Delhi on a dusty, blistering hot day in 1978. A friend and I took shelter in a tiny shop somewhere in Chandni Chowk Bazaar and were transported to a refrigerated heaven the moment the smooth, frothy, icy cold rose-flavoured yogurt beverage touched our lips. Serves four.

Ingredients
2 1/2 cups plain yogurt (try soy yogurt for a non-dairy version)
1/2 cup fine sugar
2 teaspoons pure distilled rosewater (I prefer Lebanese)
3/4 cup iced water
1 cup ice cubes, cracked
a few fragrant rose petals for garnish, optional

Instructions
Process the yogurt, sugar, rosewater and iced water in a blender for two minutes. Add the ice and process for another two minutes.

Serve in tall, refrigerated glasses with a garnish of rose petals. Chill out!

The Real Ingredient

While delectable in and of themselves, the real secret of these recipes is the love and devotion that one might put into them—a love and devotion that best manifests if one learns the art of offering food to

Krishna. As renowned scholar of Hinduism Peter Bennett insightfully writes, "Perhaps the most effective way of establishing emotional contact with Krishna is through food lovingly prepared and subsequently relished as consecrated leavings (*prasada[m]*)."[1]

The sacred offering process begins even before one goes to the store to purchase ingredients. In *conceiving of the meal*, one must have a spirit of sacrifice and selflessness—of wanting to prepare the food for Krishna's pleasure, and then to enjoy it as Krishna's remnants, only as a secondary enjoyer. This spirit, of course, is ideal, and one can certainly offer food to Krishna without it. The best results, however, will come to those who at least endeavor to make such a selfless sacrifice.

In shopping, it is critical to be aware that meat, fish, and egg products are often mixed in with other foods, and so it is necessary to study labels carefully. For example, some brands of yogurt and sour cream contain gelatin, which is prepared from the horns, hooves, and bones of slaughtered animals; certain brands of milk are prepared with fish liver oil; cheese may contain rennet, which is an enzyme extracted from the stomach of calves—but one mcan find cheese with vegetable rennet as well, which is useable. It is strongly advised to get the best quality possible for an offering to Krishna, and, to this end, I advise organic, non-GMO milk that is not produced on a factory farm, or even soy substitutes. This determined inspection of food labels and deep concern over the quality and source of ingredients can be seen as part of one's devotional endeavor.

If possible, avoid foods precooked by people who are not devotees of Krishna. This is not only because Krishna likes to receive foods that come from people who care about Him, but for other reasons as well. According to the subtle laws of nature, the cook's consciousness acts upon the food, affecting the result not only physically, but mentally as well. In other words, it impacts what the eater will get from eating the food. In this sense, food becomes an agent, of sorts, with the ability to transfer elements of the cook's consciousness to our own. This can have harmful metaphysical effects if the person preparing the food is devoid of a spiritual dimension. For this reason, as far as possible, devotees use only fresh, natural ingredients, and so should anyone trying to prepare the above recipes or others like them.

In preparing *prasadam*, cleanliness is a principle of utmost importance. Nothing impure should be offered to God, and one's kitchen work area should be kept immaculate. The cook should wash his or her hands thoroughly before preparing the food; devotees in temples often take full showers before entering the kitchen. The next principle is equally urgent: While preparing food, do not taste it—you might even try to avoid smelling it. This is part of the yogic discipline affirming that you are cooking the meal not simply for yourself but for the pleasure of Krishna, who should be the first to enjoy it. Through trial and error, the meal will eventually come out right, but not by tasting it before it is offered.

When the meal is fully prepared, it is ready to undergo the vital transformation that makes it *prasadam*. Small portions of the now cooked food should be placed on dining ware kept specifically for this purpose. No one else should eat from these dishes, which should then be placed before a picture of Krishna. While the temple procedure for offering food is complex and elaborate—with a litany of heartfelt prayers and exotic rituals—the recommended form for those at home is simply to pray, "My dear Lord Krishna, please accept this food as an offering of love." Then chant the Maha-mantra: Hare Krishna, Hare Krishna, Krishna Krishna, Hare Hare / Hare Rama, Hare Rama, Rama Rama, Hare Hare, once or twice with great devotion. Helpful, of course, is to have a spiritual master, such as Swami Prabhupada, and to offer the food through him. Technically, Vaishnava teaching asserts that God, who is pure, must be approached through one who is also pure, and thus the devotees offer food first to Krishna's pure devotee, who naturally takes this same food and offers it to Krishna. The remnants of *this* food are then properly understood as *prasadam*. However, it is also recognized that the Lord is merciful, and a humble attempt, by anyone, to offer Him something with love will have significant, positive results. It is important to remember that the real purpose of this offering is to show your devotion and gratitude to the Lord; the food itself—and the method of offering—is secondary.

Without this devotional feeling, the offering will not be acceptable. God is complete in Himself, and He doesn't need anything from us—though He wants our love. Love is the greatest of mysteries. It is the only thing in existence that is truly dynamic, a constant surge upward. The more of it you have, the more you want. Thus, God, who has more love than any other being, *wants love more than any other being*. The implications here are staggering: In love, even the Lord is never satisfied. Our offering of food, then, is a means for us to attract God by giving Him the one thing that He ardently desires—our love. Due to this intimate exchange of affection, the devotee becomes privy to God's grace. As Peter Bennett writes, "Prasada[m], a token of Krishna's pleasure and happiness on receiving the love of His devotee, is also an edible manifestation of His grace and bliss, which the devotee tastes, digests, and inwardly experiences."[2]

After chanting the Maha-mantra, which is the essence of the offering process, give Krishna a few moments to enjoy the offering. After this, you can transfer the small portions from Krishna's plate to your own, and the *prasadam* may be served. Try to appreciate the spiritual quality of *prasadam* by remembering how it connects you to Krishna in love and devotion; also remember how it frees you from the effects of karma, both good and bad, situating you in transcendence. But, above all, enjoy the tasty fare yourself, and share it with others. Bennett concludes, "Whereas food provides for the sustenance of the body, grace provides for the sustenance of the soul. Food and grace are subtly commingled in *prasada*[m]. On tasting *prasada*[m] the devotee is nourished by the grace of Krishna."[3]

Afterword
A Personal Reflection

The International Society for Krishna Consciousness is doing a superb job in letting people know that vegetarian food is healthful, delicious, and pleasing to the eye. Over the past 15 years, the Hare Krishna people have distributed more than 150 million plates of *prasadam*, vegetarian foods prepared and offered to God with love and devotion. They are master cooks, their food is stunningly delicious, and they cannot be praised enough for their success in promoting the cause of vegetarianism worldwide.

—Scott Smith, Associate Editor, *Vegetarian Times*, circa 1986

As the writing of this book comes to a close, Prabhupada engulfs my mind. It is through his inspiration and guidance that his disciples managed to spread the teachings of Krishna consciousness, along with its concomitant vegetarianism and animal rights, around the world. As Rynn Berry, author and historical advisor to the North American Vegetarian Society, writes, "Because of men like Prabhupada, the English-speaking world, which was once the most carnivorous tribe on the planet, is now converting to vegetarianism at a furious pace."[1] And so I wonder: Have I conveyed in these pages all that he would have me say on vegetarianism and animal rights? Clearly, the *prasadam* factor would be most important to him, and we have dealt with this at some length. An additional but related point would be the limitations of vegetarianism as a spiritual path unto itself. He felt strongly that while vegetarianism is important, people who suddenly learn of its virtues tend to exaggerate its merit, positioning it, in fact, where God should be. Allow me to flesh this out, if you will.

In recent years, there have been animal rights advocates who have taken to task their various religious traditions for not seeing animal rights (and its concomitant vegetarianism) as a religious imperative. These advocates look in dismay at religious institutions for neglecting the concerns of lesser creatures—beings their own religions suggest should be cared for and respected. Some are more vocal in their indignation than others—asking how it is possible for one to profess a religion if one supports unnecessary cruelty to harmless creatures. Others quietly practice their culinary spirituality, without preaching to their neighbors.

Whatever the case, more and more people see the concern for animal rights as a religious way of life—as a spiritual dynamic that is sufficient in itself. While this sensitivity to animals is virtuous for the reasons already outlined in this book, it should not be elevated to a central theological issue, and to do so would be to make it something it is not. It is important to acknowledge that our relationship with animals is only a component of spiritual and moral virtue, and not the only one. Established religious groups, like the Jewish Vegetarian Society and Christians Concerned for Animals, are well aware of these distinctions, and while promoting the cause of animal welfare, they are firm in their religious convictions, putting forward compassion for animals as a means rather than an end.

I want to be clear here. Compassion toward animals should indeed form an important component of religious practice. Jesus said that if one does good "to the least of these, he is then also doing good to Me" (see Matthew 25:34–45), a sensibility that should certainly be extended to animals. His statement points to an essential "oneness" between God and His creation, a oneness that all spiritual traditions, including Hare Krishna Vaishnavism, fully accept. However, and this is essential for both religionists and animal advocates to understand, within the theistic traditions there is simultaneously a great *difference* between God and His creation. It is this difference that Hare Krishnas tend to emphasize—for only when one acknowledges difference between God and humanity is there possibility to render loving service (*bhakti*), which is the central feature of the theistic enterprise. As one Vaishnava poet sang, "I want to *taste* sugar; I don't want to *be* sugar." In other words, it takes two to engage in loving exchange.

Further, one who places undo emphasis on the *creation* may thus inadvertently neglect the *Creator*. Such illusory, misplaced devotion, in which one's allegiance shifts from *God* to *Dog*, is a danger. Like all institutions, religious organizations are not perfect and their practitioners may not fulfill all the requirements of their religious doctrines. Those who wish to reconnect religious organizations with their teachings on animals and food need to acknowledge, however, the importance of placing the teachings within the larger context of the religion. Kindness to all creatures is, of course, a fundamental religious principle, and it is (and has been) endorsed by sages of all traditions. But kindness to all creatures is only *part of* religious practice—not the central focus, at least according to the world's major religious traditions. As Prabhupada often said, monkeys and pigeons are also vegetarian, but their spiritual insight may leave a great deal to be desired! Thus, while Prabhupada fully supports the need for *ahimsa*, his main concern is that food be offered to God with devotion (*bhakti*); he repeatedly pointed out that practicing nonviolence doesn't necessarily lead to spiritual wisdom or greater religious conviction. This is something that deeply concerned him.

Religion is by nature a holistic experience and therefore cannot be understood merely in terms of its parts. That is to say, to truly comprehend a religious tradition, one must see it in its entirety. For this reason, one has to—to a certain extent—enter into a religion in order to understand it. Even non-practitioner scholars and secular historians of religion know that to realistically assess a particular tradition, they have to participate in the world of that religion, to study it by taking part in it. Otherwise, their evaluation is stilted; it comes "from the outside" and from a partial point of view (*partial* both in the sense of choosing selective elements and in the sense of taking only one section of an organic whole). For instance, one can now take a formal Hindu vow of vegetarianism, *sakahara vrata*, available online at the *Hinduism Today* website.[2] The vow may be taken privately, before elders or parents, or as part of a temple ceremony. It reads, in part, "I accept the principle of *sakahara* as the method by which I may acknowledge my compassion, my *karuna*, for all living beings. As an act of dedication, I am resolved this day to begin (or continue) the regular practice of eating a strict vegetarian diet and not eating meat, fish, shellfish, fowl or eggs." While Prabhupada would support such a noble cause, he would be quick to add, "and I will only eat food that is first offered to Krishna with love and devotion." In this way, he is promoting a more all-encompassing and holistic approach to religion, dealing not only with individual parts—as important as they may be—but also with its essential core.

This, then, might be considered the main contribution of the Hare Krishna movement to vegetarianism and animal rights: a truly spiritual dimension. While devotees, as these pages suggest, have offered the world fine vegetarian cuisine, a detailed philosophy of cow protection, free food programs, a unique take on *ahimsa*, a deep-rooted understanding of universal compassion, elegant and successful restaurants, and some of the most colorful and celebrated cookbooks anyone has ever seen, they offered these things first to Krishna.

We might add that Hare Krishna devotees have indeed been successful. Their message comes through loud and clear. Despite years of anti-cult propaganda and occasional bad press, most people get it. If one looks even slightly beneath the surface, a plethora of Hare Krishna success stories comes to the fore, as this book has shown. We will cite only two learned examples of this. The first is a clearly articulated assessment of the Hare Krishna emphasis on eating—why the movement sees it as so important—and how *prasadam* effects an ultimate transformation in the material and spiritual lives of all devotees:

> Of all the behaviors which are of significance in Krishna Consciousness, only one is of parallel importance in secular life—eating. Dancing, singing, and the like are relatively minor aspects of American culture. Eating is not; food plays a dominant role in American life. Taking *prasadam* is not just a change in a minor activity; it is a transformation of one of the most meaningful and emotionally charged of all experiences. Instead of stressing meat, Krishna Consciousness forbids it.

Instead of emphasizing personal satisfaction, Krishna Consciousness emphasizes detachment. Instead of eating for the self, the devotees eat for Krishna. Instead of seeing food as an end toward which work is directed, the devotees see food as a means by which liberation is achieved. Thus, as the devotees eat food transformed into *prasadam*, they are themselves transformed into devotees.[3]

The second quote, which appears below, expresses an appreciation of the larger context, the ecological and agricultural wisdom of Krishna consciousness, as in the devotees' approach to cow protection and the development of rural farm communities. These insightful words come from Klaus Klostermaier, University Distinguished Professor Emeritus in the Department of Religious Studies at the University of Manitoba in Canada and Academic Director of the Oxford Centre for Vaishnava and Hindu Studies:

In its years of rapid growth in the seventies the Hare Krishna movement operated a number of farms in various parts of the world and actively propagated a very effective theory and practice of ecology based on the tradition of Gaudiya Vaishnavism. The Hare Krishna devotees repudiated the high-tech, heavy and expensive machinery that has become the main tool of agri-business especially in North America. They re-introduced oxen to plow fields and to draw carts, they revived simple, old, hand-operated farm machinery, they returned to manually planting, weeding, harvesting, and processing their produce. They rejected the use of chemicals to destroy pests and to kill plants. They developed an old-fashioned emotional linkage between the animals on the farms and the people who cared for them—and they really *cared*. They did not just treat them as inventory that had to be preserved in order to be exploited. They taught their children to love flowers, plants, trees, and to treat them as signs of Krishna's love and presence. The Hare Krishna people also propagated vegetarianism, long before others found out that it is healthier than a meat-based diet and that it is easier on the earth. They practiced organic farming and—they loved their work! They considered their gardening and farming to be an act of worship and they believed that by doing it right they not only produced beautiful flowers, fruits, and vegetables but also good karma to help the entire world.[4]

I would like to offer one final reflection—a thought that brings me back to my initial attraction to the Hare Krishna movement. Though all other religious traditions make the same point, I felt it more pronounced in Hare Krishna Vaishnavism, and for this reason, I embraced the tradition myself.

It is simply this: The *Bhagavad-gita* tells us that the wise person sees all living beings equally, for all creatures are endowed with the spark of life, the soul, and that the outer body is just that—a covering, or an external shell, for the real self. The *Gita* further tells us that God, Krishna, is the supreme father of all who live. Given these two points, let us reflect on Prabhupada's words as expressed in his talk with Cardinal Danielou and as implied in the story of ISKCON Food Relief's origins, when Prabhupada saw from his window the children and dogs rummaging through garbage for food.

To paraphrase, his thoughts run as follows: We want brotherhood, but do we consider what it means to be brothers? It means we have the same father. Only when we recognize this—that God is our common father—can we have real brotherhood. With such an understanding as a basis, we realize that if we deal with God's other children nicely, God will be pleased. But if we try to exploit or commit violence upon one another, how will the supreme father be pleased? And if God is not pleased, how can we expect peace and prosperity in the world?

Animals are also children of God, although they have less developed intelligence. They resemble human children, or perhaps those with deficient mental capacity (since children may develop into normal adults), who also do not have developed intelligence, or developed speech. Nor can they defend themselves. But in a family, the strong are meant to protect the weak. For a stronger older brother to torture or massacre a baby is a terrible crime. How upset and angry the father would be! So animals should be treated like our younger brothers or sisters, to be protected, not exploited or slaughtered so we can eat their flesh. "By Krishna consciousness," Prabhupada concludes, "by realizing that God is the supreme father of all living entities, we can actually achieve brotherhood and unity among all living beings."[5]

Notes

Introduction

1. See A. C. Bhaktivedanta Swami Prabhupada, trans., *Srimad Bhagavatam*, Cantos 1–9, 30 volumes (Los Angeles: Bhaktivedanta Book Trust, 1972–1980), 3.25.51, commentary.

2. Cow protection, vegetarianism, and more specifically *prasadam* (sanctified food) are recurring themes in the literature of the movement. An entire volume, *The Higher Taste: A Guide to Gourmet Vegetarian Cooking and a Karma-Free Diet* (Los Angeles: Bhaktivedanta Book Trust, 1983), details the specifics of such sacred vegetarian fare and compassion for animals, as do a plethora of articles in the movement's in-house magazine, *Back to Godhead* (BTG). Some of the magazine's more prominent studies on the subject would include Ravindra Svarupa Dasa, "How to Eat in Bhakti-Yoga" (1973); Vishakha Devi Dasi, "Cow Protection: Practical Necessity for a Peaceful Society" (1975); Yogesvara Dasa, "Discovering the Transcendental Taste" (1977); A. C. Bhaktivedanta Swami Prabhupada, "Slaughterhouse Civilization" (published posthumously in 1979); and Rupanuga Dasa, "Diet for a Spiritual Planet" (1980). In addition, for many years the magazine ran a regular column called "Lord Krishna's Cuisine," in which these and similar subjects, as well as numerous recipes, were artfully offered to literally millions of readers.

3. For more on Prabhupada's life and accomplishments from an insider's point of view, see Satsvarupa Dasa Goswami, *Srila Prabhupada-lilamrta*, 6 volumes (Los Angeles: Bhaktivedanta Book Trust, 1980–1983). Academic works on Prabhupada and his movement abound. Some of the more important studies are as follows: J. Stillson Judah, *Hare Krishna and the Counterculture* (New York: John Wiley & Sons, 1974); Francine Jeanne Daner, *The American Children of Krsna: A Study of the Hare Krsna Movement* (New York: Holt, Rinehart and Winston, 1976); Steven J. Gelberg, ed., *Hare Krishna, Hare Krishna: Five Distinguished Scholars on the Krishna Movement in the West* (New York: Grove Press, 1983); E. Burke Rocheford, Jr., *Hare Krishna in America* (New Brunswick: Rutgers University Press, 1985); Kim Knott, *My Sweet Lord: The Hare Krishna Movement* (Northamptonshire, Great Britain: The Aquarian Press, 1986); Larry D. Shinn, *The Dark Lord: Cult Images and the Hare Krishnas in America* (Philadelphia: The Westminster Press, 1987); Charles R. Brooks, *The Hare Krishnas in India* (Princeton: Princeton University Press, 1989); David G. Bromley and Larry D. Shinn, eds., *Krishna Consciousness in the West* (Lewisburg: Bucknell University Press, 1989); and *The Journal of Vaishnava Studies*, Volume 6, Number 2, Spring 1998, which was an entire issue on Prabhupada and his movement.

184 / Holy Cow

4. For more on Chaitanya Mahaprabhu from an ISKCON perspective, see O. B. L. Kapoor's scholarly volume, *The Philosophy and Religion of Sri Chaitanya* (Delhi: Munshiram Manoharlal Publishers, 1977), and also Prabhupada's own volume, *The Teachings of Lord Chaitanya* (Los Angeles: Bhaktivedanta Book Trust, 1974). See also my two volumes, *India's Spiritual Renaissance: The Life and Times of Lord Chaitanya* (New York: FOLK Books, 1988) and *Pancha Tattva: The Five Features of God* (New York: FOLK Books, 1994). For an academic overview of Chaitanya's life and teachings, see my paper "Who Is Sri Chaitanya?" in Edwin F. Bryant and Maria Ekstrand's edited volume, *The Hare Krishna Movement: The Post-Charismatic Fate of a Religious Transplant* (New York: Columbia University Press, 2004).

5. It should perhaps be mentioned here that the familiar term "Hinduism" is actually a misnomer. The word is not mentioned in the classical writings of ancient India, nor is it used by educated "Hindus" today, who refer to their tradition as Sanatana-dharma, or "the eternal function of the soul." The modern construct known as Hinduism is actually a medley of different religious traditions, the major ones being Vaishnavism (the worship of Vishnu, or Krishna, and His many Incarnations), Shaivism (the worship of Shiva, the demigod in charge of universal destruction), and Shaktism (the worship of the universal goddess). The Hare Krishna movement is an orthodox branch of Gaudiya Vaishnavism, or the form of the religion with roots in Bengal.

6. See Pandit Satkari Cattopadyaya, *A Glimpse into the Life of Thakur Bhaktivinode* (Calcutta: Bhaktivinode Memorial Committee, 1916), p. 59.

7. See Swami B. V. Tirtha Maharaja, *The Philosophy of Love: Ancient Wisdom of the Immortal Soul* (San Francisco: Mandala Publishing, n.d.), p. 29.

8. See Kerry S. Walters and Lisa Portmess, eds., *Religious Vegetarianism: From Hesiod to the Dalai Lama* (Albany: State University of New York Press, 2001), p. 10.

9. See Steven J. Gelberg, "Exploring an Alternative Reality: Spiritual Life in ISKCON," in David G. Bromley and Larry D. Shinn, eds., *Krishna Consciousness in the West, op. cit.*, p. 148.

10. See Satguru Shivaya Subramuniyaswami, *Dancing With Siva: Hinduism's Contemporary Catechism* (Concord, California: Himalayan Academy, 1993), p. 201.

11. See Eliot A. Singer, "Conversion Through Foodways Enculturation: The Meaning of Eating in an American Hindu Sect," in Linda Keller Brown and Kay Mussell, eds., *Ethnic and Regional Foodways in the United States* (Knoxville, Tennessee: The University of Tennessee Press, 1984), p. 207.

12. Radha is recognized in the Gaudiya Vaishnava tradition as God in female form, Krishna's eternal consort in the divine narrative of the spiritual world. Ultimate reality consists of understanding their loving exchange and, finally, entering into it.

13. Singer, *op. cit.*, p. 211.

14. Goswami Krishnajivanji, interview at Jatipura, September 14, 1979. Quoted in Paul M. Toomey, "Krishna's Consuming Passions: Food as Metaphor and Metonym for Emotion at Mount Govardhan," in Owen M. Lynch, ed., *Divine Passions: The Social Construction of Emotion in India* (Berkeley and Los Angeles: University of California Press, 1990), p. 169.

15. Quoted in *The Higher Taste: A Guide to Gourmet Vegetarian Cooking and a Karma-Free Diet, op. cit.,* pp. 51–52.

Chapter One: A Brief History of Vegetarianism in India

1. For more on Buddhism in relation to meat-eating, see Philip Kapleau, *To Cherish All Life: A Buddhist Case for Becoming Vegetarian* (San Francisco: Harper & Row Publishers, 1981), Norm Phelps, *The Great Compassion: Buddhism and Animal Rights* (New York: Lantern Books, 2004), and my book *From Nothingness to Personhood: A Collection of Essays on Buddhism from a Vaishnava-Hindu Perspective* (New York: FOLK Books, 2003).

2. Jainism is popularly considered the champion of *ahimsa* and other nonviolent philosophical perspectives. With roots in distant antiquity, the Jains were officially established 2,500 years ago with the preaching of Mahavira, a contemporary of the Buddha, though they never gained prominence in India or elsewhere. Their earliest scriptures, such as the *Acharanga Sutra,* unambiguously support the *ahimsa* ideal. For more on these aspects of Jain thought, see Christopher Key Chapple, *Nonviolence to Animals, Earth, and Self in Asian Traditions* (Albany: State University of New York Press, 1993).

3. Sunanda Y. Shastri and Yajneshwar Shastri, "*Ahimsa* and the Unity of All Things: A Hindu View of Nonviolence," in Daniel L. Smith-Christopher, *Subverting Hatred: The Challenge of Nonviolence in Religious Traditions* (Cambridge, Massachusetts: The Boston Research Center for the 21ˢᵗ Century, 1998), p. 75.

4. See Henk W. Bodewitz, "Hindu *Ahimsa* and Its Roots," in Jan E. M. Houben and Karl R. Van Kooij, eds., *Violence Denied: Violence, Non-Violence and the Rationalization of Violence in South Asian Cultural History* (Koln, the Netherlands: Brill, 1999), p. 21.

5. Lawrence A. Babb, *The Divine Hierarchy: Popular Hinduism in Central India* (New York: Columbia University Press, 1975), p. 225.

6. Maguelonne Toussaint-Samat, *History of Food,* trans. Anthea Bell (Oxford: Blackwell Publishers, 1994), pp. 100–101.

7. Explanation of the word *mamsa* appears in *Srimad Bhagavatam,* 11.5.14.

8. Judy W. Patel, *The People of India: Their Religion, Culture, and Way of Being* (New York: The Falmut Educational Trust, 2001), p. 212. For similar statistics see also pp. 300, 322, and 334. However, it must be admitted that these statistics are highly questionable. An alternate story is told in K. T. Achaya's book *Indian Food: A Historical Companion* (Delhi: Oxford University Press, 1998), where only 25 to 30 percent of India's current population is identified as strictly vegetarian, though he does not define what he means by "strictly."

9. For more on these statistics see www.harrisinteractive.com and www.vrg.org/nutshell/market.htm.

10. See the Proceedings of The National Indian Survey (2003), conducted in Delhi, Bombay, Calcutta, and Madras by the Archeological Survey of India, published as *The Pulse of India Today* (Delhi: The National Indian Survey, 2003).

11. Samak Surya, *Journey to Forgotten India: Ancient Travelers in the Land of the Ganga* (New York: William Bellows, Inc., 1995), pp. 20–45.

12. See A. C. Bhaktivedanta Swami Prabhupada, *Bhagavad-gita As It Is* (New York: Macmillan, 1972), pp. 113–14, commentary.

13. See D. N. Jha, *The Myth of the Holy Cow* (New Delhi: Verso, 2002), pp. 96–7. Rama lived in an earlier age, when animal sacrifices (according to the Vedas) were still appropriate. He also set an example for Kshatriyas, surviving in the forest (during his banishment), where he killed and ate as necessary.

14. A. C. Bhaktivedanta Swami Prabhupada, *Bhagavad-gita As It Is, op. cit.,* pp. 113–14.

15. Quoted in Erik H. Erikson, *Gandhi's Truth* (New York: Norton, 1969), p. 374.

16. S. Dasgupta, *A History of Indian Philosophy,* Vol. II (London: Cambridge University Press, 1932), pp. 508–9.

17. See Alf Hiltebeitel, *Rethinking the Mahabharata* (The University of Chicago Press, 2001), p. 202, and Arti Dhand, "The Politics and the Dharma of Conversion: Reflections from the *Mahabharata*," in *Hindu-Christian Studies Bulletin,* Volume 15, 2002, pp. 6–12.

18. See the *Varaha Purana* (8.26–30).

19. Paul M. Toomey, "Krishna's Consuming Passions: Food as Metaphor and Metonym for Emotion at Mount Govardhan," in Owen M. Lynch, ed., *Divine Passions: The Social Construction of Emotion in India* (Berkeley and Los Angeles: University of California Press, 1990), p. 164.

Chapter Two: India's Sacred Cows

1. Quoted in Suresvara Dasa, "Religion You Can Drink," in *Back to Godhead* magazine, Vol. 20, No. 1, January, 1985. I am indebted to Suresvara's article for the first few paragraphs of this chapter.

2. *Ibid.*

3. *Ibid.*

4. *Ibid.*

5. David Frawley, "The Milky Way," in *Clarion Call* magazine, Vol. 3, No. 4 (Fall 1990). These few paragraphs draw on information in Frawley's article.

6. Quoted in *The Extended Circle: A Dictionary of Humane Thought,* ed. Jon Wynne-Tyson (Fontwell, Sussex: Centaur Press, 1985), pp. 91–92.

7. Lewis G. Regenstein, *Replenish the Earth* (New York: The Crossroad Publishing Company, 1991), p. 225.

8. Jeremy Rifkin, *Beyond Beef: The Rise and Fall of the Cattle Culture* (New York: Dutton, 1992), p. 17.

9. The paradigmatic individuals representing these five levels of intimate relationship are Prahlad Maharaj, who, through loving prayers, enjoys a neutral or passive relationship with God (*shanta-rasa*); Hanuman, Rama's chief companion, who demonstrates an unwavering attitude of service toward his master (*dasya-rasa*); the Pandavas, who exemplify the perfection of friendship (*sakhya-rasa*); Nanda and Yashoda, the very emblems of divine parenthood (*vatsalya-rasa*); and Radha and the *gopis*, who are exemplary in conjugal love (*madhurya-rasa*).

10. Not to be confused with Maha-maya, the ordinary variety of illusion that keeps one distanced from ultimate reality.

11. Barbara Powell, *Windows into the Infinite: A Guide to the Hindu Scriptures* (Fremont, California: Asian Humanities Press, 1996), p. 308.

12. Quoted in Benjamin Walker, *The Hindu World* (New York: Praeger Publishers, 1968), p. 26.

13. For a comprehensive report on veganism in the Hare Krishna Movement, see Vraja Kishor Dasa, *The Vegan and the Vedas: A Detailed Examination of Veganism*

and Krishna Consciousness (Towaco, New Jersey: Krishnafest North America, 1994).

14. See the essay "Thou Shalt Not Kill," in A. C. Bhaktivedanta Swami Prabhupada, *The Science of Self-Realization* (Los Angeles: Bhaktivedanta Book Trust, 1977), p. 123.

15. A. C. Bhaktivedanta Swami Prabhupada, "Slaughterhouse Civilization," in *Back to Godhead* magazine 14.9 (1979), p. 4.

16. Cole McFarland, "The Conservation of Moral Energy: The Doctrines of Karma and Reincarnation," in *The Animals' Voice* magazine, Vol. 2, No. 4 (August 1989), p. 52. Karma is also nicely summed up in Mark Mathew Braunstein's book *Radical Vegetarianism* (Los Angeles: Panjandrum Books, 1981), p. 89, where he writes, "The Eastern law of karma might be defined in various Western ways: scientifically as action and reaction, epistemologically as cause and effect, biblically and botanically as sowing and reaping, and even economically as supply and demand." The Sanskrit word *phala* ("fruit") has an interesting karma-related significance here. The word can refer both to "edible fruits" and to "the *fruit* of one's activities," i.e., the results of a given action. In relation to sacred food, whether literally fruit or not, one can be freed of karmic reactions by tasting consecrated fare that is offered to Krishna or otherwise blessed by a holy person. Thus, with *prasadam*, "fruit" is positively modified in both senses of the word.

17. See for example J. E. Lovelock, *Gaia: A New Look at Life on Earth* (New York: Oxford University Press, 1979).

18. M. K. Gandhi, *How to Serve the Cow* (Ahmedabad, India: Navajivan Publishing House, 1954, reprint), pp. 3–4.

19. Barbara Powell, *Windows into the Infinite: A Guide to the Hindu Scriptures, op. cit.,* p. 308.

20. *Young India* magazine, October 6, 1921, p. 36. Quoted in Lisa M. Spooner, "India's Sacred Cattle," in *Vegetarian Times*, No. 50 (1981), pp. 74–77. The next few paragraphs are drawn from Spooner's article. See also Michael Perelman, *Farming for Profit in a Hungry World* (New York: Allanheld Somun & Company, 1977), p. 131.

21. Narasimha Dasa, "A Neglected Source of Wealth," in *Back to Godhead* magazine, Vol. 25, No. 3 (May–June 1991), an entire issue dedicated to "The Case for Ox Power."

22. Jeremy Rifkin, *op. cit.,* pp. 37–38.

23. R. O. Whyte, *Land Livestock and Human Nutrition in India* (New York: Praeger Publishers, 1968), p. 24.

24. Gunnar Myrdal, *Asian Drama: An Inquiry into the Poverty of Nations* (New York: Pantheon Books, 1971), p. 260.

25. Marvin Harris, "The Cultural Ecology of India's Sacred Cattle," in *Current Anthropology* (February 1966), p. 55.

26. A. C. Bhaktivedanta Swami Prabhupada, "Slaughterhouse Civilization," in *Back to Godhead* magazine, *op. cit.*

27. Much of this information is drawn from Suresvara Dasa's article "Adopt a Cow for Peace," in *Back to Godhead* magazine, Vol. 22, No. 12 (December 1987).

28. Quoted from his *Srimad Bhagavatam* commentary (1.16.18).

29. For an insightful summarization of these guidelines along with their implica-

tions, see Hare Krishna Dasi's article "Improving Our Cow Protection Programs" on the website "Hare Krishna Rural Life" (www.hkrl.com). ISKCON Television has produced a video called "Sacred Cow," and the International Society for Cow Protection has produced "Buck and Lou—Get up!," demonstrating progressive theories for comforting oxen and protecting them for the benefit of all. Paramananda Dasa, the architect of these theories, was an early champion of cow protection in ISKCON and continues to work for better bovine treatment throughout Indian and American society. In short, the Hare Krishna movement has a lot to say about Krishna's favorite animals, and it strictly follows in the long-standing Indian tradition of cow protection.

Chapter Three: Ayurveda and the Three Modes of Material Nature

1. Mark Santori, *The Many Miracles of Milk* (San Francisco: Mardon Press, 1991), p. 76.
2. See Gabriel Cousens, "Role of Vegetarianism in Yoga," in NEWLIFE magazine (November–December 2002), p. 13. Also see *Hatha-yoga Pradipa* (section 58), which tells us that practitioners of Ayurveda, yoga, and all aspiring spiritual seekers should abandon the use of flesh foods. Yogic texts such as this one inform us that meat-eating creates *vyutthita-chitta*, or a disturbed (literally "provoked") mind. To practice spiritual life properly, one needs *samahita-chitta*, or a calm mind—"equilibrium." This truth, in relation to vegetarianism, is further confirmed in Patanjali's *Yoga-sutra* (2.30), wherein *ahimsa* is described as essential for the practicing yogi. According to the *Vyasa-bhashya*, or the traditional *Yoga-sutra* commentary, *ahimsa* is here defined as "abstaining from injuring any being, at any time, and in any manner."
3. This information is somewhat dated, appearing in Lance Shringi's book, *The World According to Ayurveda* (Delhi: Barsolani Press, 1989), pp. 61–64. For more current information, please see Swami Sada Shiva Tirtha's mammoth work, *The Ayurveda Encyclopedia: Natural Secrets to Healing, Prevention, and Longevity* (Bayville, New York: Ayurveda Holistic Center Press, 1998), which does not address the statistical information given in this paragraph but nonetheless is a good resource for Ayurveda today.
4. See Will Durant, *The Story of Civilization*, Part 1, entitled *Our Oriental Heritage* (New York: Simon and Schuster, 1954), pp. 530–531.
5. Robert Murphy, *One Man's Food Is Another Man's Poison: Prescribing Medicines for Distinct Individuals* (Philadelphia: Onetime Academic Press, 2000).
6. Yolande Manson, "Ayurveda + the Blood Type Diet," first printed in the Australasian Ayurveda Practitioners Association newsletter, Spring 2002. The entire article can be found on the *Journal of Ayurveda Medical Research* website.
7. See Swami Sada Shiva Tirtha's article "Ayurveda & Anemia," on the Ayurveda Holistic Center website.
8. Shubhra Krishan, "The Ayurvedic Flavors of Health," in *New Living* online magazine (April 2003).
9. Burt Russell, *Eating for Optimum Health* (New York: Stackard Books, 2002).
10. See John Robbins, *Diet for a New America* (Walpole, New Hampshire: Stillpoint Publishing, 1987) and Neal Barnard, *Food for Life* (New York: Crown, 1993). The pertinent statistics quoted in these books are summarized in my own work *Diet for Transcendence: Vegetarianism and the World Religions* (Badger, California: Torchlight Publishing, Inc., 1997). Interestingly, Physicians Committee for

Responsible Medicine established four new food groups in 1991—whole grains, vegetables, fruits, and legumes—replacing the prior food groups, meat, dairy, grains, and fruits and vegetables, which were considered indispensable for maintaining good health. Obviously, Ayurveda prescriptions and the ISKCON diet are both rich in the currently recommended food groups.

11. Atmatattva Dasa, "Ayurveda-vedanta: The Vedanta of Life Science," in *Tattva Prakasha* Vol. 1, No. 9, November 9, 2001 (the bimonthly newsletter of IndiaDivine.com, published by Bhaktivedanta Ashram, Mysore). For more on the "10 subjects" of the *Srimad Bhagavatam* from a Gaudiya Vaishnava perspective, see Bhaktivinoda Thakura's *Jaiva Dharma*, Chapter Thirteen, entitled, "Pramana and Prameya."

12. *Ibid.* All quotes from Atmatattva Dasa in this section are also from the above article.

13. See Swami A. C. Bhaktivedanta, *The Bhagavad Gita As It Is* (New York: The Macmillan Company, 1968), pp. 293–294.

Chapter Four: "Thou Shalt Not Kill"

1. A. C. Bhaktivedanta Swami Prabhupada, Lecture on *Srimad Bhagavatam*, Canto One (1.2.9–10), Delhi, November 14, 1973.

2. This is Prabhupada's translation. Explanatory words can be found in Prabhupada's commentary on *Srimad Bhagavatam* (6.1.6), and the same text is elaborated upon by Satsvarupa Dasa Goswami in *Vaishnava Compassion* (La Crosse, Florida: Gita-nagari Press, 2001), p. 46.

3. See A. C. Bhaktivedanta Swami Prabhupada, *Civilization and Transcendence*, Chapter 12, entitled, "How to Love God."

4. I found references and explanations for "Thou shalt not kill" in the *Srimad Bhagavatam*; the *Chaitanya-charitamrita*; *Perfect Questions, Perfect Answers*; *Science of Self-Realization*; *Life Comes from Life*; *Matchless Gifts*; *The Journey of Self-Discovery*; *The Quest for Enlightenment*; *Dialectical Spiritualism*; and in countless lectures and *Back to Godhead* magazine articles. Prabhupada's other works, while not addressing the biblical command directly, certainly deal with related issues, and the commandment's essence is not far in the background.

5. Interestingly, when James (2.11), the brother of Jesus, articulates the "Thou shalt not kill" commandment, he does so while making a point extremely similar to Prabhupada's. He argues that one cannot selectively adhere to scripture: "For whoever keeps the whole law but fails in even one point has become accountable for all of it. For the one who said, 'You should not commit adultery' also said, 'You shall not murder.' Now, if you do not commit adultery but if you murder, you have become a transgressor of the law."

6. David Noel Freedman, *The Nine Commandments: Uncovering the Hidden Pattern of Crime and Punishment in the Hebrew Bible* (New York: Doubleday, 2000), pp. 110–113. For proof texts see Exodus 21.12–14 and Leviticus 24.17, 21 for capital punishment; Numbers 35.22–25 for killing by accident; and Deuteronomy 20.1–20 for Israelites being allowed to kill their enemies.

7. *Ibid.*

8. Mark Mathew Braunstein, *Radical Vegetarianism* (Los Angeles: Panjandrum Books, 1981), pp. 91–92. Rabbi Abraham Isaac Kook (1865–1935), the first Chief Rabbi of pre-state Israel and a highly respected Jewish leader, also includes animals as beneficiaries of the commandment. While speaking in ref-

erence to Leviticus 17:13, the command for a hunter to cover with dirt the
blood of an animal he has killed, Kook says, "[T]he rule to cover the blood
extends the sway of 'you shall not murder' to the animal, and the prohibitions
against mixing meat and milk and the banning of linen and wool in a garment
extends the injunctions 'you shall not rob' and 'you shall not oppress' . . . ." See
"Fragments of Light: A View as to the Reasons for the Commandments" in
*Abraham Isaac Kook: The Lights of Penitence, Lights of Holiness, The Moral
Principles, Essays, Letters, and Poems*, trans., Ben Zion Bokser (Mahwah, New
Jersey: Paulist Press, 1978), p. 321. Kook was a well-known Torah scholar, a
religious vegetarian, and author of *A Vision of Vegetarianism and Peace*.

9.   Philip L. Pick, "Jewish philosophy of vegetarianism," in the magazine of the
     EVU (European Vegetarian Union), Issue 4, 1997. Published online.

10. Reuben Alcalay, *The Complete Hebrew-English Dictionary* (Jerusalem: Massada,
     1981). For more on Alcalay's work, see my *Diet for Transcendence: Vegetarianism
     and the World Religions, op. cit*, which gives many diverse arguments for the
     legitimacy of vegetarianism in the Judeo-Christian tradition. Such arguments
     are quite compelling, though they rarely take into account "Thou shalt not kill."
     For an excellent study of these other reasons for biblical vegetarianism, see Vasu
     Murti, *They Shall Not Hurt or Destroy: Animal Rights and Vegetarianism in the
     Western Religious Traditions* (Cleveland, Ohio: Vegetarian Advocates Press,
     2003).

11. "Thou shalt not kill" appears, in various forms, in Exodus 20.13; Deut. 5.17;
     Matthew 5.21; Matthew 19.18; Mark 10.19; Luke 18.20; and James 2.11, among
     other places. In 1540, a translation of the Bible, dedicated to Henry VIII, with a
     Prologue by the Archbishop of Canterbury, reinterpreted the commandment as
     meaning, "Thou shalt not commit manslaughter." There are scholars today who
     would like to change it to "Thou shalt not commit homicide." (See David Noel
     Freedman, *op. cit.*, p. 111.) Clearly, the spirit of the commandment is "Thou
     shalt not kill," and the above adjustments lead to interpretations that go too far.

12. *The Holy Bible: From Ancient Eastern Manuscripts*, trans. George M. Lamsa
     (Nashville, Tennessee: A. J. Holman Company, 1957). This work contains the
     Old and New Testaments translated from the *Peshitta*, the authorized Bible of
     the Church of the East.

13. Rabbi Joseph Telushkin, *Biblical Literacy: The Most Important People, Events, and
     Ideas of the Hebrew Bible* (New York: William Morrow and Company, Inc.,
     1997), p. 433.

14. *Etz Hayim: Torah and Commentary*, ed. David L. Lieber (New York: The
     Rabbinical Assembly, 2001), commentary on Exodus 20.13.

15. Bernard E. Rollin, *Animal Rights and Human Morality* (New York: Prometheus
     Books, 1981), p. 6.

16. For more on the inappropriate use of land and labor involved in meat-eating,
     see Francis Moore Lappé, *Diet for a Small Planet* (New York: Ballantine Books,
     1975).

17. Keith Akers, *A Vegetarian Sourcebook: The Nutrition, Ecology and Ethics of a
     Natural Foods Diet* (New York: G. P. Putnam & Sons, 1983), p. 154.

18. *Ibid.* See also the list of pro-vegetarian philosophers—from Pythagoras to
     modern-day thinkers—in Daniel A. Dombrowski's book *Vegetarianism: The
     Philosophy Behind the Ethical Diet* (Wellingborough, Northamptonshire:
     Thorsons Publishers Limited, 1985).

19. *Ibid.*
20. *The Extended Circle: A Dictionary of Humane Thought*, ed. Jon Wynne-Tyson (Fontwell, Sussex: Centaur Press, 1985).
21. See Jeremy Bentham, *The Principles of Morals and Legislation* (Oxford: Clarendon Press, 1876), Chapter 17, Section 1, p. 311.

Chapter Five: Food for Life

1. A. C. Bhaktivedanta Swami Prabhupada, *Srimad Bhagavatam* (Los Angeles: Bhaktivedanta Book Trust, 1977), 9.21.12, commentary.
2. A. C. Bhaktivedanta Swami Prabhupada, lecture in Los Angeles, December 9, 1968.
3. A. C. Bhaktivedanta Swami Prabhupada, *Bhagavad-gita As It Is* (Los Angeles: Bhaktivedanta Book Trust, 1972), 3.14, commentary.
4. Satsvarupa Dasa Goswami, *Vaishnava Compassion, op. cit.*, p. 34.
5. In fact, Jayadvaita Swami (Jay Israel), a senior member of ISKCON, teaches a seminar entitled "Food for Death," in which he makes the point that *prasadam* distribution—the *raison d'etre* of FFL—should never be compromised; it should never devolve into mundane welfare work.
6. Priyavrata Dasa, personal correspondence, November 10, 2003.
7. See Mukunda Goswami, "No One Should Go Hungry," in *Back to Godhead* magazine, Vol. 22, No. 4 (April 1987), p. 11.
8. See Hare Krishna Food for Life promotional leaflet.
9. *Ibid.* Speech in Durban, April 23, 1997.
10. See Suresvara Dasa, "Food for Life: A Country Slice," in *Back to Godhead* magazine, Vol. 22, No. 4 (April 1987), pp. 7–8.
11. For context, Vajpayee's short speech, delivered on November 8, 2000 in New Delhi, appears below (see www.akshayapatra.org):

I am highly pleased to know that the International Society for Krishna Conciousness (ISKCON) Bangalore is launching "Akshaya Patra," a mid-day meal program for children in government-run schools in the rural areas of Karnataka's capital on November 11, 2000. The scale of the program—providing a nutritious meal consisting of rice, yogurt and *sambar* with vegetables to 30,000 students every day—is truly impressive. This is a service not only to God but also to the nation. Lack of adequate and nutritious food for children of poor families has a direct negative effect on their school attendance, their health condition, and their subsequent life as they grow up. However, it is not only their individual loss; it is also a loss to the nation and to mankind.

Making India hunger-free is one of our key national objectives. Paradoxically, even though our country has achieved record food production in recent years, a large number of our fellow-citizens still continue to suffer from hunger owing to their poor economic status and deficiencies in our food distribution system. Since the goal of 'Food for All' [an alternate name for FFL] cannot be achieved solely with the government's initiatives, it is necessary for social organizations to vastly increase their voluntary efforts.

The mass-feeding schemes run by religious establishments of various denominations can make a major contribution to the national effort by scaling up their current programs. I am confident that ISKCON's "Akshaya Patra" program will serve both as an inspiration and a practical logistical guide to other institutions interested in taking up such activities. I wish the program all success.

Chapter Six: Restaurants and Cookbooks

1. See Jon Gregerson, *Vegetarianism: A History* (Fremont, California: Jain Publishing Company, 1994), p. 98.
2. Paul R. Amato and Sonia A. Partridge, *The New Vegetarians: Promoting Health and Protecting Life* (New York: Plenum Publishing, 1989), pp. 15–16.
3. Prabhupada's letter to Dayananda, dated October 17, 1968.
4. The restaurants were first listed in *Back to Godhead* magazine Vol. 15, Nos. 3–4 (1980).
5. The "gift from the gods" quote is from Michael Bauer's article of the same name in the *Dallas Times Herald* (Friday, May 20, 1983). The *Vegetarian Times* review is from the March 1987 issue.
6. Quoted in "ISKCON in Mauritius: The Story of R. Chedumbarum Pillay" in *ISKCON World Review*, Vol. 2, No. 6 (Summer 1982), p. 7.
7. This was the front-page article of *New York Newsday* on July 27, 1994.
8. From Chez Pascale [Weekly Dining Column] in the [NYC] *Daily News* (Wednesday, May 28, 2003).
9. Prabhupada's letter to Krishna Devi, New Vrindaban, June 15, 1969.
10. *The Hare Krishna Cookbook*, compiled by Krishna Devi and Shama Devi (Los Angeles: Bhaktivedanta Book Trust, 1973), reprint 1981, back cover text.
11. See Trish Hall, "A Chef's Passage to India is Both Spiritual and Cultural," in *The New York Times* (Wednesday, August 26, 1987), The Living Section, pp. C1 and C10.
12. *Ibid.*
13. Vishakha Devi Dasi, "At Last! The Krishna's Cuisine Cookbook," in *Back to Godhead* magazine, Vol. 22, No. 10 (October 1987), pp. 10–11.
14. *Ibid.*
15. See JeanMarie Brownson, " 'Art of Indian Vegetarian Cooking' Covers a Big Subject Well," in *The Chicago Tribune* (Thursday, September 3, 1987).
16. Vishakha Devi Dasi, *op. cit.*
17. See *Publishers Weekly: The International Magazine of Book Publishing*, Vol. 232, No. 28 (July 17, 1987).
18. Lee Berman, "The Cook Shelf," in *Gourmet: The Magazine of Good Living* (November 1987), p. 72.
19. Elaine Tait, "Cookbook May Become the Vegetarian Bible," in *The Philadelphia Inquirer* (Thursday, September 10, 1987), p. 2-D.
20. *Vegetarian Times*, Issue 131 (July 1988).
21. From a personal correspondence on December 10, 2003 with Nrsimhananda Dasa (David Shapiro), founder of ITV, who produces and directs Kurma's videos. (For more on ISKCON television, see www.itvproductions.net. For more on Kurma, see www.kurma.net.)

Chapter Seven: Recipes for the Soul

1. Peter Bennett, "In Nanda Baba's House: The Devotional Experience in Pushti Marg Temples," in Owen Lynch, ed., *Divine Passions: The Social Construction of Emotion in India* (Berkeley and Los Angeles: University of California Press, 1990), p. 196.

2.   *Ibid.*, p. 199.
3.   *Ibid.*, p. 208.

Afterword: A Personal Reflection
1.   Rynn Berry, *Famous Vegetarians and Their Favorite Recipes: Lives and Lore from Buddha to the Beatles* (New York: Pythagorean Publishers, 1993), p. 165.
2.   See www.hinduismtoday.com/in-depth_issues/veggie_vow.
3.   Eliot A. Singer, in *Ethnic and Regional Foodways in the United States, op. cit.,* p. 212.
4.   Klaus Klostermaier, "*Bhakti, Ahimsa,* and Ecology," in *Journal of Dharma* 16 (July–September 1991), pp. 246–254.
5.   This last section is paraphrased from Prabhupada's recorded lectures by Giriraja Swami, "Reverence For All Life," in *Back to Godhead* magazine, Vol. 33, No. 2 (March–April 1999), p. 38.

Appendix

The following interview was conducted by Rynn Berry, for his book
Food for the Gods: Vegetarianism and the World Religions *(New York:
Pythagorean Publishers, 1998). It has been edited and excerpted for
length and relevance.*

Steve Rosen, a brilliant, tough-minded young Jewish intellectual, who had been something of a religious skeptic, attended his first Hare Krishna (Vaishnava) service in 1972 and was captivated by the preaching of its charismatic leader, A. C. Bhaktivedanta Swami Prabhupada. After closely examining the sacred texts of the Vaishnavas, Rosen embraced Vaishnava Hinduism and eventually became one of Swami Prabhupada's disciples. Since then, Rosen (now Satyaraja Dasa) has become a widely recognized Vaishnava scholar and practitioner.

The author of 12 books on Vaishnavism and related subjects, Rosen has developed an important voice in the Indian religious community. As a measure of the high esteem in which he is held by Indian scholars, his works have been issued by three of India's prominent publishing companies: K. L. M. Firma (*Archaeology and the Vaishnava Tradition: The Pre-Christian Roots of Krishna Worship*, Calcutta, 1989); Munshiram Manoharlal (*Passage from India: The Life and Times of His Divine Grace A. C. Bhaktivedanta Swami Prabhupada*, Delhi, 1992); and Motilal Banarsidass (*Vaishnavi: Women and the Worship of Krishna*: Delhi, 1996). Among his other books are *Diet for Transcendence*, *Om Shalom*, and *East-West Dialogues*. He is also the editor-in-chief of the

Journal of Vaishnava Studies, an academic quarterly that is esteemed and supported by scholars in the field.

Berry: How long have you been a vegetarian?

Rosen: I became a vegetarian in 1971 after studying the roots of various religious traditions. It started when I began to look deeply into Western religion, especially Christianity, which only goes back about 2,000 years. I then studied Judaism, which is somewhat older. Both of these religions emphasize the need for love and compassion, but rarely take it to the point of vegetarianism, at least not overtly. Wanting to delve deeper and go further back into the religious history of mankind, I began studying the various Eastern religions, which go back many thousands of years. In the course of my research, I found that common to most of the Asian religions was this sort of *ahimsa* sensibility—this notion of "harmlessness" and "nonviolence," this mood of treating others as you would have them treat you. And that's what led me to vegetarianism quite early on.

Then, taking the religious quest back to its roots, I became interested in yoga and ancient Hindu traditions that emphasized vegetarianism. This was well before I met the devotees of the International Society for Krishna consciousness [ISKCON]. I was already a practicing vegetarian when I became a practicing Vaishnava, although my commitment to the Krishna religion definitely enhanced my resolve to be kind to all creatures and to be a vegetarian.

But the point I want to make is this: I saw that there was a thread connecting all the religious traditions and, for me, this was best expressed in what is known as *sanatan dharma*, or "the eternal function of the soul"; that's what the devotees of Krishna were purporting to follow. So that's what I started to explore in the Krishna consciousness movement. Now, that particular *sanatan dharma* ideology, that particular point of view—wherever you find it, be it in Christianity or Hinduism or whatever—necessarily insists on kindness to all living creatures. Taken to its furthest and most logical end, it insists on vegetarianism.

Berry: Larry Shinn, President of Berea College, Kentucky, and an acknowledged expert on the Hare Krishna movement, observed that many vegetarians joined the Krishna movement because it gives them a rationale for their vegetarianism. Did you find this to be true in your case?

Rosen: Yes. I would say so. Here at last was a religious tradition that provided a clear connection between vegetarianism, kindness to all creatures, and the religious pursuit. As I said, I found this same principle in other traditions, but you had to look really hard for it— it was mainly to be found in the mystical traditions. Mainstream Judaism, Christianity, and Islam, for example, certainly do not stress vegetarian teachings. If anything, they would reject it. But they do stress universal compassion and love, which ultimately leads to vegetarianism, at least if such love is truly universal. Therefore, the mystical traditions that grew up around these religions do support a vegetarian way of life; but their mainstream counterparts lost sight of this. Whereas in Krishna consciousness, whether mainstream or the more mystical side, it is right on the face of it, right there as a prominent teaching.

Berry: I understand that in 1975 you were initiated by Swami Prabhupada himself, the founder of the International Krishna Consciousness movement. Did you have a sense that he was a special person?

Rosen: When I first met Prabhupada in 1972, my immediate impression was that he was a genuine saint, and his saintliness inspired me to want to improve my lifestyle. So I followed his instructions, distributed his books and spread his teachings with a view to becoming his disciple.

Berry: What were the prerequisites for becoming a disciple of Swami Prabhupada?

Rosen: One had to follow four basic principles—no meat-eating, no intoxication, no illicit sex, and no gambling. One also had to chant 16 rounds of Hare Krishna on beads. There are 108 beads on Vaishnava rosary. So one has to go around 16 times chanting the Hare Krishna Maha-mantra: "Hare Krishna! Hare Krishna! Krishna! Krishna! Hare! Hare! Hare Rama! Hare Rama! Rama! Rama! Hare! Hare!" This was the minimum prerequisite for initiation.

Berry: Did you have to repeat this refrain constantly?

Rosen: Sixteen rounds on beads as a minimum—that was for quiet, reflective meditation—and then you would chant aloud in *kir-tan*, a sort of joyous, overflowing spiritual exercise wherein you sing and dance with others. You must have seen the devotees singing like this on the streets. It's quite traditional, and it's a well-known practice all over India. There are many Vedic and post-Vedic prayers and chants like this, but this particular one is known as the Maha-mantra, which indicates that it is all-inclusive and all-encompassing. It's said that all other mantras are contained in this one mantra. It's *that* powerful. So it has a soteriological function, its meaning is very deep, and it is extremely purifying.

You see, most prayers or incantations ask for something in return. "Give us our daily bread," or something of that nature. Or, in the latter-day Buddhist tradition, you have *nam-myoho-renge-khyo*—supposedly, if you chant this incessantly, you'll get whatever you want, any material acquisition. But this Hare Krishna prayer is totally selfless. It asks for nothing in return. So its power comes from its selflessness, its purity, and it puts you in touch with the supreme pure, God.

Berry: How would you translate it?

Rosen: "O Lord! O divine energy of the Lord! Please engage me in Your service!" It means, essentially, "Whatever You want, O Lord, that's what I want!"

Berry: The great Indologist A. L. Basham said that Swami Prabhupada, in founding the International Hare Krishna movement, had established the first Asian religion in the West since the days of the Roman Empire. Harvey Cox, Professor of Divinity and Chairman of the Department of Applied Theology at Harvard Divinity School, said of Prabhupada: "There aren't many people you can think of who successfully implant a whole religious tradition in a completely alien culture. That's a rare achievement in the history of religion. Eventually, he planted this movement deeply in the North American soil, throughout other parts of the Europe-dominated world and beyond. The fact that we now have in the West a vigorous, disciplined, and seemingly well-organized movement—not merely a philosophical movement or a yoga or meditation movement, but a genuinely religious movement—introducing the devotion to God that he taught, is a stunning accomplishment. So when I say 'he was one in a million,' I think that's in some way an understatement. Perhaps he was one in a hundred million."

Rosen: Yes, that's a great quote.

Berry: He certainly was an improbable figure to have founded a religion on Western shores: he arrived in New York almost penniless in 1965. Clad in a flimsy *dhoti* and wearing rubber shoes, his only luggage was a battered portable typewriter and an umbrella. When he embarked on his long sea voyage to the United States, he was 70 years old (an age at which many people are checking into rest homes). On the outward voyage from Calcutta, he had several mild heart attacks. Yet he did the impossible: He established a branch of Gaudiya Vaishnavism in America, Europe and Asia—and it seems to have taken root.

Rosen: That's true—it was a phenomenal accomplishment! But he was not really "an improbable figure," as you say. In many ways, Swami Prabhupada was *the most likely person* to do it, chiefly because, as his biographers tell us, he spent a lifetime in preparation. He was born to devout Vaishnava parents of the Chaitanyaite school; he studied Vedic texts for most if not all of his life; he knew Sanskrit; he knew Bengali; in college, he majored in economics, philosophy and English; and he lived a pure life of loving God from the very beginning. So these things really prepared him for coming west, and for the monumental success that followed.

Berry: But he was an unlikely figure in another sense. Come to think of it, Mahatma Gandhi was an improbable figure as well. *Dhoti*-clad like Prabhupada, he weighed about 125 pounds soaking wet; yet he drove the British out of India and is considered, in some respects, the father of modern India. So that's a consideration: Very often even the most unlikely figure triumphs. The weak overcome the strong when they have truth on their side—that's the whole idea of *satyagraha*.

Rosen: Ultimately, Prabhupada's greatest strength lay in his dedication to and faith in his spiritual master, Bhaktisiddhanta Sarasvati Thakur. There were so many people who had been given the instruction by Bhaktisiddhanta to come west and to deliver the esoteric teachings of Krishna consciousness; but they considered it to be totally impossible because they'd been given to understand that people in the West were meat-eaters, alcoholics and sex-mongers. So they backed off. On the other hand, Prabhupada rose to the challenge, saying, "They declared that it was impossible . . . but I was determined to try it anyway." [laughter]

Berry: Do you think the Krishnaites [Vaishnavas] have been responsible for the spread of vegetarianism and the doctrine of *ahimsa* in America and Europe?

Rosen: Yes, very much so. In ISKCON vegetarianism is a requirement for practitioners, whereas in other traditions it is generally optional. Thus, it is an actively promoted philosophy. ISKCON has opened vegetarian restaurants in every major city of the world. They are immensely popular, opening people up to a broader conception of the vegetarian lifestyle. There are, of course, Jain and Buddhist denominations that have contributed to the popularity of vegetarianism, and certain Christian sects like the Seventh-Day Adventists have contributed as well. Perhaps I'm biased, but I would say, comparatively speaking, ISKCON has had a broader influence.

Berry: William Shurtleff told me that, when he was training as a Zen monk in Japan and working on *The Book of Tofu*, he met Swami Prabhupada, who had come to Tokyo in the late sixties to open a branch of ISKCON. So thanks to Prabhupada's zeal it has become a worldwide phenomenon.

Rosen: Vaishnava restaurants, which are lacto-vegetarian, have been thriving all over Europe, Japan, Australia, China, India, and Hong Kong, and, of course, in America as well.

Berry: India? I should think that opening a Krishnaite restaurant in India would be like taking coals to Newcastle.

Rosen: ISKCON has its own particular style of cooking and preparing sacred food that's offered to Krishna in sacrifice. In addition to the interest created by the mere fact of seeing Westerners preparing traditional dishes, devotees sometimes take traditional recipes from the culture and give them a distinctive Western flourish. Thus, the popularity is twofold.

Berry: What characterizes that style of cuisine?

Rosen: *Bhakti.* The love and devotion of the devotee—this is the main ingredient. You see, in Vaishnava devotional cooking, there are three concepts that one should be aware of: first, there is *bhoga*, or "mundane enjoyment," and this refers to unoffered food. Then you have *naivedya*, or the food that is brought before the Deity. Finally, you have *prasadam*, literally, "the Lord's mercy," which refers to the food *after* it is offered. This food is spiritually purifying and is always *sattvic*, or vegetarian and health-giving.

Berry: Is Yamuna Devi's cookbook *Lord Krishna's Cuisine* representative of *prasadam* preparation?

Rosen: Yes, in the sense that her mood in this book is devotional, but, in addition, it is a masterpiece of Indian culinary art. For many years Yamuna was Prabhupada's personal cook; he taught her his own cooking secrets, helped her collect recipes and specifically asked her to compile a cookbook. That was a great impetus for her; that's why she did it and doubtless that's why it turned out to be the award-winning cookbook that it is.

Berry: Prabhupada wanted her to do it for the West?

Rosen: For the world—even for India because, as I've said, ISKCON is unique in its presentation of Indian food. More, Prabhupada wanted her to perpetuate traditional Vaishnava cooking.

Berry: I understand that Prabhupada saw to it that his protégée Yamuna was given access to temple kitchens to which non-Westerners and non-Hindus had never been admitted. Have you, as a Vaishnava scholar, penetrated any of these temples?

Rosen: Yes, I've entered the sacred precincts of many temples that are off-limits to Westerners and non-Hindus. I've been to Tirupati, Guruvayur, Shri Rangam, and others. But, in actuality, they're easing up on the restrictions for foreigners. I think this is also due to ISKCON's presence.

Berry: Do you yourself eat *prasadam* at home? Do you consecrate your food to Krishna before you eat it?

Rosen: Yes. I offer my food to Krishna. At the same time I try to remember that the energy I get from this food is to be used in Krishna's service. This is another aspect of honoring *prasadam*.

Berry: Is it Krishna's teaching that He will not accept animal flesh as *prasadam*? Does He only accept vegetarian food?

Rosen: Exactly. That's based on various passages in the Vedic literature. Prabhupada was fond of quoting one particular verse from the *Bhagavad-gita* in which Krishna says, "If one offers Me with love and devotion a leaf, flower, fruit or water, I will accept it." Prabhupada points out that Krishna doesn't ask for meat, fish, or eggs in this verse. Of course, this *Gita* verse is not in and of itself conclusive; but there are many other parts of the Vedic literature that also point in this direction, as well as those that state it overtly. For example, in the Vaishnava epic known as the *Mahabharata* [Anu. 115.47], it is said, "He who desires to augment his own flesh by eating the flesh of other creatures lives in misery in whatever species he may take his birth." Or, also in the *Mahabharata* [Anu. 114.11], "The meat of animals is like the flesh of one's own son, and the foolish person who eats meat must thus be considered the most vile of human beings." So the *Gita* verse, taken in tandem with these other texts, inescapably points to vegetarianism. Moreover, the Vaishnava tradition has been emphatically vegetarian since ancient times. In later literature, such as Krishnadas Kaviraj's *Chaitanya-charitamrita*, vegetarianism is an implicit and recurring theme.

Actually, in that mammoth work, Krishnadas Kaviraj does something quite remarkable: In addition to delineating an incredibly complex theological system and systematically revealing Lord Chaitanya's prevailing hagiography, he describes and gives recipes for the hundreds of dishes that Lord Chaitanya found most delectable. Many of them, incidentally, appear in Yamuna Devi's cookbook.

Berry: Could you give some idea of Chaitanya's favorite recipes according to Krishnadas Kaviraj?

Rosen: Well, various forms of *shak* are described, that is, green leafy vegetables with interesting combinations of ghee and spices. All kinds of exotic rice preparations are there as well; and delicious forms of *dahl* too; the list really goes on and on.

Berry: But they're not vegan recipes . . .

Rosen: No. There *are* some that involve the use of milk and ghee, as I've said. But many of the recipes are vegan-oriented—simple but tasty vegetarian fare that would appeal to all connoisseurs of good food. Basically, there are two food groups: foods called *kacha*, which are grains, vegetables, and various foods that are boiled in water (wherein you will actually find thousands of vegan recipes). Then there are foods called *pakka*, which are prepared with cow products—again, there are thousands of recipes. These are the two basic categories.

Berry: So Chaitanya would dine on these vegetarian meals, dished up by temple chefs in the sixteenth century. How fascinating to have these culinary artifacts preserved so faithfully by his biographer!

Rosen: Well, there's an esoteric reason for that. An interesting thing about Krishnadas Kaviraj, which would kind of explain why he peppers an intensely philosophical work like the *Chaitanya-charitamrita* with detailed recipes, has to do with his ontological form; it has to do with who he is in the spiritual realm. He is a maidservant named Kasturi Manjari. Appropriately enough, this maidservant assists Radharani in the kitchen when she prepares food for Krishna. Since this is his eternal activity in the Spiritual Sky, it is quite natural that in his bodily form as Krishnadas Kaviraj he has a preoccupation with recipes and has a predilection for listing foodstuffs and feasts in his *Chaitanya-charitamrita.*

Berry: Interesting. You are suggesting that Chaitanya's biographer, Krishnadas Kaviraj, was the reincarnation of a sous-chef in the kitchen of Krishna Himself!

Rosen: In a manner of speaking, yes. In his original spiritual form, he is the assistant of Radharani in the kitchen. And so this affects the way in which he approaches his service as a writer of Chaitanya's biography in this world. This is even brought out more clearly by the fact that Chaitanya's other biographers—and he's had several—don't delve into the recipes or give a detailed listing of the preparations at all. But Krishnadas sure does! He meticulously describes all the different kinds of feasts that Lord Chaitanya attended; he tells how to prepare the various dishes, and he lingers lovingly over every detail of its preparation.

Berry: I should think that after having been Radharani's kitchen assistant, Krishnadas would have achieved *moksha*, or liberation from the wheel of rebirth. Wouldn't being reincarnated as Chaitanya's biographer have been a bit of a comedown?

Rosen: Not at all. Here's the first thing that needs to be understood: As Radharani's assistant, there is no higher goal—he was already beyond *moksha* and established in his natural constitutional position in the spiritual world. He's one of the inner circle of Krishna's associates and so he is considered eternally liberated. That's the first thing. Closely linked to that is another, related idea: his incarnation as Chaitanya's biographer can be seen as *lila*, or pastime, enacted merely for the Lord's pleasure.

You see, people are born into this world for diverse reasons. Conditioned souls need to learn certain lessons and are forced to take birth as a reaction to their *karma* or materialistic activity. Through proper conduct and the Lord's mercy, they ultimately achieve *moksha*, or liberation. However, liberated souls also take birth in our world, but their reason is different: they come to help others and to assist the Lord in His mission. So this is one way to answer your question.

From another perspective, it can be seen like this: Lord Chaitanya is considered the most confidential and powerful *avatar* of Krishna. The Gaudiya Vaishnava tradition proclaims that Chaitanya *is* Krishna, but in His most intimate feature. So, since Krishnadas was Chaitanya's intimate devotee and biographer, he moved closer to the Godhead. Direct service to Lord Chaitanya is the ultimate form of *moksha*, even for souls who are already liberated. So this is seen as a very exalted thing. This ultimate form of liberation—*seva*, or service to God—is delineated in the *Bhagavad-gita*.

Berry: I want to ask you something about the *Gita*, since you just mentioned it. In the *Gita* there are several passages which stress *ahimsa* as one of the eternal verities. Would you say that the *Gita* is a seminal work for the Vaishnavas?

Rosen: Yes. The *Gita* comprises chapters 25 through 42 of the *Bhishma-parva* section of the *Mahabharata*, and the *Mahabharata* is considered one of Vaishnavism's main texts. In regard to *ahimsa*, the *Mahabharata* says *ahimsa para dharmo*: "nonviolence is the highest duty." This emphasis on nonviolence can be found in all major religions as well.

Berry: You've become something of a scholar in the field of comparative religion, too, having written *Food for the Spirit* (now *Diet for*

Transcendence), *Om Shalom, East West Dialogues, inter alia.* As a spokesperson in the field of comparative religion, how would you account for the fact that the religions of the East, such as Buddhism, Jainism, Taoism, and Hinduism, tend to promote *ahimsa* and vegetarianism, whereas the Semitic revelatory religions of the West, such as Christianity and Judaism, condone, if not encourage, the taking of animal life and the eating of their flesh?

Rosen: I think it's because in Western religion there tends to be an emphasis on *loka-hita*. This is Sanskrit terminology; it means "kindness to one's own species."

Berry: This would include Islam as well.

Rosen: Especially Islam. Western religions emphasize *loka-hita* more than Eastern religions. The newer religions emphasize *loka-hita* more than the ancient religions. Islam is only 1,300 years old. Since it's a newer religion, it accentuates *loka-hita*, which is a fundamental, beginning spiritual ethic: "First you have to be kind to yourself and your own kind; then you can extend it to others." Now, in the older religions, and especially in the East, they stress *sarva-bhuta-hita*, which means "kindness to all living things." It's a more inclusive ethic—it includes one's own kind as well as all other living entities. This is the compassionate sensibility that is stressed in ancient India's Vedic texts, and especially in the Puranas and the *Gita*. This is one of the things that attracted me to Vaishnavism: it promotes this more inclusive, embracing ethic. It encourages love for *all* creatures; vegetarianism is implicit.

Furthermore, the Eastern religions, especially the various forms of what has come to be called "Hinduism," also stress the principle of *aham brahmasmi*—"I am not this body but, rather, I am spirit-soul." This very spiritual perspective includes a sense of bonding with all that lives, an interconnectedness with all life forms. They are spirit, and so are we. So we have much in common with all creatures in God's creation. People who adhere to an Eastern religious tradition will tell you in all candor that "I am not this body—I am something beyond this body." Of course, this notion can be found in the Western religious traditions as well; every spiritual path will include some sense of experiencing our identities as different from the body. But it's a question of emphasis. In the East, it is a rigorously elaborated upon and highly valued sensibility. Especially among Brahmins, these spiritual ideals are markedly evolved.

Berry: By chance, as I was making my way here this afternoon, I was reading Norman Lewis's book called *A Goddess in the Stones*—it's about his travels in eastern India. In it, he recounts an incident that vividly illustrates the point you are making. He describes the reaction of a little Hindu girl on learning that there are people in the world who actually eat fish. Let me read it to you: "Fish had been introduced and ingenious wicker traps were offered for hire in which several, not exceeding two inches in length, had been caught and transferred to tins full of water. These were being examined by a pretty and expensively-dressed little girl, who, I was to learn, had never seen a live fish before. 'And what will they do with them?' she asked her father. 'They will eat them.' he told her. She seemed to turn pale with horror, and was on the verge of tears. The father explained smilingly, 'She is very gentle by nature. You see, we are Brahmins. We do not eat living things.' "

Rosen: Yes. Instinctively, she realizes that the only difference between her and this poor fish, who is going to be eaten, is the body; spiritually she realizes that she and the fish are one, parts of God, and should not be exploited or abused in any way.

The interesting thing to me is that in the West this would be considered an esoteric teaching, whereas in the East this is a most *exoteric* teaching. As Prabhupada would often say, "The common street sweeper in India knows that he is not the body." By contrast, in the West, people are generally not conscious of the distinction between body and soul in their everyday life.

Berry: This may be related to the Indic idea or belief in *samsara* or the transmigration of souls. The Western religions do not support such a belief. Is that a fair statement?

Rosen: No, this is not really an accurate assessment. In my book *The Reincarnation Controversy: Uncovering the Truth in the World Religions*, I argue that, just as with *ahimsa*, the principle of reincarnation is accepted by both Eastern and Western traditions. Although practitioners are generally unaware of it, Western religion for the most part accepts the doctrine of transmigration, even if it's only religious mystics, or those who study the "esoteric teachings" of Western religions, who would admit this to be true. In the East, transmigration is common knowledge and is pretty much accepted across the board. But make no mistake, *samsara* is definitely there in Western religion.

You have the example of orthodox Judaism—generally those who adhere to this system of religious belief will deny the doctrine of reincarnation. However, those Jews who know their own mystical tradition, Kabbalah, will inevitably come up against texts that lend support to the idea of transmigration, and they will even become acquainted with a lengthy work known as *Sefer-HaGilgulim*, which is largely devoted to elucidating the truth of reincarnation. The Hassidim and other orthodox Jewish sects are aware of this, and they accept that a person can be reincarnated in the shape of a stone, an insect, a plant, an animal, and so on, until one perfects one's life and learns one's lessons. But the mass of Jewish people do not know that transmigration plays a role in Jewish teaching.

In Christianity, the idea of reincarnation was consciously suppressed. If one studies the 25 ecumenical councils one will find that at the Second Council at Constantinople, in 553 C.E., Emperor Justinian, with the approval of Pope Vigilius, ordered that all references to reincarnation be stricken from the Bible and from post-biblical Christian literature. So most Christians are unaware of Christian reincarnationist teaching.

Berry: Weren't they trying to stamp out Origenism—the teachings of Origen of Alexandria? The emperor and the pope made common cause against Origen because his teachings on reincarnation threatened the establishment.

Rosen: That's right. The pope was afraid that if Christians in general believed that they had many lifetimes in which to perfect themselves, they would not treat death as such a grave issue. (Forgive the pun.) If they had more than one life, they might not be serious about following Christian directives and scriptural injunctions. In a word, they couldn't be threatened with hellfire and damnation after a single life. With this in mind, the powerful leaders of that period decided to tell the mass of people that they had only one life—and that after this they would go to heaven or hell. Finished. This, they hoped, would make serious Christians.

Berry: You were saying that *ahimsa* and *samsara* are esoteric doctrines in the West but are known to the man in the street in the Orient. What about vegetarianism? It strikes me that this has also been an esoteric practice in the West, but commonplace in Asia.

Rosen: Until recently one had to go to an occult bookstore to find information about vegetarianism or reincarnation; they are considered counterculture subjects in the West, or at least they were up until the last 20 years or so. But in India these have long been topics with which the common man is conversant, and speaks about very easily.

Berry: This is a bit off the point, but I was wondering if you've read Jeremy Rifkin's popular book, *Beyond Beef*.

Rosen: Yes. It's an excellent work.

Berry: Do you agree with his view of Indian history?

Rosen: No, not exactly. For the most part, he seems to accept textbook Hinduism, the kind that was popularized by Indologists who were largely Christian missionaries—biased, with a secret agenda, to say the least. In chapter five of Rifkin's work, he mentions that Hindu Brahmins were largely performers of animal sacrifices, and that it wasn't until the rise of Buddhism that *ahimsa* principles were adopted by the Hindus. This is simply untrue. Rifkin's main reference is Marvin Harris, an anthropologist who does not draw on primary sources. If one studies the original texts, in Sanskrit, one finds that *ahimsa* was promoted in the earliest portions of the Vedic literature. This can be found in the *Rig Veda* (10.87.16), for example: "One who partakes of human flesh, the flesh of a horse, or any other animal, and deprives others of milk by slaughtering cows, O King, if such a fiend does not desist by any other means, then you should not hesitate to cut off his head." Or consider the *Yajur Veda* (12.32), which says, "You must not use your God-given body for killing God's creatures, whether these creatures are human, animal, or what have you." Or the *Atharva Veda* (17.1.4): "One should be considered dear, even by those in the animal kingdom." So, contrary to popular belief, the *ahimsa* principle can be found in early Vedic sources, even if there was a parallel Vedic allowance for animal sacrifices.

Now, it is true that the Buddha refuted the hypocritical Brahmins of his time who were engaged in needless animal sacrifices in the name of religion. But other Brahmins spoke out against these hypocrites as well. It's not that *ahimsa* was peculiar to Buddhism; it was there in Hinduism all along. Even Vedic texts that recommended animal sacrifices did so with numerous caveats, and they were clear that these sacrifices were certainly not meant for our present age of Kali.

Only misled, bogus Brahmins bastardized the tradition and taught that it was appropriate to conduct animal sacrifices in Kali-yuga. But this was an aberration that was not condoned by Vedic texts.

You see, in India, there are 18 Puranas, ancient scriptures—six for those in the mode of goodness, six for those in passion, and six for those in ignorance. The scriptures for people in the mode of goodness adamantly eschew the use of flesh foods—*and* animal sacrifices. Only the scriptures for those in passion and ignorance condone meat-eating and, rarely, animal sacrifices—and both in regulated fashion only. It is meant to wean practitioners off these things. A similar phenomenon exists in the Bible, for example, where the kosher laws are described.

So while I feel that Rifkin's book has a lot to offer, I think he didn't really do his homework in regard to Eastern religion, and this is reflected in his fifth chapter, which is called "Holy Cow," I believe.

It's my opinion that Westerners in general don't really understand the reason for Eastern vegetarianism, so Rifkin's analysis is not surprising.

Berry: It would appear that Westerners become vegetarians largely for narcissistic or health reasons; whereas, in Asia, especially in India, people seem to be vegetarians for spiritual and ethical reasons. Is that a correct assumption?

Rosen: Not entirely. Practitioners in the East are also aware of the health benefits conferred by a vegetarian diet, and, conversely, Westerners often become vegetarian for spiritual reasons. But, to focus on the Eastern religions: If one studies ancient Ayurvedic texts, one will find it very clearly stated that it is better to be a vegetarian not only for religious, ethical, and moral reasons but also for medical and nutritional reasons. It is always better to do things in full knowledge than to do things without knowing the purpose. That's acknowl-edged in all Indic traditions. But the central reason for Eastern vege-tarianism, especially for Vaishnavas, is twofold: first, a Vaishnava can-not bear to see the suffering of others. They feel an intense love for all living beings, and cannot harm anyone—let alone eat them! Secondly, a Vaishnava can only eat foods that are offered to Krishna in sacrifice, and as we've mentioned earlier, Krishna will only eat vegetarian foods. These two reasons are deeply ingrained in Vaishnava culture, and have been an integral part of Vaishnava consciousness long before the rise of Buddhism. So, yes, the two main reasons are ethical and spiritual.

Berry: You were raised in a non-practicing Jewish family, and after converting to Vaishnavism, you've become an expert in the field of comparative religion. Has your interest in Judaism been rekindled by your study of other religions?

Rosen: Very much so.

Berry: Can one be a practicing Jew and a Krishnaite at the same time?

Rosen: The average Jewish theologian would say no. They would say that it's not possible because Hinduism is idolatrous and polythe-istic. But the conception of *sanatan dharma* that is set forth in the Vedic literature is quite monotheistic in that it sees Krishna as the supreme God—the *same* supreme God that is mentioned in biblical literature. And, as far as idol worship goes—there is a huge difference between worshiping a Deity of the supreme and worshiping an idol of some lesser god, fashioned by one's own imagination. I've actually written quite extensively on this. You see, what Vaishnavism, or Krishnaite religion, emphasizes is this: getting at the essence, finding God, and this is the same basic idea that is there in Judaism and in all major world religions. So, I would say, yes, one can actually be a good practitioner of any faith and still be a Vaishnava. But one must dig deep, and must look into the essence of one's religion. In fact, if one does so, one will find that the practice of Vaishnavism can enhance one's faith in many ways, whatever one's sectarian affiliation may be.

Berry: Can you draw any parallels between Judaism and Vaishnavism?

Rosen: That's the subject of a whole book, and your readers can turn to *Om Shalom*. But, as an example, the word *judaism* comes from *judah*, which means "to exalt the Lord" or "to glorify God." So if one could, for a moment, divorce Judaism from its ethnological dimension, the essence of Judaism is to glorify God. The connection to Vaishnavism, then, is obvious, for the goal of Vaishnavism, too, is to glorify God. In this way, if one looks at the essence, one can find great harmony in these traditions.

Berry: Muslims and Hindus in India have such divergent views on vegetarianism, don't they?

Rosen: Sure. And you can even see such differences of opinion in the various Hindu sects, too. You have Shaivites and worshipers of Kali, for example, who often sacrifice animals and eat flesh—they call this animal sacrifice *bali*—and then you have the Vaishnavas, who are scrupulous vegetarians and who are kind to animals.

Sometimes worshipers of Kali offer a goat to the goddess in sacrifice, for she is said to be propitiated only by red blood. Vaishnavas who enter Kali temples often bring an offering of red flowers to appease the goddess by the similarity in color. To this day, there is an unscrupulous class of Kali priests who run a lucrative slaughterhouse business in the name of religion. Not so for the Vaishnavas....

Berry: Would you say that a goodly number of Hindus indulge in meat-eating as a result of this form of Kali worship?

Rosen: Well, animal sacrifice, or *bali*, is now on the wane. Thankfully. There's evidence that Calcutta's most famous Kali temple, known as Kalighat, now sacrifices fewer goats per year than ever before. This is setting a standard in the less popular temples, too. All Kali temples that are associated with the Ramakrishna Mission have prohibited animal sacrifice, and it is prohibited by law in the temporary shrines erected throughout Calcutta during Kali Puja. So there is something of a "vegetarianizing" of the Goddess going on. Rachel Fell McDermott, a Harvard scholar now teaching at Columbia University, has been doing a good deal of research on this subject.

Berry: But in the Vedic texts—is there ever an allowance for meat-eating?

Rosen: Well, certain medicines include animal products, so, yes, for medicinal purposes—but a true Vaishnava, and especially a

Brahmin, will never take these things. Also, in Vedic culture, there was some allowance for a *kshatriya*, a member of the warrior class, to eat meat, but this was only in very special conditions—when he was living in the forest, preparing for battle. And even then, he would do so only under certain regulations, and then he would have to kill the animal himself, uttering the *mamsa* mantra in the animal's ear. This mantra basically says, "As I eat you now, in a future life, you may eat me." This was to inculcate in the meat-eating *kshatriya* a sensibility of karmic or causal truth. There is a severe reaction for killing animals, or eating meat, and this was widely known in ancient India. Actually, in India, it is *still* widely known, and meat-eating is frowned upon by most believing Hindus.

Berry: What about the *ashvamedha*, or the horse sacrifice, that one reads about in histories of ancient India?

Rosen: The *ashvamedha* was one of many royal sacrifices. Three were most prominent: the *rajasuya*, the *vajapeya*, and the *ashvamedha*. Again, this was for *kshatriyas*, and they were very complicated sacrifices that would ensure entrance into heavenly planets, although not necessarily into the kingdom of God. The *ashvamedha* involved a complex series of events that lasted over one year. Essentially, it called for over one hundred horses, but only one was chosen as the main object of sacrifice. What is not generally mentioned in relation to this sacrifice, however, is that the horse was not only killed but was immediately brought back to life—immediately rejuvenated by the power of the mantras that were chanted by the priests. If the priests could not produce a young horse out of the fire sacrifice, then they were forbidden to perform the sacrifice at all or to kill the older horse in the first place. Incidentally, the whole ceremony is off-limits in this age, since there are no qualified priests who can properly chant the mantras.

Berry: Wasn't there some sort of sexual ritual between the horse and the queen?

Rosen: [laughter] Well, modern scholars have assumed as much. The ceremony called for the queen to lie down behind a drawn curtain with the horse that was to be sacrificed. This was to soothe the horse, to calm the poor animal. Sexual innuendoes are not really there in the texts, and there is no evidence that any perverse activity was actually part of the ritual. Anyway, I must reiterate that these sacrifices are not recommended for this age. There are schisms, however—not among Vaishnavas, but among other Hindu groups—saying that it can still be done. It should be pointed out, though, that the vast majority of practitioners and Vedic scholars insist that the *ashvamedha* and similar sacrifices were meant for a previous age, and that the modern sacrifice, for Kali-yuga, our current age, is the chanting of the holy name. This is now the recommended process of God-realization.

Berry: What about the rift between Advaita philosophy and non-Advaita philosophy? According to Indologist A. L. Basham, when he visited Benares, which is the sacred city associated with Shiva worship and Advaita religious philosophy, the Advaita Brahmins who pride themselves on having gone far on the path of *Raja yoga* and Shankarite meditation tend to be very arrogant and self-important because they feel that they have successfully merged their *atman*, their soul, with *Paramatman*, the supreme soul, or God. Basham notes that they strut about the streets of Benares like *dhoti*-clad gods. Far from exhibiting a fading away of self, they display a refined egotism that reminds him of the self-absorption of the Theravada Buddhists.

On the other hand, Basham says that when he visited Vrindaban, which, as you know, is that city in northwestern India that is associated with Krishna worship and non-Advaita or theistic Hinduism, he found the Vaishnavas to be friendly, unassuming, and forthcoming. Basham ascribes their friendliness and lack of holier-than-thou attitude to their being dualists who worship a personal God, holding themselves separate from God (unlike the Advaitavadis of Benares, who see themselves as one with God). Identifying with God, however one rationalizes it, seems to run counter to humility.

So we have these two cities—impersonalist Advaita Benares and personalist non-Advaita Vrindaban—representing the polarity that exists in Indian religious philosophy. Do you agree with Basham's critique?

Rosen: Yes, to a certain degree. I think it's very well stated, too. Advaita philosophy is very much akin to Theravada Buddhism. Chaitanya Mahaprabhu preferred the non-Advaita or dualist system because under the Advaita system there is no opportunity for rendering service to God. He prefers being distinct from God and thus being able to pay his adoration to a personal deity.

Berry: What about reincarnation and liberation? Do these various systems perceive the ultimate goal in different ways?

Rosen: There are various nuances of difference in these things, depending on which Advaita group you are talking about and which Vaishnava group you are talking about. Generally, in the Advaita system you continually reincarnate until you achieve *moksha*, "release," which, for Advaitans, means becoming "one with God," a position from which one generally falls. For Buddhists, the goal is *nirvana*, or enlightenment, but this, again, is not really an ultimate goal: What do you do in your enlightened state? The Vaishnavas say that the ultimate liberation is developing love for Krishna and, after death, attaining His supreme abode. This is the perfection of *moksha* and *nirvana*. You experience release from material bondage and are situated in your eternal constitutional position. What's more, you exist in eternity, knowledge, and bliss, so you have enlightened activity in Krishna's service and relish it for all time.

Index

abortion, 46
Abrams, Jerry, 139–142
Adiraja, 121
Adopt-a-Cow Program, 56–57
Advaita philosophy, 213–214
aestheticism, 8–12
Africa, 121–123
Agarwal, Gopal and Sally, 132
ages of the world, 24–26, 57, 209, 213
agni (fire of digestion), 65–66. *see also*
   digestion
agriculture, 39, 51, 58, 100, 179–180. *see
   also* farms
aham-brahmasmi (self as spirit-soul), 205
ahimsa (harmlessness)
   animal rights and vegetarianism and,
      16, 130, 144
   in Eastern religions, 17, 20–23, 177,
      204–205, 208–209
   Hare Krishnas and, 6–7, 32, 46, 188,
      200
   in the West, 196, 208
Akers, Keith (*Vegetarian Sourcebook*), 110
Akshaya Patra, 127, 191–192
Alcalay, Robert (*Complete Hebrew-English
   Dictionary*), 87–88
Amato, Paul, 131
animal rights
   Hare Krishna philosophy and, 16, 130,
      144, 180
   Hare Krishnas and, xvi–xviii, 5–8, 128,
      175
   religions and, 176
   utilitarianism and, 110
animals
   companion, xvii

relationship with God, 76, 180–181,
   206
souls of, 85, 103–109
suffering of, 86–87, 110–111
animal sacrifice, 17–27, 80, 208–209,
   211–213
animal slaughter, 26, 75–90, 103–111. *see
   also* slaughterhouses
anrishamsya (non-cruelty), 32. *see also
   ahimsa* (harmlessness)
Anthropological Survey of India, 27–28
Aquinas, St. Thomas, 106–107, 110
arishtam, 69
Arjuna, 9, 37–38
asceticism, 8–12
ashvamedha (horse sacrifice), 24, 212–213
Atharva Veda, 60, 63, 208
Athi-yoga, 67
atman, 213
Ayurveda, 44–45, 51, 59–74, 209

Baird, David, 147
Balabhadra (William Dove), 58
Bala Books, 148–149
bali, 211. *see also* animal sacrifice
Ballarmine, Cardinal, 108
Basham, A. L., 198, 213–214
Bentham, Jeremy, 111
Berry, Rynn, 175, 195–214
Bhagavad-gita
   on material nature, 71–72
   practices, 9, 33, 66–67, 69, 204
   on souls, 104, 105
   Vaishnavas and, 4
   values, 21, 30–32, 180
   on vegetarianism, 202

215